D0898177

KING GEORGE'S KEYS

"Halt. Who goes there?"

"The Keys."

"Whose Keys?"

"King George's Keys."

"Pass, King George's Keys. All's well."

The sentry's challenge and the passwords in the Ceremony of the Keys, as observed at Gibraltar in the time of King George VI, during whose reign and that of King George V most of the author's Colonial service was performed.

KING GEORGE'S
KEYS

A record of experiences
in the overseas service of the Crown

SIR ROBERT STANLEY
K.B.E., C.M.G.

With a Foreword by
the Right Hon. Viscount Boyd, C.H.

JOHNSON

LONDON

© SIR ROBERT STANLEY

First published 1975
ISBN 0 85307 133 0

PRINTED AND MADE BY
CLARKE, DOBLE AND BRENDON LTD, PLYMOUTH
FOR JOHNSON PUBLICATIONS LTD
11/14 STANHOPE MEWS WEST, LONDON S.W.7

CONTENTS

Contents

EPILOGUE : MR. SPEAKER

ILLUSTRATIONS

---

1. Traditional salute by followers of the Emir of Bida at the Greater Moslem Festival (Id al-Kabir).

2. Pagan village in the Niger province of Nigeria.

3. Merchant adventurers of the Niger.

4. Venus Rocks near Paphos, Cyprus. (Author's daughter with companion).

5. The author as Colonial Secretary, Gibraltar.

6. *R.C.S. Nareau.*

7. Ellice Islands girls in dancing dress.

8. The author as Speaker of the Mauritius Legislative Council.

(The illustrations will be found in an album between pages 112 and 113)

FOREWORD

by

THE RT. HON. VISCOUNT BOYD, C.H.

————————

THE Colonial Office as an independent Department lasted for one hundred and twelve years. The average life of its Secretaries of State was twenty-four months. I survived for over five years and was therefore able to travel a great deal and visit most of the territories of which Sir Robert Stanley writes so engagingly.

How vividly he recaptures the never to be forgotten sights and sounds of Northern Nigeria—the contrasts in light and shade and colour, the wonderful birds and the great waterways of the Niger and the Benue, and how sensitively he recalls those who lived there, not least in his moving passages about the Mymuye people. And how skilfully his journeys come to life again. "Sofari sogoodi", Sir Winston Churchill said at the end of each day's safari in East Africa. I suspect Sir Robert felt the same, after a long march when revelling at sunset in Africa's moment of glory.

Then come fascinating glimpses of three very different Colonies in war time. First he went to Cyprus, where, secure under British Sovereignty, Greeks and Turks lived happily together; then to Barbados where, as throughout the Caribbean, Island pride and insularity foredoomed the later Federation; then to Gibraltar for a critical administrative task. After the war he went once more to Africa, this time to Northern Rhodesia, now Zambia. Here he found, as I did later on, that the main racial problem stemmed far more from the insistence of white trade unionists in the Copperbelt to retain their privileges than from any efforts by white farmers to retain theirs. He won the affection and respect of Sir Roy Welensky and the unofficial members of the Legislative Council at a critical moment in that country's history.

A*

ix

After serving under eleven Governors and in five territories he had his own command; he became High Commissioner for the Western Pacific territories, one of the most romantic and rewarding but arduous jobs in the service of the Crown. Here, though rigged out this time in gubernatorial cockfeathers, he reverted once more to his favourite role and became a District Officer again. He went to the islands while they were still recovering from the emotional and physical effects of the Japanese invasions. He set up house in Honiara, "the place where the winds come first". He was seen to be immensely hardworking, efficient, kindly and tactful, and he loved his job and was fascinated by the beauty of the islands. He will long be remembered, not least by the various islanders who performed for him their ancient and elegant dances.

Throughout his career, I am sure, like Santayana's Englishman he carried the English weather in his heart wherever he went, and it became a cool spot in the desert—a steady and sane oracle among all the deliriums of mankind.

He was spared violent political changes in the Colonies he served. It was never his fate to receive from an overworked Secretary of State a cable which was meant to start "My immediately preceding communication", but which arrived "My immediately preceding Constitution".

Sir Robert Stanley has an honoured place in that company of Colonial Officers through whose devoted and unselfish lives some thirty independent sovereign States are now in voluntary association in the British Commonwealth.

AUTHOR'S PREFACE

THIS book is about people and places I have known and events with which I have been concerned during thirty-five years' service in the overseas territories of the Crown. Where it seemed appropriate I have provided contemporary scenery to give colour to the narrative. I have not devoted space to discussion of principles, because principles are better acted upon than talked about—they are part of an accepted code—and policies, though all designed to achieve the common aim of good government, had necessarily to depend upon circumstances in individual territories: circumstances that were what the beliefs, customs and ways of life of the people had made them.

I have called the book *King George's Keys* because those keys and, more recently, the keys of Queen Elizabeth II—the keys that could so proudly meet the challenge of Empire—enabled me to pass through many doors, and by so doing to come close in understanding and sympathy to those within. I entered in a good many guises: as a District Officer with side-roles as policeman, magistrate and coroner; as a head of Secretariat and Government spokesman in Legislative Council with quasi-ministerial responsibilities; as an acting Governor and, in my own right, as a High Commissioner and a kind of Admiral of the blue ensign with overall control of a fleet of Government vessels and jurisdiction over island dependencies extending three thousand miles across the Pacific.

I have also appeared in a full-bottomed wig as Speaker of a Legislative Council. In these various capacities I have travelled many thousands of miles and found myself among all sorts and conditions of men: Emirs in fine robes of ceremony, heralded by trumpeters and saluted by galloping cavalcades resplendently apparelled and aglitter with the scintillations of brandished spears;

simple pagan folk who gave me shelter within the smoke-blackened walls of their huts of mud and thatch; elder statesmen and prentice politicians in Legislative Councils; Melanesians in their quiet and lovely islands and, upon their distant atolls; Polynesians with whom I have rubbed noses in customary greeting. I have known many missionaries and been greeted by an unconverted former cannibal.

In 1925, when I was appointed as a cadet in the Administrative Service of Nigeria, that part of His Majesty's dominions that was sometimes described as the British Colonial Empire had every appearance of stability and permanence. Thirty years later, when my term of office as High Commissioner for the Western Pacific expired, the steadfast rock upon which this little Empire within an Empire had seemed to rest was soon to become overlaid by the shifting sands of change.

The transformation, which began after the partition of the Indian sub-continent in 1947, was rapid; but was not fully apparent until after my retirement. Although in Northern Rhodesia (now Zambia) forces were at work which were to lead to the creation and eventual dissolution of the ill-fated Federation of Rhodesia and Nyasaland, I never had to face the special problems of service in any administration whose days were already known to be numbered. Until shortly before my retirement the word "colonialism" had not acquired sinister connotations, nor had accusing fingers been pointed at what have been described as "colonial attitudes".

Nevertheless, in a volume of this kind some general comment on the topic may be looked for, and there are one or two historical aspects of the argument that seem to me to be particularly relevant. What I have to say applies mainly to the British colonial record in Africa.

In the first place, and concerning the original assumption of colonial responsibilities, it is necessary that policy decisions should be judged within the framework of the era to which they belonged. It was after his retirement in 1919 as Governor-General of Nigeria, a territory that affords as good an example as any of a colonial situation during the early years of this century, that Lord Lugard (then Sir Frederick Lugard) published his celebrated enunciation of the Dual Mandate imposed upon Britain in those portions of tropical Africa for which she had accepted responsibility as trustee; on the one hand, for the advancement of the subject races; and, on the other, for the development of their material resources for the benefit of mankind.

The verdict of students of history of different nationalities, Lugard wrote, was "unanimous that the era of complete independence is not yet visible upon the horizon of time." Scarcely in his most far-ranging conjectures could he have imagined that within a few decades the world would so have changed that the obligations of trusteeship, whatever they might have been, would have to be interpreted in an entirely new context, and that a strange new figure—Africa unbound, articulate and confident— would come striding like a giant into the arena of international relations. Lugard was a man of his time, an imperialist in the worthiest sense of that provocative word, a brave soldier and a wise and very human administrator. His visions and those of men like him were not those of today; but he helped to raise Africans in their many thousands from their knees and to cast aside their burdens.

The tragic experiences through which Nigeria has passed since her independence vividly illustrate more recent arguments of the critics of our colonial administration in Africa. As, for instance, that the settlement of boundaries on the basis of national claims to "spheres of influence"—those shadowy shapes that seemed to owe more to geometry than to geography— resulted, as it frequently did, not only in the erection of arbitrary barriers dividing tribal societies, but in enclosing together within artificially created limits other communities whose historical and cultural backgrounds were wholly different one from another; that the forms of government that were introduced were not necessarily those best suited to the needs and political evolution of African societies that might one day cease to enjoy the guidance of a protecting Power; and, finally, that there was inadequate preparation for the independence that was granted.

There is a deal of substance in much of the criticism of this kind. On the subject of racial diversity as one of the causes of the apparent instability of the Nigerian Federation soon after independence the Federal Government itself has been outspoken. "Nigeria was plagued", it was stated in an official publication* issued in 1968, "by a deep-seated imbalance in its political structure, an imbalance which stemmed from the inequality of its components and which placed one of the regions in a stronger position over the others." And another passage in the same publication refers to "The slow pace of social integration among the various population groups."

It is not surprising that in emergent African States there should have been departures from the "Wesminster Model." African leaders depend just as much as those elsewhere upon the goodwill and support of the people; but the notion of an officially recognized Opposition does not conform with traditional African ideas, which would have found another name for shadow cabinets, and with which, moreover, a combination rather than a separation of Presidential prerogatives and executive powers is more in accord. Events have also shown that a leader is unlikely to feel secure unless he is assured of the loyalty of the Army.

Be the considerations of policy that determined the pace of independence what they may, it is undoubtedly true that during most of my own service, and certainly between the two World Wars, expatriates employed by Colonial Administrations had little reason to suppose that some of them might become redundant before the expected date of their normal retirement.

"The great purpose of the British Empire", declared Mr. Malcolm MacDonald in the House of Commons in December, 1938, "is the gradual spread of freedom among all His Majesty's subjects in whatever part of the world they may live. That spread of freedom is a slow, evolutionary progress. . . . It may take generations or even centuries for the people in some parts of the Colonial Empire to achieve self-government. But it is a major part of our policy, even among the most backward peoples of Africa, to teach them and to encourage them always to stand a little more on their own feet."

The day of lowered Union Jacks and golden handshakes had not yet arrived.

* Nigeria 12-State Structure The only Way out.

In a future that may be yet distant some aspiring Gibbon may, with imperial talent directed to an Imperial theme, succeed in presenting the world with a comprehensive panorama of the British Empire in decline. It is too soon, in my opinion, for the undertaking of such a monumental task.

"Let us", said Sir Winston Churchill in his famous call to the nation on the eve of the Battle of Britain, ". . . so bear ourselves that, if the British Empire and its Commonwealth last for a thousand years, men will still say, 'This was their finest hour.'" That prospect of Imperial survival was swiftly to fade; but one thing is certain. Like that of Rome, the story of the British Empire, its visions and achievements, its follies and failures, its ordeals, sacrifices and triumphs, its days of shadow, its hours of peril and its moments of glory, will illuminate the pages of history as long as men preserve and value the traditions and the testimony of the past.

To my wife
whose constant support and precious companionship
illuminate the memory of so many shared experiences
this book is dedicated

Part One

Apprenticeship

"Education never ends, Watson. It is a series of lessons, with the greatest for the last."

SIR ARTHUR CONAN DOYLE, *The Red Circle.*

CHAPTER I

THE CALL OF THE COAST

IN 1924 I was a junior member of the editorial staff of Reuter's London office, which was something of a nursery for ambitious young journalists. There were possibilities that I might one day be sent to one of the Company's branches—in New York, Paris, Rome or the Far East—but, notwithstanding these prospects, service of a different kind in quite a different country lay closer to my heart's desire.

It was not the first time I had changed course. After leaving school I had spent a year at the "Shop" and three years as a Gunner subaltern—in Palestine for a short time during the concluding phase of Allenby's campaign and, later, with a pack battery in India. Prospects of promotion for junior officers were not encouraging in those days, and I resigned my commission with the intention of going to South Africa to work on a farm— a plan which came to nothing. After that, I spent some months in New York as tutor to the two young sons of Helena Rubinstein (that celebrated lady and her husband were old family friends) and, while there, found spare time employment on *The Brooklyn Daily Eagle*, now defunct but then an evening newspaper of wide circulation. I had hoped to find a future in the States, but if America held any promising opportunities for me I was too imperceptive to discover them.

I could not complain that Reuters lacked such opportunities in those days when television was unknown, broadcasting was still in its infancy, and the first news to reach the world of an earthquake, an assassination or a *coup d'état* might be heralded by the little scuffle of sound made by a message-bearing container from one of the cable companies as it fell like a plummet from its delivery tube into our editorial midst.

The work was brimful of interest, for the Company's role,

reputation and extensive coverage gave it a unique position in journalistic affairs. Close to Fleet Street, but not part of it, it stood with one hand keeping a finger on the financial pulse of the City, while the other ranged over the continents hither and thither in search of whatever was newsworthy. The increasing responsibility with which I was entrusted placed me from time to time in sole charge of the editorial work during the interval between the departure of the night editors at 6 a.m. and the arrival of the day staff four hours later. If big news should break within that period it was up to me to handle it, and the possibility that on my way home my eye might catch a word or two on a newspaper placard which owed their presence to messages I had disseminated an hour or so earlier lent piquancy to my task. All this should have been encouragement enough for youthful ambition, but the call of Africa was still insistent and, in the end, compulsive.

I cannot recall precisely when my thoughts began to dwell on the possibility of a career in tropical Africa. The editor of a left-wing Barbados newspaper once wrote of me in a valedictory article that "he worshipped the glorious British Empire on which the sun never sets, but he realized that the colonies should no longer be regarded as luscious meadows on which imperial kine had grazing priority". I think he wished to indicate that in his opinion I had done my job as Colonial Secretary with fairness and impartiality, but his assessment of my imperial sentiments was more picturesque than accurate.

Certainly I had never regarded the colonies as a field for the exploitation of privileged interests, and whatever my feelings about the British Empire might have been, they could scarcely be described as idolatory. I grew up in a generation which, I would say, regarded the Empire as being as much a part of the established order as the penny post or the piles of golden sovereigns that I used to see upon the counters of the bank where my father cashed his cheques. One had only to glance at the great red spaces on the map of the world to appreciate the Empire's ubiquity and its magnitude, and I have no doubt that I was not alone in taking its permanence as much for granted as the post office and the currency.

As for the dependencies with their widespread geographical distribution and their diversity of peoples I shared an ignorance that, except among those who had personal associations with them, was fairly extensive. Who, after all, could reasonably be expected, without reference to a gazetteer, to indicate the whereabouts or to explain the status of such entities as Negri Sembilan, Faridkot, or the island known since the last world war as Guadalcanal?

Some of the names were familiar to me by reason of their appearance in a stamp album, with spaces provided for specimens of all the postage stamps in the world that had been issued at the time of its publication. I also recall a package of stamps among which was a set issued by the Oil Rivers Protectorate. I did not take much trouble to find out the precise location of these rivers or why they were so called. Perhaps, with recollections from early childhood of the great, grey-green, greasy Limpopo, I was attuned to the idea that it was of the nature of some rivers to be oily, as some springs, one was told, were hot or sulphurous and certain lakes bitter.

In any case the description fitted in with my rather vague notion of equatorial Africa as a land of dark and sluggish streams infested with crocodiles and surrounded by impenetrable jungle. This mental picture must have owed much to Edgar Wallace's popular stories of Sanders of the River, which about this time captured my attention, and in the more adventurous flights of my boyish fancy I imagined myself in the role of one exercising lonely authority at riparian palavers to which submissive chiefs had been summoned to hear the decrees and receive the justice of the White Man. Later, at the age of twenty, I came across a copy of Winwood Reade's *The Martyrdom of Man*, and from those fascinating pages I was able to visualize, not only the colour and movement of the daily scene, but the warp and weft of African society as it used to be in the regions through which the Niger flows.

But although the idea had been with me for some time it was not until after my return from America that a Colonial Service career presented itself as a realizable possibility. One day—it was in January 1923, shortly after I had started work at Reuters

—I made my way during my lunch hour from their offices, then in Old Jewry, as far as London Bridge and stood looking down from the parapet at the ships in the Pool as they lay with hatches uncovered alongside the many-mansioned warehouses. In my pocket was a letter from the Under Secretary of State for the Colonies informing me that the Duke of Devonshire proposed to select me for appointment as a cadet in the Administrative Service of Nigeria and asking me whether I was prepared to accept the offer; and in my mind was a conflict. I had come to the river, to this scene which always fascinated me, because it belonged to a world in which, though it excited me, I had no part, and rather as a man who is trying to resolve his thoughts will sometimes play with his pipe before he lights it with mind made up I needed a catalyst to enable me to reach a decision.

The letter in my pocket had come as a surprise to me. Some weeks earlier I had applied for a Colonial Service post and had been interviewed at the Colonial Office; but, lacking the not essential but desirable qualification of a university degree, I had no serious hopes of success. Then had come the Reuters opportunity, I was in low water financially and I pursued it—prematurely, as it was now apparent.

The conflict was between the strong attraction of the offer I had now received, with its challenging invitation to action and adventure, and, to some extent at least, my reluctance to give notice to employers who had just restored my self confidence when it was at a low ebb by giving me a chance to prove myself. This reluctance might well have been overcome—I was still on probation at Reuters—but I could not ignore the uneasiness which my mother had expressed at this turn of events. Since my father's death while I was in Palestine I had spent much time abroad, and she was far from happy at the possibility of my departure now for what was still known as "the white man's grave". The prospect of her distress turned the scale.

So for the time being the noes had it.

Nearly two years later I was able to reach with a clear conscience the decision I eventually made. I had served a faithful apprenticeship at Reuters. My mother's apprehensions about the

Coast had been at least partly assuaged. The favourable reply to my renewed application to the Colonial Office reached me on Christmas Day.

In the months that intervened before my departure from England there was a good deal to be done.

I was my own man, free to make what I could of an inspiring opportunity and possessed by all the enthusiasm of youth.

Before sailing for Africa selected candidates for administrative posts were required to undergo a three months' course of instruction in such subjects as criminal law, evidence and procedure, Mohammedan law, tropical hygiene, elementary surveying and the Colonial system of accounts. The instructors included retired Colonial civil servants distinguished in their respective spheres, and the lectures themselves, delivered at the Imperial Institute—that dignified repository of colonial display—in lecture rooms of imperial dimensions, were practical, interesting and nicely laced with humour. Thus in one of a series of talks on ethnology it was explained to us that the animism of primitive societies embraced all kinds of objects, and that railway locomotives, when first introduced into certain parts of Africa, had been regarded as a species of bullock, believed to be overloaded because it squealed before starting.

In the time available it was impossible for such a course to provide more than a brief introduction to some of the more important aspects of our work in the field, but at least it helped us to appreciate how extensive and various those duties were likely to be. Our education proper would begin on the day we reported for duty and it would continue all the years of our service.

At the same time it was necessary to equip and provide sustenance for the body as well as for the mind. The shopping list was a long one. Tropical clothing, camp kit—often for months on end to be one's only furniture—lamps, bedding, cooking and eating utensils and at least a few months' stock of such basic commodities as flour, tea, sugar, soap and some tinned milk, with as much addition in the form of biscuits, jam, sardines and the like as the palate craved and the pocket could afford. All this and much more in the way of unimpressive but entirely indispensable trifles. There would be no little shop round the corner where one could buy a pair of bootlaces or a packet of razor blades. As for provisions, apart from items obtainable from the depots established here and there by the principal trading companies for the purchase of agricultural produce and the sale of goods selected to attract African custom, there was little to be found in the Nigerian outback, and the uncertainty of communications made it most advisable to maintain a well stocked store cupboard.

Many of the articles of clothing and equipment in a recommended list furnished by the Colonial Office seemed to have been selected for their prophylactic virtues. They included a topee and spine-padded bush shirts to protect the head, neck and back from the harmful rays of the sun; dark glasses to protect the eyes from glare and dust; high ankle boots and gaiters or puttees to protect the feet and legs from the bite of venomous snakes, and an electric hand-lamp with a long-life battery to reveal the presence of these and other hazards when walking about at night; mosquito boots, worn after dark to protect the ankles from the assaults of the malaria-carrying anopheles, and a mosquito net for general protection when asleep. The topee, of Cawnpore pattern, required as an accessory a waterproof covering to protect it from the heavy rain which, if not deflected, would soon reduce it to a sodden shapeless mass of pulp.

There was a real need, as I discovered, for all the items I have mentioned. I bought them all, as well as two airtight uniform cases (a protection against damp and vermin) and a steel bath and cover with a removable wicker lining. This bath turned out to be one of the most useful purchases I ever made. On trek it could be used as an additional container for linen and clothing, and when the weather was favourable for an evening meal out of doors it served, when partly filled and placed near a lamp adjacent but not too close to the table at which one was eating, as a trap for the nocturnal swarms of flying ants, which were lured by the light in their thousands to watery destruction. Its most original and valuable function, however, proved to be that of a raft, in which capacity it was successfully used to ferry trekking loads, and on one occasion my wife, across bridgeless streams swollen by flood and too deep to be forded.

On the 13th May, 1925, I arrived at Euston to begin my journey. It was here that, for all practical purposes, a West African tour began, for the few inches that separated the running-boards of the boat train from the edge of the station platform made a gap wide enough to divide two continents. Once on board, one had become part of the company of government officials, traders and missionaries which made up the expatriate world of the Coast.

Everything about the Euston departure platform helped to facilitate this sudden transition. On every side were barrows piled high with cabin trunks, uniform cases, canvas valises and amorphous bundles of unpredictable content labelled colourfully for Lagos, Freetown, Sekondi or Accra. My fellow passengers stood about in small groups, those of us who were newcomers being easily distinguishable by the pinkness of our not yet sallowed cheeks and the comparative respectability of our overcoats, which lacked the outmoded and rather seedy appearance such garments assume when left unworn for lengthy periods in a tropical climate.

It was a mainly masculine gathering—the Coast was not kind to European women—but I noticed one or two wives with dried-up complexions, and a fair-haired girl whose smart coat and skirt, new shoes and modish hat suggested that they might have been part of a recently purchased going-away outfit. A firm of tropical outfitters, to whom I was starting my tour somewhat heavily indebted, had sent their representative, who with unobtrusive but undeflected perserverance moved about from one client to another, presenting each with a long envelope containing invoices typed in quadruplicate for the satisfaction of baggage-masters and customs officials. At the far end of the platform were a number of men and women in the uniform of the Salvation Army. As the train pulled out they began to sing a hymn, presumably with the zealous intention of encouraging and inspiring a colleague on his way to the Mission field; but in that smoke-dimmed and slightly chilly atmosphere the Christian chorus sounded more like a dirge than a song of praise. I gave a last glance at the retreating platform. In the distance the fair-haired girl in her going-away outfit stood by herself, a lonely figure bravely waving a white handkerchief.

I settled down in my corner seat and wondered what lay ahead of me. This time there could be no turning aside.

Chapter II

A MOSLEM EMIRATE (1)

THE most vivid of my earliest recollections of Nigeria are of persons and personalities. One of the first Africans to impress himself upon my memory was a man whose identity I could by no means have discovered. He belonged to the crew of one of what, at first glance from the decks of the M.V. *Adda*, looked like a miniature armada of war canoes, but turned out to be a small fleet of swiftly paddled surf boats setting out yeastily through the strong swell to unload cargo or disembark passengers in the absence of a harbour or of any other form of transport between ship and shore.

We were approaching the open beaches of Sekondi. This was before the construction of the harbour works at Takoradi, a little further along the Coast, and passengers left or boarded the ship in a "mammy chair"—a boxlike contrivance accommodating four persons seated two a side facing one another. The expertise in the lowering operation consisted in avoiding an impact between a descending chair and a rising surf boat—a conjunction that could be unpleasant and dangerous.

In spite of the sometimes heavy rolling of the ship it was remarkable how little loss or damage seemed to result from this somewhat hazardous system of lighterage, but occasional mishaps were unavoidable. As I watched, an unusually big wave lifted up the bows of a surf boat and swung it over to one side just at the moment when a sling filled with trunks and a uniform case had been released of its contents. Most of the pieces were swiftly seized hold of and held fast by the crew while the boat righted itself, but the uniform case, eluding their grasp, toppled over and slithered into the sea. In a flash one of the paddlers jumped overboard in its wake and holding it up on the surface with his head apparently submerged, trod water until his com-

11

rades, reaching out from the boat, were able to relieve him. Such were the speed and skill of this manoeuvre that I doubt whether the contents of the case suffered in the least degree from the accident.

Before reaching Lagos I was notified by telegram that I had been posted to the Niger Province, one of the eleven administrative entities into which what had once been the Protectorate of Northern Nigeria was, at the time of my arrival, divided. These Northern Provinces, as they were collectively called, covered territory whose history and physical features were very different from those of the South.

The Coast had always presented barriers—to explorers, to traders, to missionaries. Malarial swamps, whose noxious vapour or "bad air" was for long believed to be responsible for the appalling loss of life caused by the anopheles mosquito before the discovery of quinine; the navigational hazards of a maze of uncharted waterways; and danger from ambushes and the war canoes of villagers to whom slave-raiding parties had given good reason to be suspicious of strangers of whatever colour. But the North, guarded though its boundaries were by desert, had for centuries been accessible to traders from oasis to oasis along the caravan routes and, across the semi-arid tracts of the Western Sudan, to migrants and nomadic wanderers.

By those approaches, filtering through the centuries from the medieval Sudanese kingdoms to the North, came Islam, whose discipline received a powerful stimulus early in the nineteenth century from the puritanical zeal of one, Othman dan Fodio, a Chief and religious leader of the nomadic cattle-owning Fulani tribe. Raising the standard of revolt, he summoned his lieutenants to a *jihad*, a holy war. A clarion call to the Faithful, for whom death in battle would ensure instant admission to Paradise.

These Fulani leaders established a rule over the Hausa States of the region that was to last a hundred years, and it was upon their administrative capacity and authority that Sir Frederick Lugard, as he then was, relied in making them the instruments of his policy of indirect rule when, in 1900, the territory became a Protectorate under his governorship.

From Lagos there was a journey of more than four hundred

miles to the headquarters of the Niger Province at Minna, and thence by branch line to the curiously named town of Badeggi, fifteen miles from Bida, my final destination.

Bida was the headquarters of the principal administrative Division of the Province, and it was also the capital of what had been the ancient kingdom of Nupe, now classed as an Emirate and constituting one of the many Native Administrations which, headed by recognized chiefs, had been everywhere established. By virtue of language and racial type the Emirate was a recognizable and sizable piece of the vast mosaic of tribal communities which made up the pattern of Nigeria. Early contacts with British administration had provoked conflict at Bida, but except for the witness of one or two small pieces of cannon, discreetly relegated to an ornamental role, those days were no more than a memory in the minds of older men. The Emirate had a population of perhaps a hundred thousand, and the city itself might at one time have sheltered twenty thousand or more inhabitants; but in 1925 the number was certainly less. Under the *pax Britannica* the highways and byways were safe from marauders, the people were no longer afraid to live outside the towns, and the unrepaired gaps in the slowly crumbling walls that had been built for their protection gave sufficiently convincing testimony that fear had departed from the land.

Towns like Bida were nevertheless still important as centres of native industry and commerce, and as the administrative headquarters of Emirates. They were the home, not only of the Emirs and their courtiers and retainers, but of a watchful company who, for motives worthy and less worthy, clung to the skirts of royalty or wrote with their fingers in the dust of the palace precincts. Within them was the confraternity of tradesmen and craftsmen—butchers, blacksmiths, carpenters and wood carvers, makers of harness, riding boots and slippers, tailors and embroiderers, spinners, weavers and dyers, workers in glass and brass—whose livelihood lay in the vicinity of crowded market places.

All these, with a small floating population including traders and travellers—the terms were almost synonymous—and, now and then, a strolling jester displaying the rags and baubles of his mock regalia, or an itinerant band of professional hoe-dancers. Exciting performers these—to be seen sometimes at public festivals in their swirling skirts, casting their long-bladed implements high into the air, where they flashed like fountains in the sunlight, and catching them with incredible dexterity when they fell. Finally, like an open sore on an otherwise healthy body, there was the piteous residue of the needy and the afflicted.

The British presence was maintained by a small Government station under the charge of a District Officer and, since Bida was an educational centre, by a Provincial school and an Arts and Crafts school, each directed by a European Superintendent. The wife of the Arts and Crafts Superintendent and a missionary priest were the only other Europeans, whose number was thus increased by my arrival as assistant to the District Officer to the grand total of six. There was no doctor and there were no Government police. The enforcement of law and order throughout the Emirate was effected by the Native Administration through the District Headman and the *dogarai,* a kind of native constabulary, conspicuously uniformed in red gowns and turbans, who, with a sash and scimitar replacing the whip of hide they carried, would not have looked out of place in the Baghdad of Haroun al Raschid.

They combined their peace keeping duties with those of bodyguard to the Emir and were a colourful addition to his retinue on ceremonial occasions. The whip was a symbol of authority, used occasionally to warn or threaten, but never in my experience to chastise.

For aid in sickness the population relied sometimes upon the services of two or three trained African dispensary attendants, but usually upon native specifics and the will of Allah. Fully qualified medical aid was available in the person of the Provincial Medical Officer at Minna, to whom in dire circumstances a telegraphic summons could be despatched. Then, if the doctor was not visiting some remote part of the twenty thousand square miles of country over which his responsibility extended, or there was no critical situation demanding his presence at the Provincial hospital, and if a train happened to be running on the day when he was wanted, and the patient or patients could be reached speedily by rail or road, there was a chance that assistance might be obtained before it was no longer needed. The "ifs" were discouraging, but there was no undue despondency.

The Superintendent of Education left on leave within a day or two of my arrival, and the care of all local educational affairs devolved upon his colleague, Bob Carruthers. I cannot recall, if I ever knew, the extent of Carruthers' professional qualifications, but if there had been such a degree as Master of Crafts he could have taken it with honours; he was an expert at all things mechanical and a prince of handymen. He was an energetic Scot with a capacity for robust criticism, freely but never unfairly bestowed, which had earned for him the nickname of *"ruwan zafi"*, meaning "hot water"; but he was also a painstaking instructor demanding high standards, and his whole heart was in his work, though he was inclined to be impatient of the forms and observances of indirect rule and sceptical of the progress to be expected under such a system.

One day he came into my office in a state of some indignation and proffered a slip of paper, which I recognized as a voucher form used for authorizing payments from Native Administration funds for miscellaneous items. In principle, disbursements of this kind required the prior approval of the Emir in his capacity of Native Authority, but the vouchers were authenticated by the signature of the District Officer or, when expenditure on educational account was required, by the Education officer concerned. This practice was desirable in order to avoid or minimize mistakes and irregularities in the Native Treasury, where notions of financial control were, to say the least of it, little advanced; but as a positive indication of the validity of the transaction an addition had recently been made to the form by the insertion of the words *"da yardan Sarki"* (with the Emir's approval) immediately before the instruction to pay. This innovation, it appeared, had been too much for Carruthers' sense of practical realities. "Now what d'ye think of that?" he demanded—the question was clearly rhetorical—*"da yar-r-dan Sarki"*—emotion lent vigour to his r's—"and have I to go and ask permission from the Emir's palace every time I'm needing a set of piston rings or a wee spanner for the workshop?"

Daintree, the missionary, was a man of more placid disposition, sincere and selfless like all his kind, but somewhat overburdened, one felt, by his sense of vocation. He tended to speak
in a declamatory and didactic manner, even while conversing at
a sundowner, when, firmly clasping in one hand a glass charged
with some innocuous mixture, he would leave the other slightly
poised as if to emphasize by gesture the infallibility of a personal
conviction. I have sometimes wondered whether his mildly
pontifical manner was a form of escape from the lonely dedicated life he led. As Bida was a Mohammedan Emirate he was
not permitted to preach or proselytize at large—such was the
Government's policy—but he might receive and minister to those
who of their own free will resorted to his compound.

The Emir accepted his presence with good humoured
tolerance, and one or two others may have listened to him with
polite interest, but I doubt whether he made any converts to add
to the few faithful members of his little household. In the South,
Christian missions, after many years of devoted service, had an
inspiring record of achievement, but the onward march to the
North was yet to come. One would like to believe that earnest
labour, even in a field of such restricted opportunity, was its own
reward; for, matched with the call from the minaret, so solitary
a voice was no more than a whisper.

The District Officer, J. J. Emberton, was captain of our little
community. Calm and equable at all times, he ruled his small
kingdom with a mixture of firmness, tolerance, commonsense
and humour that made him liked and respected by everybody.
For me he was a kind and patient tutor, teaching not so much
by words as by example, and supplying just that combination of
discipline and friendship of an elder-brotherly kind that an
experienced and conscientious colleague was best able to dis-
pense.

On the morning after my arrival in Bida I was taken by
Emberton to the Divisional office and introduced to Mr.
Johnson. Although it was at Bida that I first met him, his
counterpart was to be found, courteous, patient and perservering,
the lonely inhabitant of a little world of brown-paper-covered
files and termite-infested correspondence registers, at any one of

fifty Divisional headquarters throughout the length and breadth of the territory. His name was not always Johnson; it might be Williams or, more stylishly, Faulkner or Broderick; but he was as unmistakable as the scarlet-coated sentries outside Buckingham Palace and, in his very different sphere, just as dependable. He was the clerk in charge of the Divisional office—of any Divisional office—an essential component of the Provincial Administration. He was more than a type; he was an institution.

He was always recruited from the South—from Lagos, possibly, or quite often from the Gold Coast—for in those days the Northern Provinces produced few Africans able to speak English and qualified to undertake responsible clerical duties. Convention demanded that on duty he should wear European dress. His trousers seldom lacked a crease, and his coat, folded over the back of a chair, could be quickly slipped on if he should be summoned to the presence of the District Officer. His striped shirt might be a little frayed at the cuffs, or even darned upon the shoulder; but his tie was neatly tied, and his shoes, selected from the illustrated catalogues of distant emporia, were immaculately polished.

Bida's Mr. Johnson spent most of his working hours sitting at a jaded typewriter, which rested on a somewhat rickety table usually wedged under one leg to prevent oscillation on the uneven floor of beaten mud. On the seat of his chair, to give the required elevation for the manipulation of his aged and temperamental machine, were placed a couple of weighty leather-bound tomes, which might have been volumes of the Domesday Book, and fulfilled much the same purpose. These mute but fact-laden witnesses to the researchful industry of an earlier generation of administrative officers were gradually disintegrating under the influence of dust and damp; but the information they contained soon became obsolete as population shifted, land was abandoned or rotated and wealth fluctuated, so it didn't matter very much. Government did not have much money to spare for the needs of out-station offices, and we could not afford to buy filing cabinets; but nests of empty four-gallon kerosene tins, laid sideways with tops removed, made convenient termite-resisting substitutes, and these receptacles also housed the stocks of printed forms of pay-

B

ment and receipt vouchers, as well as for the continuous supply of statistical returns that it was part of the duties of Mr. Johnson and his colleagues in superior places to prepare, despatch, receive, file and put away until such time as they too should yield to the dissolving influences of nature.

Mr. Johnson showed no signs of being depressed by the lack of up-to-date equipment. His demeanour was always correct and his outward bearing serious, as befitted the responsible position of one upon whom, during the frequent absences on tour of the D.O., depended the smooth running and efficient conduct of routine station business. Only in the privacy of his small two-roomed Government quarter would dress and deportment be relaxed. There, in the evening, clad in a loose garment, he would recline at ease in a deck-chair, dreaming perhaps of his distant country and the prospects of promotion, while his wife coaxed the fire under the stew-pot for the evening meal, and one or two plump semi-naked children played industriously with a rusty cigarette tin or hobby-horses contrived of cornstalks.

I have described him as lonely. Lonely, indeed, he must have felt in the remote bush stations where there were no compatriots to share his hours of leisure; for he was an expatriate among an alien community towards whom he had enough education to feel superior, and with whom there was no incentive or encouragement to fraternize—a community, moreover, in the eyes of whose own leaders he was a stranger of no standing, an *akawo* (accountant) imported by the white man to perform duties of secondary importance, a person of no influence, living in segregated accommodation, whose goodwill it would be irrelevant to cultivate, and with whom no social contacts were practicable or appropriate. That Mr. Johnson was able in such an unpromising atmosphere to secure the compliance of the humble many and at least the tolerance of the aristocratic few was a tribute to the tact and dignity that seemed to be native to his character.

As I look back it is not difficult to discover in those qualities, as in his sometimes bewildered, always earnest, application to duty, no less than in his personal habits of dress—the well tied tie and the highly polished shoes; yes, and the loose garment of his easy hours—a symbol, a coin of new mintage among changing currencies, and perhaps a notion both of the shape and the quality of things to come in a new Africa in which an emancipated and politically conscious Mr. Johnson must still labour to achieve his destiny.

Chapter III

A MOSLEM EMIRATE (2)

AFTER visiting Mr. Johnson we entered the D.O's own office. This was a long single-storied building, constructed, like the clerk's office and most of the Government houses of the station, of sun-dried bricks, and thatched with grass supported on poles cut from the raphia palm—an economical form of structure when the materials, free for the taking, were already at or within walking distance of the site, and a labourer's daily wage amounted to no more than a few pence. It consisted of one room with a mud floor, surrounded by a verandah where the Government messengers would sit, usually gossiping in what they hoped were inaudible tones, but with an ear cocked for a summons. Here, too, complainants and petitioners seeking an interview with the D.O. found shelter from the sun or rain while awaiting their turn. On the interior walls were nearly always one or two silent witnesses of all that went on, the beady-eyed little gecko lizards, surely made of india-rubber, that lay in wait for the hapless insect that should stray unsuspectingly within range of sudden seizure by a rapacious tongue.

We were greeted at our approach by an elderly, dignified person wearing a white gown and turban with, pinned to his breast, a badge in the semblance of a crown, the insignia of his rank; this was Mohammedu, the political agent. I thought the title somewhat grandiloquent for what seemed to be an office of comparatively humble status; but the political agent gave valuable service in an era during which the "political officer", as an administrative officer used to be called, felt the need in his dealings with African chiefs and their subordinates of an independent source of information which, whether biased or not, could assist him in assessing the value of plaints and submissions that might be coloured by fear, jealousy, ambition or greed. It was useful, too, to have the market gossip and to know that if some scandal arose he would have an opportunity of appreciating the many-sidedness of truth. The system had obvious possibilities of abuse, but I am sure that many political agents successfully resisted temptation. They were usually promoted messengers with long records of probity and faithful service, and they had more to lose from Government displeasure than from local unpopularity. At the same time they were loyal and constant in their devotion to their own chiefs.

An example of such devotion that I shall not forget was the behaviour on one occasion during my second tour in Nigeria of my own political agent, whose name was Ahmadu. He was a little burdened by the weight of years and flesh, but his grave and unrevealing countenance was appropriate to a guardian of confidences and a detector of intrigue, whose shrewd judgement had also to be a filter-bed of rumour. I arrived one evening at Wushishi, a town which gave its name to a small Emirate within whose boundaries was the old Protectorate capital of Zungeru, at that time headquarters only of a Division, of which I was in charge. The Emir of Wushishi was an old man; he had been sick for a long time and was believed to be dying. As I entered the town I looked in vain for his representative, whose little caval-cade always came out to welcome me on my arrival and conduct me to the rest-house. Such a neglect of the observance of customary civilities could be due only to some very exceptional circumstance. There was an unfamiliar, rather uncanny, silence. I missed the sounds and visible signs that at such an hour would have been usual—the pounding of yams in a mortar for the evening meal, children at play, perhaps an old man, staff in wrinkled hand, standing in a doorway. The one long street seemed deserted, as if the population had been called away.

I reached the rest-house and sat down to wait while my servants, who had travelled ahead of me, set about preparing a bath and a meal. Suddenly, with a dramatic impact upon the silence outside, there came a high-pitched drawn-out cry, as of a banshee: it was that of a woman wailing. It did not need the averted eyes of my steward-boy to tell me what had happened.

"See if you can find Ahmadu," I said to him.

A few minutes later Ahmadu was seated before me, waiting in silence for me to speak. His face was impassive, as always, and he betrayed no unusual emotion.

"Ahmadu," I began, using the idiom appropriate to the decease of royalty, "I fear the Emir is lost to us."

And then a surprising thing happened. The old man's composure vanished on the instant; he gave a great cry and tears sprang into his eyes. He beat his breast, and his body swayed in anguish. Embarrassed and ashamed of myself for what had obviously been too abrupt and maladroit an opening, I waited until he had recovered himself and then dismissed him with a few words of sympathy.

Somebody has been waiting during this disgression who is worthy of notice. This is the Emir's messenger, who makes a daily visit to the *Barriki* (a term recalling the early days when administrative headquarters included a military detachment) to read and deliver the Emir's replies to the D.O's requests and enquiries and to take note of any fresh business. His task is exacting and sometimes delicate, for he has to watch two political barometers and bear tidings that must not, if he can help it, be displeasing to either of those to whom he has to make his reports. He could be blamed by the Emir as a bad diplomat for anything that might anger the D.O., and, so he fears, be suspected of incompetence if the Emir should be unresponsive to some proposal that the D.O. has instructed him to communicate. But he has learned in the course of many interviews to interpret signs and choose his moments.

His name is Angulu, which means "vulture", and he received it, as I was afterwards told, because he was a youngest child, conceived when his mother thought to have no more children, and brought to the womb as unexpectedly as a vulture drops to an awaited feast from what seems to be an empty sky. He is a slightly-built man, judging by the slim fingers and thin wrists that emerge from the folds of his ample gown to rest lightly on the leather satchel that contains the letters from the Emir he will presently read and the pen with which he will record any enquiries or instructions. His dark, watchful eyes are alert and intelligent, and as he waits in the shade of the verandah for

Emberton to give him audience his mind is active. His thoughts, as in retrospect I imagine them, might be illuminating.

To what stratagems, he asks himself, will it be necessary to have recourse today? Perhaps, as the little judge has arrived, it will be a favourable moment to break the news that the Emir has not yet provided some local timber for the Arts and Crafts school whose delivery was promised for last week, and that a sum of £20, representing part of the town tax has disappeared on its way to the Native Treasury. (The timber has, in fact, been diverted to the Emir's palace to satisfy an urgent private priority, and replacements have been arranged; but this is information not to be divulged. As for the missing tax money, everybody knows—everybody that is except, it is hoped, the D.O.—that the responsible official has been under pressure from the Agent of the local branch of one of the principal trading companies to settle a long outstanding account for the exact sum involved, and has been threatened with legal proceedings if it is not immediately paid.) There may be something to be said for taking the bull by the horns. Presentable excuses can be tendered for the delay in delivering the timber, and it is unlikely, in any case, that the tax deficiency can escape discovery for long, so why not get credit for prompt disclosure? The big judge, who usually displays tolerably good manners, will surely not think it fitting to betray anger in front of his young new assistant. On the other hand, if nothing is said there is just the possibility that there will be time for Peter to be robbed in order to accommodate Paul, and things can be straightened out at leisure. Better, on the whole, to remain silent.

Anyhow, reflects Angulu, it is more than ever tiresome to be obliged to watch words, to parry awkward questions and to have to rack one's brains swiftly for acceptable replies in these days of the Fast. It is not yet noon, and already he is beginning to feel thirsty. Last year the rains broke before the beginning of Ramadan, and the air was cool. Now for many seasons this difficult moon will move through the most exhausting phases of the hot weather. The Christians are fortunate in not being required to observe such disciplines. But no, that is an impiety. They are obviously not a community who take their religion or their Prophet seriously. How else can it be accounted for that whereas every educated Moslem is versed in the teachings of the Prophet (Peace be upon him) and the tenets and practices of the Faith, the Christians are so uninstructed that no more than a mere handful of them—and they, apparently, judging by the way in which they are segregated from their fellows, of no esteemed caste or particular account—are qualified to expound doctrine and practise ritual, and so to claim the title of *Mallam*. Perhaps it is because the Christian paradise is so lacking in appeal that few seem to consider it worth while to qualify for admission. One has never heard that it offers any cup of purest wine, or any dark-eyed houris "chaste as hidden pearls" to be the loving companions of the faithful ones. Not that the white men seem to have much to do with women, anyway. Perhaps in that they show some wisdom.

"Angulu."

It is the voice of Mohammedu, clothed in the authority of the big judge, and the cry of "Lion!", with which Angulu responds, is an acknowledgement of that authority. He makes his entry, pausing at the threshold to perform the customary salutation to a superior, sinking down upon his heels, with body inclined slightly forward and finger tips resting on the ground, a courtesy that when observed, as it was, in Arab dress seemed to me to be more graceful and less obsequious than a bow.

Yes, there is the little judge, his pink cheeks fresh from the sea. Angulu smiles inwardly as he finds himself recalling the old superstition that these fair-skinned people came from the ocean. How strange they still look, these counsellors and rulers of princes, in their casual and frequently abrupt attire, and how careless they are of their dignity, perched uncomfortably like sacks on the precarious little platforms they call chairs, instead of composing themselves decorously upon the ground, as Nature intended.

Proceedings open with verbal salutations introduced by another "Lion!" as Angulu sits down in front of us.

"Greeting, greeting!" This from Emberton.

"Lion." These repeated "Lions." are a mark of deep respect.

"Greeting, greeting!"

"May God prolong your life !"

"Amen."

"The Emir salutes you."

"How is the Emir ?"

"We thank God." (i.e. for his health, which in these preliminary interchanges must always be assumed to be good. The Emir may, in fact, be far from well—even on the point of death—for all that such a customary enquiry will reveal. By the same convention at this stage all news is good news. Tidings of misfortune, if any, must wait upon the conclusion of the introductory courtesies.)

"May God prolong the life of the Emir."

"Amen."

It is time, at last, to get down to business. Emberton extends his hand towards me.

"Behold the little judge. He has come from England to help us."

It appears that, according to protocol, I too am a lion. My expression is probably more sheepish than leonine, but I try not to look self-conscious, and reply with a grave "amen" to Angulu's prayer for my long life.

There is a pause. Angulu fingers his satchel. It is for the D.O. to speak.

"That is well, Angulu. Now, touching this question of the timber that the Emir promised should be delivered ?"

"Lion." The epithet now expresses polite non-committal attention, and avoids a premature utilization of excuses, which would be wasteful if it should turn out that they are not necessary.

"The timber should have reached the school last week. It has not yet arrived."

The excuses, it seems, will be required. Angulu produces them. As the D.O. knows, there has been sickness in the neighbourhood. The men cannot work because their limbs tremble. Small beads of perspiration begin to appear on his brow, as if in sympathetic response to the mental picture of anguished labour unequal to a heavy load. Very soon, he continues, in a few days. . . . Emberton cuts him short.

B*

"I saw some loads of timber outside the Emir's palace yesterday. I am glad that, in spite of sickness, difficulties are being overcome."

Angulu sighs. This unfortunate habit of the big judge's of walking about in the town at unbusinesslike hours is a continuous embarrassment and may lead to serious trouble one day.

"Now I should like you to tell the Emir that I went to see the *Maaji* yesterday."

If Angulu's ears were visible beneath his turban we should see them prick up at this. The *Maaji* is the official in charge of the Native Treasury. What will come next? Can it be that Mohammedu, that wretched fellow. . . ? Angulu glances swiftly at Mohammedu, who is seated in the attitude of a Buddha in apparent contemplation of the palms of his hands. His face is quite expressionless.

"I told him," Emberton goes on, "that I thought surprise checks of the cash in the Treasury should be carried out more frequently. For the Emir's private information, I propose to make one the day after tomorrow. This, of course, is between the Emir and myself."

Angulu is relieved. He knows that Emberton knows that his intention to carry out a survey will not be kept secret. Meanwhile there are forty-eight hours in which to make such temporary financial adjustments as will prevent the tax deficiency from being revealed.

His suspicion that the D.O. knows the facts, and his surmise as to the source of that knowledge, are close to the truth; but Emberton's intention on this occasion is to give a warning. It was no part of the duty of an Administrative Officer to condone or ignore irregularities in a Native Administration, but one of the many lessons I was to learn was the need for patience in such matters.

It did not need the detective ability of a Sherlock Holmes to discover malpractices, and it was not difficult for an erring official to be replaced; but there could be no certainty that his successor would not in turn succumb to temptation, and if the whole machinery of native government was not to grind to a standstill under the burden of too exacting standards it was sometimes necessary to overlook venial offences, and occasionally, even with more serious lapses, to warn rather than to punish. The D.O's job, in short, was to play his disciplinary cards with discretion and to be sparing in the use of trumps.

With the sticky patches behind us, the rest of Angulu's business is soon disposed of. He withdraws after a valedictory obeisance, and with a not too friendly glance at Mohammedu, who is pensive and unheedful, mounts his horse and rides off, troubled by his increasing thirst and wondering how best to proffer to the Emir the slightly damaged fruits of the morning's diplomacy.

Almost obscured by the deep shade of the large fig tree outside the office is a sombre little group of petitioners or complainants, waiting patiently to tell their troubles to the D.O. Their turn has now arrived, and summoned by Mohammedu the first of them enters. He is a senile person, evidently infirm, who advances with uncertain steps, grasping for support the shoulder of a younger man, presumably a relative. After a good deal of short-sighted fumbling he produces from the recesses of a soiled gown, once white, which has become grey and, in places, threadbare with age, a creased and tattered strip of paper, which he passes to Mohammedu for Emberton's inspection. This is the notice of assessment, handed out by the District *Mallam* (scribe) to each taxpayer at the beginning of the tax-collecting season.

This tax, or tribute, was an annual liability, substituted for the numerous imposts that, before the days of British administration, had been extorted by the Fulani rulers from all who could be compelled to pay. It was based on estimates of the average profits of different wealth-producing classes: a craftsman, for example, or a butcher, usually gained more than a farmer, and a trader was, in most people's experience, better off than anybody else.

Each village was notified of its total liability, calculated in accordance with the numbers in the several categories of those liable to pay, but individual assessments were made by the Village Head and elders, who took account of private circumstances. It was a rough and ready system, but it worked well enough in a society to whom the complications of accounting were unknown, where capital was valued in terms of acres and livestock, and the size and level of granaries that could not be concealed were the nearest equivalent of a current account. At the annual re-count of population that was made for the purpose of arriving at a lump sum assessment the blind, aged and infirm were separately enumerated. These categories were exempted from taxation, and there were usually plenty of candidates for inclusion in them; but local knowledge and the vigilance of jealous neighbours were safeguards against feigned disabilities.

The assessment slip that Emberton now scrutinizes indicates liability for the payment of a sum of ten shillings, a figure somewhat higher than the average overall incidence for the Emirate. From all appearances it might well seem that this petitioner, who is obviously in poor shape, has a good claim to be exempted from further taxation altogether. And surely nothing but a keenly felt sense of injustice could give to so feeble a frame the strength to undergo the fatigue of a journey from his outlying village to the *Barriki*. But appearances can mislead. The old man may derive profit from some trading enterprise in which he is a sleeping partner. Or the notice he has received may have been given to him as the head of a compound in which there are able-bodied members of his household who have not been individually assessed. On the other hand there is the possibility of genuine error. The possibilities, in fact, are numerous and investigation is clearly called for. Emberton promises to examine the matter and makes a note to get a report through the Emir from the petitioner's district. The two take their departure: it may be only imagination that suggests that the step of the elder is less unsure as he leaves the office than when he entered it a few minutes earlier.

Now comes a woman who is a stranger to the neighbourhood. She is a visitor from the South, and a compatriot, it appears, of Mr. Johnson, who ushers her in and, since she speaks neither English nor Hausa, the *lingua franca* of the North, remains to act as interpreter. Her husband, she explains, is employed as a mason on some repairs to railway buildings at Badeggi. For some time she has been concerned about him. He is abstracted in his behaviour and does not seem to care about his food. He refuses to confide in her, and she is sure he is guarding some disturbing secret. She fears that he may be the victim of witch-craft.

This suggestion, startling as it sounds, is not one to be lightly discounted, and the story may contain the seeds of tragedy. Not so long afterwards, at Zungeru, I was summoned early one morning by an urgent message to view the gory remains of just such a temporary visitant to the station, who had chosen the "happy despatch" to secure release from his mental sufferings. I shall not forget the anguished face—the staring eyes and the lips drawn back in a snarl of agony—and the long knife clutched in the death-stiffened fingers. From enquiries arising from the inquest that, as coroner, I had to hold, it came to light that the dead man had been a carpenter, also in Railway employ, and had learned that enemies in his own country, in pursuance of some malevolent purpose, had placed a death spell upon him. This knowledge so preyed upon his mind that the fatal design was in fact accomplished. The Bida case had no such tragic conclusion. Careful enquiries revealed no grounds for suspecting any threat of bodily harm, and it seemed likely that if any spell had been cast it had been by a pair of dark eyes and not by any distant sorcerer.

By the time all our visitors were disposed of it was well past midday. Office hours in the North continued until 2 p.m., but a D.O's work was never done. Emberton went off to the Arts and Crafts school to see Carruthers about the repairs for which the misdirected timber had now been retrieved, and, left to myself, I examined the official correspondence that had arrived on the mail from Minna. It had already been seen by Emberton and passed to Mr. Johnson, who had filed it in brown-paper jackets and brought it back for attention. There was not very much : two or three letters from Provincial headquarters, and one from the Private Secretary to the Governor relating to baggage and supply arrangements for a visit that His Excellency proposed shortly to make to the Bida Division in the course of an extended tour.

Included in the correspondence from Minna was a copy, forwarded by the Resident for information and observations, of a circular letter from the Secretariat at Kaduna seeking information about the conduct of Fulani initiation ceremonies, which, according to certain reports reaching the Lieutenant Governor, had resulted in one or two instances in the infliction of serious injury to the neophytes. These ceremonies were part of the traditional practices of the "cow Fulani", who still pursued their nomadic way of life, moving across the countryside from river to stream with the procession of the seasons from days of thirst to days of flood, and sheltering at night in primitive grass huts surrounded by their cattle within the protection of a thorn hedge. The Fulani boys, after reaching puberty, had to undergo the ordeal of a severe whipping before they could claim adult privileges or their manhood could be recognized. To this test, endured with fortitude, the lads submitted themselves eagerly, and any attempt on humanitarian grounds to modify the punishment would have been likely to meet with scornful opposition by young and old alike. On the other hand, practices that had resulted or might result in permanent injury could not be ignored, and before deciding what steps should or could be taken the Government would consider it essential to obtain the fullest and most reliable evidence it could get.

From the letter from the Private Secretary, to which I turned finally, I learned that the Governor's transport would consist of two cars and three lorries, each of three tons capacity. The scale of baggage regarded as necessary for the maintenance of proper comfort and dignity on a tour of this kind was no concern of ours, but the weight of the vehicles to be used might create a few difficulties, since, except on the short link to Badeggi, there were no stretches of permanent all-season road in the Division. The roads built by the Native Administration were used hopefully for most of the year, but bridges, contrived out of bush timber and lacking both steel and masonry, which attenuated funds were inadequate to provide, were light, unsubstantial affairs, designed for easy replacement if inundated and swept away, and without any guaranteed safety factor. Our Native Administration vehicles were all in the light class, and it would be inconvenient, to say the least of it, if one of the visiting three-tonners, responding possibly to the stimulus of His Excellency's domestic equipment and the gubernatorial reserve of liquor, were literally to fall out of the convoy as one of our too frail carriageways collapsed.

The problem was solved by down to earth methods. We shored up the bridges of doubtful stamina with stout props of timber, and culverts were inspected by crawling beneath them in search of weaknesses. The Governor's visit passed off without misadventure, though one or two of the bridges sagged slightly at critical moments.

CHAPTER IV

A MOSLEM EMIRATE (3)

THERE are no street lamps in Bida, and shortly before dawn the city lies, silent and peaceful, guarded only by the celestial authority of the stars. As yet there is no silver in the East, but drifting through the unpeopled streets there comes a breath, too slight to stir the derelict and crumpled stalks of maize that straggle across the waste places here and there among the family compounds in which the people live. The first sound to break the silence of sleep is the high-pitched wail of a blind beggar groping through his endless night as he calls for alms in the name of Allah. At this hour there is none to pity him, unless it be the watcher in the minaret who, as soon as there is enough light to distinguish a white from a black thread, will call the Faithful from sleep to prayer.

Presently there is fire in the sky, and the morning star looks down upon the early stirring of man, woman, child and beast and the smoke of resurrected fires curling slowly upwards from the roof-tops. The first witness of the sun is a shiver of reflected light from the glossy surface of a courtier's gown. Its owner is one of those in attendance upon the Head of an outlying District, who has slept outside the city walls and risen early to reach the palace in obedience to a summons from his overlord. With a rustle of accoutrements and a scrambling and scuffling of unshod hooves the little cavalcade prances through one of the city gateways and turns towards the Emir's compound. On its way it passes the blind beggar and, at a word from the District Head, one of the company reins in his horse and turns, stooping from his saddle to drop one or two coins into the uplifted begging bowl. This little scene is watched only by a plum-bellied infant, which, having escaped momentarily from maternal surveillance, stands holding with one hand for better balance to the side of the doorway through which it has emerged and gazing with large serious eyes at the riders as they pass. Almost immediately the child's mother arrives in pursuit and with scolding accusations retrieves the wanderer, tucking it, naked and unprotesting, firmly under one arm before returning with it to domestic safety.

Very soon the pattern and tempo of daily life are everywhere resumed. Bida, and towns like it, did not, at the time of which I write, at all resemble any European city. There was a wide central thoroughfare, unpaved and plentifully strewn with pot-holes and depressions, which became little reservoirs of mud or dust according to the season. This "main street" provided frontages for the principal public buildings—the workshops, the Treasury and the Court House of the *Alkali,* or Judge,—adjacent to which on either side was a maze of alleys and passage-ways so narrow that only with difficulty would they permit the progress of a laden donkey assisted by slaps, prods and appropriate exhortations. The passages ran between the mud walls and fences of woven grass that formed the boundaries of the family compounds, for it was a wall or a fence, not a roof, that defined the limits of the living quarters of each family, and within the space so enclosed, keeping company with corn bins that looked like beehives and one or two massive water jars, each of which might have sheltered one of the Forty Thieves, would be several small round huts, adobe-walled with conical grass thatches, usually windowless and each with a single entrance.

Every one of these was allocated to a specific use, which might be sleeping, cooking or storage, and their number and dimensions depended on the size of the family and the wealth and dignity of its head. Where there was more than one wife—a not very general state of affairs despite the Moslem sanction of polygamy, for young brides were certainly worth their weight in cowries, the ancient currency, if not in gold—in such case the senior lady of the establishment, the "mother of the house" as she was called, must be provided with separate accommodation and all the consideration due to her superior status. Ingress to a "house" of any consequence would be through another round hut with entrances back and front, but without doors and providing against intrusion no defence greater than that required to preserve privacy :

there were sometimes cases of petty thieving, but burglary and housebreaking had no place in the catalogue of conventional crime. This entrance-hut—the Hausa *zaure*—was used during the day for repose and gossip, and at night, if needed, as a guest chamber for visitors.

Forming a kind of city centre was the market-place, upon which converged daily most of the human traffic of the capital and its vicinage. Not a mart for the easing of heavy purses and the satisfaction of extravagant tastes : here were no costly stuffs, no rich ornaments, no exotic delicacies; no cloth of gold, no silver vessels, no "jams meticulously jarred", nothing at all that had travelled any golden road. But, spread on grass mats that took the place of market-stalls, were all the fruits of the soil and the crude yet vigorous examples of the craftsmen's disciplines. Here were maize on the cob, shading from ochre to primrose; grains of millet, a rusty brown, sold by the "cash bowl" in heaped half-pennyworths; the elephant-coloured yam that took the place of the potato, and the sweet potato tasting like chestnuts; the ground-nut cakes and the sweetmeats; small red, rather bitter, tomatoes and long leathery beans, with okra and egg plant, used one and all to impart flavour and piquancy to the staple dish of guinea corn porridge. Here were the butchers' stalls, whose ineffectual overlay of muslin strips did little to impede the appetite of blood-hungry flies and bluebottles. Close-by were gobbets of fat-spluttering meat grilling on a miniature palisade round a charcoal fire, and, not far removed, calabashes of Fulani butter, with others of wild honey gathered from hives of hollowed bark. Lilliputian mounds that looked like heaps of cigarette ash were piles of powdered antimony, favoured by the women as an eye cosmetic, and, laid out alongside them, were small imported looking-glasses, gimcrack and rubbishy pieces, wherein to contemplate bedizened lids and lashes : the same display included necklaces of large blue beads made in Bida from discarded bottles.

In another direction was an assembly of four-legged stools, large and small, carved out of solid blocks of timber and decorated with cunningly chiselled patterns : these also were a Bida speciality, and, next to them, were farm implements—hatchets and short-handled hoes designed for use in a stooping posture. Elsewhere were bridles, riding boots and slippers of dyed leather, green and red. Last and least, minute bundles of three or four matches tied together with strands of wool and sold to those who could afford no more than a tenth-of-a-penny piece to possess the gift of Prometheus. All this presented to the eye in impressionistic contrasts of light, shade and colour beneath a pallid, almost cloudless, sky, drained of its azure by the heat and dust : a sea of shining faces of every hue from copper to chocolate, with once in a while the unnatural leprous-looking countenance of an albino : a pattern of humanity without outline or definition, but animated, like children in a crowded playground, by the freedom and vivacious drama of the moment. Heard from a distance, the babel that arose from this restless concourse was like the tumult of a river in spate, and from streets near-by flowed tributary streams and rivulets of sound—the ring of iron on anvils, the hammering of brass, the incessant pounding of goatskin bellows suggesting a rapid beat of muffled drums, the dry cough of adze on undressed timber, the cudgelling of newly dyed cloth to instill it with its fashionable gloss.

To a city already awakened to such scenes of industry I accompanied Emberton two days after he had given warning to Angulu of his impending inspection of the Native Treasury. This focal institution, known in the Arabic phrase as the *"Beit ul Mal"*, was housed in a substantially walled building containing a strong room for the custody of the large proportion of Native Administration funds that was held in cash. Into its coffers was received, with only very occasional losses by way of evaporation, the flow of tribute from the Districts and the *jangali,* or cattle tax, levied upon the Fulani herds. These payments, or rather what remained of them after the Government had taken its half share, formed the bulk of the Native Administration revenue, from which were defrayed the salaries of the Emirate officials and the other costs of the services they administered. In wealthy Emirates, such as Kano and Katsina, each of whose populations exceeded a million, the Emir drew the princely emolument of £5,000 a year; but in Bida the stipend was fixed at a more modest figure. Such sums seemed large in comparison with our own by no means ungenerous salaries, but the calls on an Emir's privy purse from relatives, retainers and hopeful hangers-on were as numerous as they were incalculable. At the lower end of the salary roll were the *dogarai*, who had to be content on only thirty shillings a month, a sum not so insignificant as it sounds when one recalls that an average family could subsist adequately, if somewhat monotonously, on the staple diet of millet porridge and vegetables for about threepence a day.

The office of *Maaji* was usually filled by a venerable person, selected for probity and public standing rather than for any special proficiency in book-keeping—a qualification which, indeed, few could claim—but in Bida at that time the incumbent was a comparatively young man, who some years earlier had been a star pupil at the Provincial school. To a flair for figures he added an elegance of manner and a distinctive taste in dress, which on that occasion revealed itself in a silky turban and a gown of saffron coloured brocade whose billowing folds would have furnished material for the presentation dress of a debutante. Born of another race, and into a different age and environment, he might have figured as an exquisite of the Regency about to make his bow at the Court of St. James's, or offering a gold and enamelled snuff-box to an intimate of Beau Brummel.

As was to be expected, the inspection of the Treasury revealed no irregularities. Shillings and two-shilling pieces were poured out onto tables in clouds of metallic dust from bags, each containing one hundred pounds worth of coin, and laboriously counted into stacks, which were then arranged into wooden trays. Serpentine coils of pierced nickel pennies and halfpennies were then unwound for our examination and a count was made of the boxes that contained the "tenths". Since these had been sealed by the West African Currency Board they could be accepted at reputed value. Finally a large leather-bound volume, in whose dog-eared and ink-stained folios the daily receipts and disbursements were recorded, was produced for initialing. This was the cash book, neatly ruled off and balanced to the exact amount of the cash we had counted. It was almost too good to be true.

Our next appointment was with Justice in the person of the *Alkali*, who, as Judge of the Native Court, administered the

Sharia, or sacred law of Islam. The Court House was a large square chamber with a lofty arched ceiling and floor raised a few inches at one end to form a judge's bench; but in all that here took place there were few resemblances, either physical or in concept and procedure, to an English court of law. The Law was not, for the Moslem, a corpus of man-made statutes superimposed upon a base of ancestral tradition, but a revelation of the will of God in the words of the Creator, communicated to the Prophet by the angel Gabriel, and subsequently amplified and embellished by the schools of jurisprudence in accordance with traditions established by the acts and judgements of Mohammed and his immediate followers. The code thus formulated was no narrow one; it was an encyclopedia of religious and civil deportment for the instruction of all and sundry concerning every detailed aspect of public and domestic life. Here were the canonical injunctions to prayer, fasting, alms-giving and pilgrimage. Here were the punishments for theft, brigandage, homicide and rebellion, and the prohibition of wine, betting and the use by males of personal jewellery. Here was guidance in the distribution of slaves and booty taken in war. Here were the rules for marriage, divorce and inheritance; authority for the organization of camel races, and the use of toothpicks or the perfuming of the mouth, so as to give to prayers a sweet odour.

The law of evidence, as expounded in the treatises of jurisprudence, was no less elaborate, and was intimately concerned with the capacity of a witness, who might be objected to on the grounds, among others, that he lived with a son who drank wine, that he was distracted and looked about him at prayer, or that he traded in flutes and drums. It is doubtful whether the *Alkali* of Bida took heed, or was even aware, of the greater number of these precautionary niceties; but of one form of procedure, designed to obtain settlement of a dispute when witnesses were lacking, extensive use was made. This was the taking of the Koranic oath, administered to a defendant in cases in which a plaintiff could not produce evidence to substantiate his allegations. If in such event the defendant swore by the Koran that he was blameless or had no liability the case was dismissed. There was much virtue in this simple procedure. In a society in which the sacred book was held in highest veneration, and belief in the divine wrath that could fall upon the transgressor was correspondingly firm, perjury was not an offence to be committed lightly. If the defendant had any scruples or mental reservations he might elect to "turn the oath", as the phrase went, by requiring the plaintiff to swear to the truth of his depositions. It would then be for his accuser to do a little conscience searching: if the plaintiff accepted the challenge judgement was given in his favour; otherwise the matter went no further.

Even with the convenience of such an effective short cut to adjudication the *Alkali's* task, under such a complex and far-reaching code, must have called for remarkable feats of memory and a superabundant skill in separating the grain of truth from the chaff of circumstance. The Judge, according to the jurisconsults, must be gifted with sagacity and a mature mind, and should be apt in the interpretation of the law and in deducing its application; he should be conscientious; possessed of means (since poverty too easily allows itself to be tempted); of well known and respected family; free from debt; and in his character dignified, calm and kind; but not too sharp or searching of eye, lest he be led into judging people by their physiognomies.

I do not know how many of these attributes the *Alkali* of Bida possessed; but as he came forward to greet us in his rather drab gown and turban he certainly looked dignified and calm, and I suspect that beneath his rather serious judicial aspect, heightened as it was by a pair of silver-rimmed spectacles and a flowing grey beard, there was a sufficient store of benevolence to mix with wisdom and sagacity. Accompanying him was an elderly assistant, clasping not without difficulty beneath one arm a volume so capacious that it might have embosomed all the doctrines of the Schools, but was in fact the Court Record book, in which the essential particulars of each cause were entered, to be eventually transcribed into the judicial archives. Most of the *Alkali's* work was concerned with cases of debt and divorce—the latter unhappily frequent and brought almost always by forsaken wives. There was little serious crime, and the few cases that occurred were usually dealt with by the Emir's court.

The *Alkalis'* courts of Nigeria, for all that they differed so widely in character and procedure from the courts of summary jurisdiction to which, in our own judicial system, they were the nearest approach, were an efficient institution, respected by Moslem and pagan alike; and nowhere more clearly than in the everyday working of these courts were the authority and discipline of Islam revealed. Islam, in fact, was still enlarging and consolidating its realm, advancing unobtrusively into pagan areas like the flickering rim of a bush fire that, after its first devouring onslaught, creeps forward almost unobserved to win new ground, sending up here and there a slithering tongue of flame as, one by one, fresh tussocks of grass and thickets of undergrowth are captured and transmuted. The missionaries who spread the Faith were armed neither with sword nor oratory; they carried no tracts and were indeed unconscious of their role; they were the Hausa folk who, ever ready to explore new fields of enterprise, came first with bags of salt or beads to trade for shea nuts or the seeds of the locust-bean tree, and then, with the permission of the local pagan chiefs, to farm the land. In this way small family settlements took root; and these became the nuclei of larger communities, including members of local tribes who were attracted by the comparative prosperity of the newcomers, the dignity of their dress and the superior standards of their way of life. And so, little by little, the fetish huts fell into ruin, the sacred groves grew lonely and the clay idols were forgotten. Ancestral voices grew fainter as the men exchanged their goatskins and monkey fur for gowns of homespun, and the women made dresses to replace the bunches of leaves or the girdles of beads with which simple adornments their modesty had hitherto been clothed.

It was an understandable transformation, and it was not difficult to appreciate why the die seemed so often to be loaded in favour of Islam and against Christianity. It was, after all, a simple creed —"there is no God but Allah, and Mohammed is his Prophet"— invested with no miraculous clothing, and unvexed by bewildering metaphysical dogmas. "I am commanded to serve Allah and to associate none with Him. To Him I pray and to Him I shall return." Here was the Koranic command to surrender to God— the simple meaning of the word "Islam". There was, too, the explicit clarity of the rules relating to prayer : no Mohammedan could ever be in any doubt as to how he should say his prayers, or the times at which to say them. It was a religion for simple hearts and single minds; a coat of many colours clothing the nakedness of the barren places and the poverty of the paganism that it overlaid; therefore comformable and sympathetic to the pagan tradition of the Africa it came to conquer. In effect, a passport of entry into a new and better world in which the believer could become one of a classless brotherhood, whose gift was dignity and whose essential discipline was submission to the divine will. Christianity had messages of hope, comfort and compassion; but who was there to show a way that all might follow? Not the missionary societies, selfless, devoted, ardent as their field workers might be. When not only every high-road but every little alley of Islam was named and signposted, how could the uninstructed expect to discover in that other country a straight and narrow path whose destination might be clear enough but as to whose precise route there was so little agreement among the many who preached salvation. Roman and Anglican, Methodist, Plymouth Brother, Seventh Day Adventist, a score of others: good men and faithful to their calling, but where was the evidence of their unity or their brotherhood? What code of conduct, what word of purpose did they recite together?

Our last visit that morning was to the Emir's palace. This was an out-sized example of the mud-wall type of compound, covering perhaps an acre of ground. In front of the high prison-like walls was open space enough for the gathering of large crowds and the manoeuvres of the scores of horsemen who, robed in all the finery that purses or their credit could command, came on the great Moslem festivals from all parts of the Emirate to join in the general celebrations at the capital. The most spectacular of these was provided by the District Heads when with their mounted retainers—one party following another—they galloped up with raised and brandished spears flashing in a torrent of light and colour to salute the Emir as, clothed in white robe and turban with a burnous of white silk, he sat enthroned on a dais before the palace gates, attended by trumpeters, each with his eight-foot-long *kakaki,* an instrument resembling a coach horn, which might be sounded only with royal consent.

The massive gates, which gave the sole entry into the palace precincts, opened into a lofty chamber of solid construction combining the functions of guard-room, waiting-room and news centre, from which, nicely compounded of fact, rumour and gossip, emanated the nearest equivalent of what might be described as an unwritten daily Court Circular. Here, in the bad old days, would have been found that influential intermediary without whose aid no petitioner for royal grace or favour could hope for audience, an official known, appropriately enough in the Hausa term, as *kofa,* meaning "door"— a door that would open more smoothly on well oiled hinges.

We were met on arrival by the *Sarkin Dogari,* the Chief of Police, whose hurried and almost belated emergence, with one hand completing the adjustment of a gaily striped turban, was due, as I now suspect, to the sudden interruption of a noonday interlude of unofficial repose. Emberton gave a message to be conveyed to the Emir, and we were at once conducted through the entrance and across a courtyard to a detached building with a whitewashed interior, furnished only with a carpet and two chairs—evidently an audience chamber. I looked around me as we made this brief journey for signs of the daily life of the palace, but there was little in the few scattered huts and unpeopled space surrounding them to satisfy my curiosity: no Arabian Nights glamour; no splendid courtiers or obsequious minions; no passage of messengers on mysterious errands; no veiled countenances or covert glances; no backstage secrets of any kind; not even a trace of the misguided timber that should have reached the Arts and Crafts school. The general atmosphere was disappointingly drab and dreary.

The Emir arrived almost immediately and, after shaking hands somewhat flabbily, seated himself on the carpet in front of us. I confess that for a few moments my sense of dissappointment persisted. I had thought perhaps to find a patrician character with features cast in the mould of ancient Rome; or else, possibly, some Doge-like personage aristocratically apparelled in the robes of his authority.

The Etsu Nufe—such was his traditional title—was not in the least like either of these mental pictures. Broad shouldered, heavily built, almost clumsy in his comportment, with coarse, blunt features bearing no trace of lineal refinement, and attired in a plain white gown without embroidery, he might have passed as an ex-champion of the prize-ring had it not been for something inscrutable in his eyes and a certain dignity, as of one accustomed to command, that was, if anything, accentuated by his weighty carriage and brusque, unstudied movements. And as the interview proceeded—it was confined to conventional civilities and some words of introduction—I soon became conscious of a concealed power and a reserve of authority that gained rather than lost potency from the unostentatious reception accorded to us and the unaffected manners of our host.

Unendowed as the Emir might be with physical attractions, he was, as I was quickly to discover, able to inspire loyalty and command obedience among the thousands that he ruled. And this devotion was spontaneous. One day I accompanied him on an informal visit to the market. At every point the crowd surged forward, surrounding him with eager, smiling faces, while the babel of chaffering tongues suddenly changed into delighted shouts of recognition and excited cries of "Lion." "Lion."

Such was the Etsu Nufe, an African chief in the old tradition, one of the many by means of whose intelligence and administrative ability Lugard's policy of indirect rule was being put to the test.

Chapter V

DISGUISES FOR DAEMONS

A S I look back to Nigeria from the farther end of the Valley
of the Shadow I see a country of two disciplines. One is the
law as established by statute and custom, the foundation of the
administrative fabric. The other is a dictatorship of natural
forces and daemonic powers, not susceptible to rational description, whose instruments are wonder, awe and superstition, with
prescriptions also for mirth and festivity, for the regime is
not hostile to merriment, and, for those with eyes to read them,
many proclamations of beauty. In some areas, and particularly
in the realm of custom and among pagan peoples, the two
spheres of governance approach or overlap; but from the
unwritten codes fantasy is never very far away.

In those days of the twenties and the thirties of which I write
the cruelties and terrors of the past were no longer remembered,
and the tragedies of the future lay far beyond the horizon. But
superstition was not dead, and it was the fear of supernatural
sanctions that enabled the rulers of the primitive order to maintain their authority. Among them, however, there was one at
least who had no covenant with fear or punishment. A blithe
spirit, who often accompanied me on my journeys through the
bush, she was undoubtedly a dryad. She kept herself invisible,
but in the season of blossom I knew by the white robes she left
upon the many flowering trees that I was not far from her
presence. At other times she would call upon the birds to assist
her in the stage management of her sylvan affects : the cock
weaver-bird in courting array of navy blue and scarlet; the
roller in dress of pale blue with russet trimmings; a flock of
parrots streaking through the tree-tops like a flight of green-and-
red-feathered arrows. And larger birds as well: the hornbill
gliding in awkward undulations, like a schoolboy's paper dart,

as if over-weighted by its long pendulous beak; a bustard running swiftly with wings flapping to gather speed enough to lift its twenty-pound weight into the air; and herons, solitary by the banks of streams and in reedy swamps or, during the breeding season, in numerous and noisy company among the branches of a favoured nesting tree. Often, towards the hour of sunset, she indulged her noisy mood, this woodland sprite, by conducting choruses of the elegant little laughing doves, blue-grey and copper-bronze in colour, that seemed almost to shout their clamorous cu-cu-cu-*coo*, cu-cu-cu-*coo*, timed like the letter V in the Morse alphabet, or the opening bars of Beethoven's Fifth Symphony, in a continuous cascade of defiant jubilation. And then, as I approached, she would command them to flight, and there would be a beating of wings, charmingly described in the metaphor of an obscure Hausa poet as the joyous hand-clapping of young maidens running into the forest. But as the light faded she would grow weary of this sport and wander about among the trees, changing their form and drawing away their colour, or draping them in mist, so that they became ethereal and mysterious like Chinese paintings, and sometimes fancifully shaping the tops that rose above their fellows as silhouettes against the darkening sky into all sorts of quaint or eerie likenesses : a swan, a dancing bear, an old man leaning on a stick, one of Snow White's seven dwarfs, the Devil talking confidentially to somebody in a top-hat. . . .

Among the invisible powers there was one who had great authority and spoke a language that all understood. This was a genius whose signal was the sound of distant drums. Drums beating for the communal hoeing of fields and the clearing of grass-encumbered highways; drums to advertise the killing of meat on market day; drums for dancing and merry-making beating with endless repetition through the night; drums for death and lamentation.

Mysteriously related to the genius of the drums was a spirit of like disposition who ranged the country of the pagan tribes and spoke to them in a language of immense antiquity. I remember well the first occasion on which I became conscious of his spell. It was during a tour I spent in the Province of Adamawa, a remote part of the territory some hundred miles up the River Benue from its junction with the Niger, and close to the boundary with the Northern Cameroons. The Province had a large pagan population, including the Verre tribe to whom I paid a visit shortly after my arrival.

The Verre country lay in the hills just beyond the southern limits of the Benue valley, and only a day's march from the river. The hills were not very steep, and the valleys were intensively cultivated for the raising of a species of dwarf millet that grew well in poor and shallow soils. Since the crop seldom attained a height of much more than twelve inches it gave to an enclosed landscape a grassy aspect that was not at all tropical in appearance and, by a stretch of the imagination and the addition of a few olive trees, might almost have been part of a Mediterranean setting. What could, in fact, at a distance have been mistaken for olive groves proved on closer view to be the walls of spiny euphorbia that protected the numerous clusters of small round dwelling huts from the unhindered intrusion of man, beast or weather. It was a closely populated neighbourhood, and at frequent intervals our party was awaited by a compact group of men and women, drawn up with almost military precision, who, to welcome us, burst into song as we approached. They were almost naked, and their heads, whose tight curls were plastered thickly with red mud, looked like nothing so much as unripe blackberries. But if their appearance was barbaric their singing was strange and lovely. Their resonant voices rose and fell in eddies of sound that at one moment were like the sigh of wind in grass or the hush of surf on empty sands, and at another swelled into a torrent of full throated harmony. Their song was universal and ageless; it belonged to the mountains and to the sea, to sunrise and twilight, to the night and to the stars. It could have been a hymn to Bacchus when the harvest was rich and golden with the fulness of the year. Woven into these ritual choruses came the sonorous sounding of a hartebeeste horn. A haunting, rather sad sound it seemed : a sound to stir some vague nostalgic longing, or perhaps, heard suddenly in the silence of a sacred grove, a panic dread.

I should not be surprised if the spirit who lingered here were none other than the great God Pan himself, dispossessed so many centuries ago of his Arcadian groves and seeking refuge among the timeless hills of unawakened Africa.

Then there were the elemental spirits. One was Fire: his ceremonial fanfare was like the crackle of musketry, and his grant of dignity a sea of crimson surging through the yellow grass; but, after he had passed, the bright stubble still remained golden among the ashes, as if to prove that beauty was indestructible; and very soon young green shoots thrust upwards from the blackened soil, and one saw that there had been, not a holocaust but a cleansing and a preparation for the renewed offering of Earth's unceasing gifts. Then came Rain, supreme arbiter of growth, by the measure of whose indulgence, sparing, prodigal or capricious, the bounty of Earth herself must be apportioned. Small wonder that among supernatural powers claimed by pagan chiefs those of Rainmaker were held in utmost veneration. And after Rain came Harmattan, a dry wind from the desert to the North, that for the appropriate season commanded the changes in the daily scene. Every stream that during the rains had been a torrent or a cataract dwindled to a chain of motionless pools, or dried up altogether; the long grass became an investment of bronze and, finally, of gold; and in the villages the granaries of millet were full to the brim with the harvest. Mornings at first were crisp and invigorating, the noonday temperature was agreeable, and at night it was pleasant, when on trek, to sit out of doors in the rosy glow of a log fire, conscious of the presence of the wild creatures that animated the surrounding darkness and of the quiet, eternal stars overhead. But as the year moved on the days grew hotter, and the landscape was shrouded in a grey haze of dust that softened the fierce glare of the sun on the parched earth, while it invaded the throat and nostrils and irritated the eyes. Then came Fire again, hastened by the Fulani who wanted early grazing for their cattle, and the cycle was repeated.

I doubt whether the railway engine, that overworked bullock of the anthropological lectures, deserved the status of a daemon; but, together with its attendant coaches and waggons, it was certainly held in popular esteem, not more for its magical tractive powers than for the opportunities it provided for social distraction and free entertainment. By 1925 the Nigerian Railway was no longer an innovation in the areas it served: it had become part of the pattern of native life. Popular for its original purpose with the Hausa traders of the North, many of whom made long journeys to sell or exchange their produce or home crafts in profitable markets, it came also to be used as a pedestrian highway through extensive tracts of country where it was easier, as well as being a discouragement to the now rarely encountered highwayman, to walk beside the sleepers in a wide sylvan corridor, cleared of trees and high undergrowth, than to follow a narrow, tortuous and frequently overgrown path through the bush. New words and expressions had come into the Hausa language to describe the railway and its appurtenances. The permanent way was "the long metal", or simply a single word expressing the idea of length. A railway bridge was called "girder", the English word. A train was a "land canoe": doubtless its smooth, gliding motion, observed at a distance when wheels and undercarriages were obscured by vegetation or long grass, was responsible for this adaptation. (In later years an aeroplane was known as a "sky canoe".)

But it was towards the bush railway station that, upon the comparatively infrequent arrival of a train, all steps were turned. On those occasions the station precincts became a market-place and a social centre for the neighbourhood, which turned out—man, woman, child and infant—to derive what pleasure or profit it could from the brief presence of the "up" or "down through mixed", that made its journey twice a week in each direction. This designation meant that the train carried both goods and passengers, and that, barring engine failure, derailment, washouts on the line (not infrequent during the rains), or obstruction due to other acts of God or man, it would eventually arrive in one piece at its final destination of Kano or Lagos. The waiting passengers, patiently seated on the ground in the cleared space that took the place of a platform, were usually the most composed of the expectant crowd, which one or two of the local *dogarai* would endeavour to control. A task executed, in the absence of any railed enclosure with more zeal than confidence of success; for the people had come to enjoy themselves; they had no cinema, no village cricket, no Punch and Judy show, so they came to the railway station.

One such occasion recalls itself as I write. The police are pursuing with cries of wrath, and whips raised to threaten evasive shoulders, an elusive covey of small urchins whose trespass has been too brazen to disregard and whose capture and expulsion would temporarily restore the dignity of flouted authority. But while the Law is minatory and ineffectual, officialdom seems able to exact some sort of obedience as it emerges in the person of the stationmaster, dressed in no little brief authority with brass-buttoned khaki jacket and badged cap of office. He steps forward to the edge of the track and imperiously waves back those who have ventured too close for safety to the path of the clanking and snorting locomotive that, followed by three passenger coaches, a brake van and one or two open trucks, now enters the station limits and a few moments later comes to a standstill, hissing thirstily beneath the dripping hose of a water tank.

All attempt to impose further restraint is now in vain. Confusion reaches its climax in a babel of laughter and shouted conversation, punctuated by excited cries of recognition as friends press forward to greet alighting travellers. Tin trunks, corded boxes, large enamelled basins piled with pots and pans and tied up with squares of cheap printed cotton, rolled-up grass sleeping mats bulging with the secrets of the wardrobe, calabashes, gourds, provisions for the journey wrapped in leaves, a dozen other petty accessories of travel are lowered from or hoisted into doors and windows while their owners climb down to mingle with the noisy, gesticulating throng or clamber up to claim vacated seats. Strolling by in the finery of a new white gown, whose ample breast and wide, flowing sleeves are futuristically decorated with green and yellow embroidery, comes a tall figure that might have stepped from an illustrated catalogue of native dress. One might be excused for mistaking him for a prosperous merchant, or perhaps a Native Administration official of some standing; but he is, in fact, the head steward of an Administration Officer's household, who, while off duty, has exchanged his working attire for go-to-market clothes to meet friends and hear the news from all and sundry. Close behind this elegant person is an African about whose occupation and origins it would be difficult to make any kind of conjecture, but whose remarkable appearance illustrates the perverse effect of a flamboyant taste in dress on a racy attempt to keep abreast of the times. This reveals itself in khaki shorts, a green shirt open at the neck, a dilapidated dark blue schoolboy blazer, brown sandals and socks, suspenders and a canary coloured cap that would do justice to any jockey. Surprisingly, he greets the stationmaster as an old friend, and the two walk together for a short distance hand in hand like children.

Next come women, Nupe and Yoruba from the middle-Niger belt, striding gracefully from the hips with the superb carriage that an African woman acquires from balancing a pitcher or a bundle on her head as she walks along. They squat on the outskirts of the crowd and set down their merchandise of comestibles; for this is the bush equivalent of the refreshment room. Here are bananas and plantains, ground-nut cakes, sweetmeats compacted of seeds of the locust-bean tree with honey, and smoke-blackened slabs of dried fish, a delicacy I never sampled but which, judging by its widespread popularity, must have tasted much better than it looked. Farther on is another group : Fulani women these, easily recognizable by their light complexions, slender, graceful build and long plaits of hair, resembling sticks of liquorice, that fall saucily to their shoulders. They display their calabashes of butter or of sour milk with the cooked balls of guinea-corn flour that are moistened in the milk and eaten with it. Buying and selling are everywhere accompanied by the customary by-play of shrugging shoulders, deprecating gestures of the hand and little bursts of ironical laughter, but all with the greatest good humour, until the transaction concludes with the passing of a few nickle coins. When there are no more customers the women replace upon their heads whatever remains unsold, rise carefully from their squatting posture in order not to disturb a delicate balance, adjust the lengths of cotton fabric or dyed homespun that serve not only the combined functions of skirt and bodice but also to bind to their backs the silent large-eyed babies by which they are always encumbered, and with a skilful shrug of the buttocks shift

c

the unprotesting infants into more comfortable positions as they move off.

A hand-bell is rung loudly and vigorously. A cheerful person with a bare torso and skirtlike garment tucked in at the waist, who seems to be some sort of assistant to the stationmaster, doubles up in hilarious appreciation of a facetious passenger's parting jest. As the train slowly gathers speed little naked boys run along beside it, turning cartwheels. An unwary hen scurries with terrified squawks to the asylum of the nearest undergrowth. The through-mixed is once more upon its way.

CHAPTER VI

DISTRICT OFFICER

I HAVE sometimes been asked to which of the numerous over-seas posts I held in the course of my service I became most attached. It was not a question to be answered without a good deal of reflection. One had to weigh frustrations, anxieties and disappointments against the satisfaction of successful achievements, the consequences of mistakes one had made against the value of the lessons one had learned from them, and, as far as Nigeria was concerned, the necessity, imposed by climate, for lengthy periods of separation from wife and family against the call of a country whose every unbeaten track led to the discovery of something rare and strange. But, judging as dispassionately as I can, I would affirm that it was in Nigeria that, despite the problems created by climate, I spent some of my most rewarding years.

Rewarding especially in two ways: and firstly in terms of responsibility. It is true that in other territories as I gradually ascended the ladder of promotion I was called upon to make decisions that covered increasingly wide fields of public policy, but nowhere more than in Nigeria as a D.O. in substantive charge of a Division was I more completely my own master. In the senior secretariat posts to which I was later to be appointed— Colonial Secretary of Barbados, Colonial Secretary of Gibraltar, and Chief Secretary to the Government in what was then Northern Rhodesia—I was, for many of my working hours, a prisoner within four walls, my call to action was a trayful of files or a pile of despatch boxes, and my daily dealings were comprehended in discussions round a table or in a flow of words directed to patient stenographers.

Even as a Governor, though I was freed from much of the tyranny of the desk, my movements had to be comformable to the necessity to preside over meetings, to attend the public functions and social gatherings at which the Governor's presence was customary, and for the entertainment of visitors who might expect to receive his hospitality. In the Nigerian bush there were no such distractions. No exhibitions, no flower shows, no school speech-days and prize givings. The only public celebrations were the annual Moslem festivals. Instead of despatch boxes there were only Mr. Johnson's brown-paper-covered files, and the contents of an incoming mail could usually be digested in half an hour and disposed of in a morning. There were certainly plenty of meetings, but they consisted of discussions with the Emir at mutually convenient times or in the villages with Village Heads and Elders.

Of course there were rules, regulations and standing orders with which I had to comply, as well as principles and precedents by which I had to be guided, but none of these laid down a time-table, and within reasonably broad limits the interpretation of these codes and practices was a matter for my discretion and commonsense. In the existing circumstances it could not well have been otherwise. At Zungeru, the headquarters of the Division of which I was in charge during the whole of my second tour, communication with Provincial headquarters was, owing to the proximity of the railway, comparatively speedy. But this was exceptional.

In the Muri Division of the Adamawa Province, where I spent more than a year in charge at a later period of my service, conditions were very different. There was, indeed, a telegraph office which could be reached in an hour from my headquarters at Jalingo by the only stretch of all-season motorable road in the ten thousand square miles of my extensive domain, but for the traveller to or from the Provincial capital at Yola the easiest, but none too easy, land route through semi-mountainous country meant a journey of up to seven days. By water, *via* the Benue, some time could be saved if the river was not too low. In any case I was usually on tour for from two to three weeks each month and by the further interval required to reach me during such periods detached from the control of higher authority. If there should arise some unforeseen problem requiring urgent investiga-

tion, or in which my presence would be helpful to th
Authority—perhaps a quarrel between rival claimants to
fishing rights which might result in violence if not adju
or the failure to account for his revenue collecting transactions
by a District Head who, in the local phrase, had "eaten his tax",
or even, as occasionally happened in a pagan area, a resistance to
authority in the person of an Emir's messenger who had arrived
on some unpopular errand—in any eventuality of this kind the
need was to act at once and to report as the situation might
require as soon as it was practicable to do so. In an emergency I
could not call the police or the fire brigade. I *was* the police and
the fire brigade.

The other rewarding aspect of my Nigerian service is less easy
to describe. It was the experience of living in body, mind and
spirit a life which fulfilled the needs and purpose of the whole
man; an experience which involved a kind of religious intercourse with all the moods of Nature, and created a fellowship
with all the actors in the divine comedy—the proud and the
humble, the ragged and the resplendent, the sophisticated and
the simple, the craftsman and the husbandman, the merchant
and the beggar—who appeared upon the stage in their pre-
destined roles.

Even a condensed citation of the numerous duties of a District
Officer would be tedious. The reference to them in *The
Dominions Office and Colonial Office List* for 1940—a robust
volume of more than 900 pages, with forty maps, which
comprehends dispositions and establishments as they were at the
outbreak of war—is commendably laconic. The functions of an
Administrative Officer, it says, "if employed in a district . . . are
of a magisterial and political nature, and he is the immediate
agent of Government in his District." Further, "his responsibilities
extend to all departments of the Administration which have no
local representative". In all its implications a pretty tall order.
In the performance of magisterial duties it was rather in
chambers—if the parallel be permitted—than upon the bench
that a *"Jogi's"* functions were exercised. A District Officer had
to review all cases that came before the Native Courts, and had
power in criminal matters to quash a conviction, to reduce a

sentence or to order a re-hearing. But outside the larger Government stations with their mixed populations it was rarely, and usually only in cases in which non-natives were involved, that he was called upon to adjudicate in his own court. This gave me no cause for regret. In the absence of a police detachment, it was necessary for the D.O. himself to initiate action for the apprehension of a suspected offender who was not subject to the Native Court jurisdiction, and one could not proceed to trial without some preliminary examination of evidence, which if regarded as sufficient to justify prosecution must inevitably raise a presumption, however tentative, of guilt. At the same time it would be incumbent upon me if the accused lacked legal assistance, as he probably would, to do all I could to ensure that his case was fairly presented. The combined roles of prosecutor, defending counsel, jury and judge, made an incongruous mixture, though, on the whole, the system worked a good deal better in practice than it looked on paper.

There were few Government Departments which had representatives permanently stationed at any District Officer's headquarters, but members of certain Departments came and went to undertake specific tasks. Education officers travelled many scores of miles to open or inspect the scattered elementary schools that, as their number grew, would become the first nurseries of a new generation of political leaders. A schoolroom of mud and thatch could be built at the expense of a few pounds, and a few pounds more would provide a minimum of essential equipment, but trained teachers were almost beyond price, and only a tiny proportion of those who might have benefited could hope to become literate. Agricultural officers worked patiently and often with success to introduce new cash crops, such as cotton and ginger, where soils were suitable; but among communities so little advanced that they had never discovered the wheel, and where even a plough was an object of suspicion, recommended improvements in farming methods were not received with enthusiasm, and one could feel sure that by the "adult male hoe" —the term used in the tax registers to designate the husbandman —the battle for the defence of tradition against innovation would be fought to the last furrow.

A Department which I cannot pass by without special mention, and amongst whose officers I made some good friends, was that of the Lands, Mines and Surveys. Surveyors were employed on trigonometrical work in the Niger Province in the years I spent there, and their road to the high places took them far from the beaten track. One of them was Arnell, a convivial soul, whose good fellowship on the rare occasions when he appeared at a headquarters station I thought of as the natural complement to the isolation he must have felt on his lonely excursions into a no man's land of rarely trodden bush paths and arduous ascents. In imagination I see him leading his line of carriers with their loads of camping impedimenta and esoteric equipment through stream, swamp and forest, sometimes waiting while a way is hacked with machetes through matted thickets of grass and undergrowth, sometimes clambering up a slope of growing steepness, hindered by roots and boulders, but always pressing closer to the height that was his territory. I think of him, too, standing on a rocky summit in the shadow of an approaching storm, his sights upon the distant hills, until he was struck down by the thunderbolt that destroyed him.

I did my best as an amateur in such roles as Inspector of Schools, Health Inspector and Agricultural Assistant to tie up loose ends and exercise a watching brief on behalf of the professionals, but by far the most important of my "political" duties was the touring of my Division, to which I devoted the greater part of my time; for it was in the villages, not the *barricki,* by the spoken, not the written, word that the essential business of the day was attended to.

During my second tour, and for the greater part of my subsequent service in the Protectorate, I was fortified by the presence of my wife. We were married during my first leave, but for an unconfirmed officer (confirmation was approved, subject to satisfactory reports, at the end of three years' service) special permission from the Resident of his Province was necessary before his wife could join him. I had not completed the prescribed period when my wife came out, but as I had already been placed in charge of a Division it was presumably thought that I should make the grade, and I had no difficulty in obtaining the requisite approval together with leave to travel to Lagos to meet her and bring her up country.

The D.O's house at Zungeru was two miles down the line from the railway station, but the track itself passed within a hundred yards of my front door. It was late at night when we arrived and in the absence of any road vehicle the transport of luggage required some organization. Difficulties were overcome with the help of a co-operative Foreman Platelayer, who suggested that we and the luggage should be conveyed by his trolley. As soon as the boat train had resumed its northward journey, leaving the way clear for the next forty-eight hours or so, the trolley boys manoeuvred their vehicle onto the rails, the luggage was piled up on board and we embarked. It was an original way of beginning our travels together. The sight of our dark platform gliding through the night with its load of black shadows and the animated silhouettes of the crew bending from the waist with the rise and fall of the propelling handles might well have been a cause for astonishment if there had been any other witness to our progress than the trees and the stars.

My wife was able to be with me in all the stations to which I was subsequently posted and accompanied me to some villages in the more remote part of the territory where, to the best of my knowledge, no white woman had ever been seen before. Our travelling was nearly always on horseback, and for these expeditions she wore a bush shirt with khaki breeches and puttees, and a topee, not unlike my own in shape, which effectively concealed her hair; so that upon our first arrival in one of these villages the inhabitants may well have assumed that in the white man's country there was little in the way of dress to distinguish the sexes, or may even have wondered, until their conjectures were later dispelled by her appearance in more womanly attire, whether the report of a D.O. with the strange habit of appearing everywhere with a wife had not been inaccurate, and my smooth-skinned and slightly built companion was not in fact a smaller and less mature kind of "little judge".

During these journeys we were presented with an intimate picture of the Africa through which we travelled – a picture of which many details would have escaped us if we had had to walk instead of being able to ride, for the additional elevation was just sufficient to open up a prospect that would otherwise have been impeded by the tall grass that during most of the year grew to heights above eye level.

Not that, except in the hillier parts of the territory, there was much arresting scenery. No such spacious panoramas as greet the traveller in the highlands of East Africa. The undulating, featureless country was covered by a vast green mantle of orchard bush, whose trees, with one or two noble exceptions, achieved no great stature and were of rather ungracious appearance, and until one began to grow wise in the ways of the forest there was little to relieve the monotony of the narrow paths that linked villages sometimes as much as ten miles apart. But sometimes the surroundings were bizarre. Liberally scattered through the bush were giant anthills of red laterite, thrown up by the ubiquious termite: they were sometimes as much as twenty feet in height, often narrowing to a point so as to suggest the spires of miniature cathedrals. Another extraordinary spectacle was the monstrous baobab with its huge shiny barrel of a trunk, pinky-lilac in colour, and its gesticulating, root-like branches. A grotesque creature, responsible for the humorous legend that on its original appearance it excited the interest of the Devil who, after plucking it up for closer inspection, became so enraged by its disproportions that he flung it violently back into the ground, where it remained embedded upside down.

And if one looked beyond these oddities, searching not only with the eye but with the ear for the messages of the passing scene; if one observed the caprices of light and shade and the subtle variations in form and colour that signalled changes in the character of the sylvan growth; if one listened to the sound of water in hidden streams, trying to judge from sibilant whispers how swift and deep might be the crossing one approached; if one detected the rustling of leaves or the sudden swaying of a branch that might betray a scampering escalade of monkeys; or if one watched during the early rains for the first flaming blossoms of the locust-bean tree; all these and a hundred other witnesses were there to reveal the secrets of the life around one and tell the time of the months and seasons.

c*

We always made an early start, and well before sunrise the carriers had roped up their loads and we were on the move. Our departure from a village involved quite a lot of movement. A little ahead of us rode the District Head with his scribe and one or two other mounted attendants who, whenever space permitted, would spur their horses forward in a series of short prancing sallies, ending in an exuberent curvet, in order to display their enthusiasm for protocol and impress bystanders, if any, with the proconsular importance of the occasion. On foot were followers of lesser degree, the Headman of the village and *his* attendants; and in their wake a straggle of unidentifiable underlings, minions of the minions, carrying on their heads the rolled up sleeping mats that encased the travelling wardrobes of their masters, and in their hands kettles of water for ablutions before prayer or when relieving nature on the march. Perhaps, also, a *dogari* in his red gown, lending colour and an additional flavour of authority to the ensemble. The procession, in fact, was something like a dragon, with the spectacular portion at the head. Somewhere in the region of the creature's belly were my wife and myself, maintaining what I deemed to be a prudent distance from the equestrian activity of the advance party; for equine excitement is infectious, and I made little claim, my wife still less, to any skill in horsemanship. With us was always my faithful political agent, and, except when I was accompanied by the Chief of an "independent" District, a representative of the Emir, through whom, in conformity with the policy of indirect rule I would be careful to channel any instructions that might be needed when interviewing local dignitaries.

This envoy occupied an indeterminate position in the order of march and usually rode by himself, attentive but aloof, as if to emphasize the detachment of his interpretative role. The tail of the beast, composed of our domestic servants and the carriers, was more intent upon progress than protocol, and took advantage of the brief delay that occurred when we took leave of the Village Head at his boundary to detach itself from the main body and press forward to our destination. As we always travelled at a walking pace it was usually there first.

For a tour lasting three weeks or longer we might require as many as twenty carriers; for in addition to our camp equipment, provisions and personal necessities I had to take office requisites, ranging from law books to paper-clips, and perhaps some specie boxes if tax collection was to be undertaken. All told, the party might easily total between thirty and forty persons, and in sparsely populated areas we sometimes had to bring with us foodstuffs, such as yams, to avoid straining the resources of local markets or, like the locusts that sometimes descended in voracious multitudes, jeopardizing the reserve of village food supplies. When the necessity for this precaution arose, it inevitably swelled our numbers still further.

Since those days I have often reflected, not uncritically, upon the contrast between the way of life of the British official surrounded by all the things he needed for efficiency, comfort and recreation—his furniture and domestic equipment, his clothing for all occasions, his grocer's array of tinned provisions and delicacies, his shotguns, golf clubs and gramophone records—and that of the Africans among whom he lived. I have called to mind the Hausaman, setting out upon some trading venture in the dry season when the millet harvest was reaped and the parched soil could be left until seeding time. A lone traveller, burdened only with his mat and his bundle of merchandise. His passport the fellowship of Islam; for he was sure of a night's shelter at the house of any Moslem before whose entrance he arrived with the solemn invocation of peace: *"salaam alaikum!"* That was his staff of faith; and if his simple homespun was scarcely a gown of glory it almost certainly concealed a small leather case, suspended from the neck and enclosing a scrap of parchment inscribed with a verse from the Koran—his bottle of salvation. We could have learned some lessons in humility from such an example; but in my day the white man unencumbered with his peculiar accessories would have been regarded as an oddity and commanded little respect. Africans, in my experience, expected some pomp and circumstance to be associated with those who claimed to speak with authority. Indeed, I think it likely that because we rarely wore uniform, dressed simply and were apparently scornful of personal adornment, we were sometimes handicapped in our approach to those who, in the matter of our attire, would have regarded some display, with appropriate sparkle of buttons or accoutrements, as proper to the maintenance of official dignity.

The carriers were nearly always professionals, provided by an unofficial "official" to be found in every Government station, the *Sarkin Alaro,* or Chief of Transport, who almost certainly took an unofficial commission on their meagre earnings. But the rake-off cannot have been too excessive, for there were always plenty of recruits, and never any complaints from those he summoned. I remember them on the march: a merry, noisy, joke-cracking, tatterdemalion crew, full of zest and good companionship; their workaday dress, more often than not, the mere vestige of a gown hanging in strips over their baggy but abbreviated trousers, but a vestige they would never have discarded for the bare torso of the pagan or the singlet of a Christian. Each remained faithful to his allotted burden—uniform case, chop box, bed bag, camp tables, whatever it might be—and became expert at securing it, balancing it on a small headpad of twisted grass, and manipulating it through the natural hazards of the daily stage. They were brawny as buffaloes, muscular as leopards, stout-hearted as lions and resourceful as . . . professional carriers. I do not know whether they loved their work; but I think that a man who could match his wits with every mood of Nature; who could carry his sixty pounds of servitude, protecting it as if it had been the ark of bulrushes, for twenty miles over paths sandy, rocky, waterlogged or slippery, but seldom smooth and easy, advancing at one moment with cautious, experimental steps through the breast-high current of a swollen river, and at another inclining his movements to keep balance on the sloping side of a granite outcrop, always cheerful and laughing at each difficulty as if it were the best joke in the whole repertoire of Nature's comic muse; I think that such a man, humble in status as he was, might well be on the way to finding happiness.

Despite their keenness to be first at the post, we did not let them get too far ahead of us on the road; for it was never wise to be widely separated from one's loads, especially during the rains when a cloudburst could transform a fordable stream into an avalanche of water in a matter of minutes, and if the carriers had preceded us to the far side there would be hours of waiting, deprived of all creature comforts, for the flood to subside.

No less essential to this bush-errantry, as indeed to every other phase of our Nigerian experiences, was our domestic staff. They were never too tired, even after a four or five hours walk through heat, rain or dust, to minister to our needs and comforts; and in this, as in all other ways, they gave us devoted service through our years in the country. Mustapha, our head steward, was proud of his status of major-domo. When we were at headquarters he regarded it as a matter of personal honour to ensure the efficiency of preparations for our modest entertaining, and before a dinner party he would survey the table with an artist's eye in order to satisfy himself that knives, forks and glasses, augmented, if necessary, by borrowings from neighbours (customary at larger stations in comparatively junior establishments such as ours) were adequate, and that it was decorated with a few gay leaves or blossoms.

There was also our indefatigable cook, known to his compatriots as Ibrahim, but in the households of those in whose service he had learned the ways of the white man by the less sonorous alias of Jimmy. He was a cheerful little fellow with grizzled hair and wrinkled countenance, who walked with a limp due to an accident in childhood that made one leg a little shorter than the other; but his impediment in no way impaired his mobility, and on trek he was always the first to arrive at the rest-house and get his fire going. He was perhaps more successful as a *chef de cuisine* (his aide was known as "cookoo-matey") than as an unassisted cuisinier; for although adept at organizing the preparation of a meal in a leaky kitchen with damp firewood and an improvised kerosene-tin oven, his culinary range was limited to about twelve recipes, which included half a dozen ways of cooking chicken. Dependable, full of spirits, never happier than when working under difficulties, sharp as a needle and honest as daylight, he was prepared for every contingency and a pillar of strength in moments of domestic emergency.

When the District Head was with us we were often regaled by

one or two musicians and, possibly, a professional eulogizer. I confess that, at least to my alien ear, the music never sounded very musical. It consisted of incessant drumming, accompanied by a monotonous refrain emanating from a sad-toned wind instrument that sounded like a bronchitic bagpipe. The tunes ranged over never more than three or four notes in a minor key, and were repeated over and over again, two or three variations apparently exhausting the whole of the performer's repertoire. The drum was nursed under the left arm of the player, and caressed rather than beaten with a flipper-like motion of the hands and wrists, such as one might employ to demonstrate to a performing seal. The eulogizer's task was literally to sing the praises of those whom the king delighted to honour, in this case my wife and myself. This he did in a mournful sort of wail that matched the "bagpipe" very well, but seemed more like a lament than an encomium.

And so, a little before noon, we reach the village of our destination. It is a good deal hotter than when we started and the procession has lost much of its original *élan*. The District Head's retinue is subdued, and the bounce, I am glad to note, has gone out of the horses. The bagpiper seems to have blown himself out; but the eulogizer, spurred to his task by the hope of an attentive audience, continues his praises. "We greet you, oh great Judge, we greet you!" And then, observing a row of small children and a line of female heads inadequately concealed behind a grass fence, "Oh, pay attention to his commands!" At this moment I have no commands to give; which is just as well, for the children are unimpressed and, bashfulness overcoming curiosity, the girlish faces behind the fence disappear suddenly, leaving only the sound of girlish giggles.

But here is the rest-house and, before it, a giant fig tree with its grateful shade from which another Village Head emerges to welcome us. Round about are the carriers, still in first class fettle and impervious, it would seem, to fatigue, putting down their loads and helping the servants to sort out our boxes and bundles. Jimmy has a fire going, and while waiting for the kettle to boil is doubtfully examining a selection of local eggs, holding them up to the light to discover which ones are addled, and ready to reject any whose elongated shape indicates that, as has once happened, a temporary shortage in the farmyard has been made good by a thoughtful inclusion of crocodile eggs. Soon there will be tea, effectively disguising the amber tint and pungent flavour of the village water supply. Then a bath, followed by lunch (*poulet Jacques*) and in the drowsy hours of the afternoon I shall fight off sleep by attending to any official correspondence that Mr. Johnson may have deemed to be of sufficient importance or urgency to send on to me by runner.

The rest-house itself was nothing more than an enlarged African hut of typical mud and thatch construction, with an encircling verandah, two doorless entrances instead of one, and a couple of windows without frames, glass or shutters. There were, however, good and bad rest-houses. The better ones had well beaten floors that did not crumble like pie-crust as one stepped upon them, were not riddled with white ants, did not admit sun and rain through holes in the roof, and were not infested with bats. If all or any of these defects were so pronounced as to discourage occupation it was possible to accept the hospitality of the Village Head and sleep in his *zaure*.

Towards evening there would be a meeting with the District Head, the Village Head and the Elders to discuss local affairs—the condition of the crops, if it was the growing season, and the outlook for the harvest; the holding of the annual census; the progress made in tax collection. All these topics were closely linked, since it was upon the estimated bounty of the harvest that the tax assessment depended. Those whom I questioned understood this very well and were careful not to mislead me by giving too optimistic an appraisal of prospects. Apart from the mild excitement generated by our arrival there was little public interest in our presence. The *Jogi* came and went, and at the next visit or the visit after that they would notice a fresh face. The Village Head would be asked the same questions and give the same answers: their stake was in the land, their fortunes in the keeping of the seasons, their destiny in the hands of God. But though one had little to give that could make richer their way of life, there were signs and appearances from which one could usefully learn: the demeanour of the headman and the respect which he appeared to command among those who attended him; his precision in the observance of customary courtesies; the state of the approach paths to the village, whether cleared or overgrown; the general aspect and state of repair of the village (not omitting the rest-house), whether tidy and well kept up, or semi-derelict and littered with decaying vegetable refuse. Indications, one and all, from which one might judge whether or not the community was in good heart, and whether the reins of authority were in capable hands or had become slack.

When all matters requiring examination had been gone into and, as far as might be, disposed of, the day's work was done, and before darkness descended my wife and I would take a stroll to the outskirts of the village. It was not far to go. The main street was a double line of compounds flanking the temporarily widening track we had followed that morning. There might be a small market-place with a few shade trees beneath which those with leisure could sit and gossip. Sometimes a village school building; more rarely a dispensary whose stocks might need replenishment. There was not much human traffic, but one might come across some children, watched by naked toddlers, intent upon a game of hopscotch. And all about us familiar sounds of village life were audible : in desultory snatches of conversation; in the heavy pounding of yams in their wooden mortars; in the grinding of corn into flour upon a slab of stone. Tasks, these, for the housewife, who, when visible, appeared to be quite unimpeded by the weight of the latest born infant swaddled to her back by the tight cloth cradle that was rocked, agreeably no doubt to its occupant, by the regular swaying motion of the mother.

Soon we would reach the end of the millet patches that fringed the village, and here, before turning back, we would pause for a while, where the bush began, to watch the transformation of the forest. For now was Africa's moment of glory, when the glow of the sinking sun fell full upon the labyrinth of tree trunks and the myriad spears of the tall grass, making luminous and rosy each separate scroll of twisted bark, and lighting up the leafy canopies above as if the stars had marvellously dropped from heaven and become a shimmering haze of gold and amber leaf and blossom. We waited until the light began to fade and the colour had gone from the earth, and then began our walk back to the rest-house. From the village as we approached there drifted the call to prayer, and Mustapha was coming to meet us with a lighted lantern.

Chapter VII

PAGAN PEOPLE

NIGERIA was never a "white man's country" in the sense in which, for example, the "white highlands" of Kenya used to be so regarded. White men went to the Coast as explorers, traders, missionaries, administrators and civil servants in great numbers, and as officers to command locally raised Forces, but never as settlers. Multi-racial problems such as those which complicated constitutional advance in more temperate zones of British-occupied Africa did not therefore arise. But to frame constitutions is one thing, and, as the events of recent years have all too tragically emphasized, to achieve national unity is another. Nigeria was lacking in essential ingredients of such unity: there was no identity of race, no tribal cohesion, no common language, religion or culture, no Homeric epic to summon heroes from the past, no saga whose echoes did not die upon the distance. The Nigeria I knew was no more than a name, and that a name which, at least in the North, meant nothing to any African one could meet upon the road. "What is your country?" one might ask him, and "I am a Beri Beri", "I am a man of Kano", or "I come from Sokoto" he would reply. What was remarkable was not this evidence of diversity but, as far as the North was concerned, that a mosaic of so many dissimilar pieces could be so securely held together by a purely administrative cement.

Despite diversities, within the Emirates the rulers appointed by the British Administration had, by and large, secured the allegiance, not only of the Hausa speaking populace and other Moslem communities, but of the many pagan tribes within their boundaries. In the Muri Division of the Adamawa Province there was a predominantly pagan population, including some forty thousand members of the Mumuye tribe, a remote, secluded people living a life of rugged simplicity among

66

and sometimes on the tops of their almost inaccessible granite hills, and indifferent to, if not scornful of, the comforts and conveniences of civilization and the changing face of the outside world. It was while my wife and I were travelling in a District inhabited by the Mumuye tribe that one day I received disconcerting news.

It came from the Village Head who was waiting for me at the end of our first day's ride from my headquarters at Jalingo. There was bad sickness in the neighbourhood.

"What kind of sickness?" I asked. "What happens to those who take it?"

Violent headache, I was informed, was the characteristic symptom. The Village Head raised a hand to the back of his head and rolled his eyes in mock anguish. In most cases, he said, death ensued rapidly. Many had already died.

I did my best to recall the notes I had made during lectures on tropical diseases during my training course at the Imperial Institute. Could this, I wondered, be an outbreak of cerebrospinal meningitis?—a scourge by no means unknown in Nigeria, though more to be expected in the dry season than during the rains, which were now upon us. I sent off a note by runner to Provincial Headquarters asking for the advice of the Medical Officer and suggesting that he made a visit of inspection, and messages were despatched to the Emir of Muri and the Native Authorities of contiguous areas advising them to proclaim the trade routes into the District closed until further notice. I also had word passed to the Heads of all villages in the neighbourhood to warn everyone against unessential intercourse with their stricken fellows, and urging them to try to ensure that the deathbeds of those who had perished were burnt.

For the protection of those with me I instituted a parade twice daily, at which the carriers, police escort and servants were made to gargle with salt and water. Even against the background of tragedy I could scarcely restrain a smile at the spectacle of our little band in their haphazard motley of gowns and uniform standing in a circle with heads thrown back and legs apart in the stance of a professional weight lifter while they dutifully gurgled and spluttered in a chorus suggestive of the rapid emptying of a cellarfull of bottles. The performance was, no doubt, regarded by casual passers-by as unusual, and yet another instance of the white man's unpredictable eccentricities.

These measures taken, we moved on towards the afflicted villages in the hope that medical aid would follow. To this day I do not know whether my amateur diagnosis was accurate or my makeshift precautions correctly taken, for the Provincial Medical Officer with a population of half a million to minister to was urgently occupied elsewhere and unable to investigate our distress. Night after night we heard the musical obsequies and the death drumming for departed souls; and when, at the next annual count of population, the District scribe sat down with the villagers to bring his tax lists up to date he crossed off from the records the names of four hundred Mumuye who would not again be liable to any earthly assessment.

These Mumuye people were less tuneful than the Arcadian choristers of Verre, but the country they inhabited, except for the sterner aspect of the terrain, was very similar. There were the same grassy-looking fields of dwarf millet and, prominent against the rocky amphitheatre of the boulder-clad hills, the same compact groups of cactus-guarded dwellings that looked like congregations of monstrous toadstools. Goats browsed optimistically on the scant vegetation of the hillsides, and hungry-looking pye-dogs snarled and turned tail as one approached. Once we passed a nest of snakes writhing by the side of our path—a repulsive sight, The tribesmen we met on the road were incurious and went by without any sign either of greeting or hostility. Each carried a bow and a quiver of arrows, poisoned at the tip, as I was informed, with strophanthus. The lobes of their ears, pierced in infancy and stretched artificially, hung down in loops to chin level. A few staggered under the effects of millet beer, and once or twice, as we came close to a habitation, the sound of chanting voices accompanied by drums and stringed instruments disclosed the venue of an organized symposium. At work in the fields, hoeing among the yam patches, there were women, who ignored us as completely as the men. They wore scant aprons of leaves, but no other clothing or adornment.

For generations the Mumuye, with other hill pagans of the

Upper Benue had defied the Fulani from the vantage-ground of their fortress-rocks. In this and other semi-mountainous neighbourhoods the invaders had gained little authority or influence, and wherever there were hills of any size the war on the unbeliever had, for all practical purposes, ceased at the foot of them. For the flag-bearers of Islam were essentially horsemen. Mounted, and armed with spears or swords, they possessed in their speed, mobility and superior equipment an obvious advantage over the naked tribesmen who fled before them. But to ascend on foot in pursuit of the infidel to a mountain retreat was an exercise for which they were ill prepared; the flowing robes of the Faithful were not well adapted for the business of climbing a steep hillside or forcing a passage through a cactus hedge, and their arms and accoutrements were a hindrance as well as a burden. They became an easy target for the stones and poisoned arrows showered down upon them by the agile and unencumbered defenders of the heights; and it is not surprising that they had little stomach for such adventures.

One branch of the Mumuye tribe formed a District under an independent Chief, but those of whom I am writing had recently agreed to "follow" the Emir of Muri, to whom they were well disposed. The inherent despotism of his ruling caste was tempered by a liberal perception of the need for tolerance and understanding in the exercise of princely prerogatives, and he had an appreciation of human strength and weakness appropriate in the father, as report had it, of a hundred sons. The compact with the Mumuye was, in effect, a kind of gentleman's agreement whereby the "followers" accepted the authority of the Emir and were prepared to pay tax (provided the assessment was not unreasonable) when demanded, on the more or less implicit understanding that in all other matters they would be left alone to arrange their own affairs. They had, indeed, a Chief of their own, but the mainspring of his power and authority was priestly and magical, for he was none other than the rainmaker of the Mumuye tribe, able with his supernatural gifts to tap the precious reservoirs of heaven; and there was little likelihood that his skill and reputation would decline, for since his abode was a deep valley close to the high watershed of the Northern

Cameroons—an area of abundant rainfall—the prospects of a satisfactory response to his rites and incantations were excellent.

The Emir had invested him with the customary symbols of authority, a gown and turban, but he seldom put on these unfamiliar garments, in which he would indeed have presented a droll aspect, for he was a gnomelike little figure of a man, less than five feet in height, and preferred like all his people to go naked save for a loin-cloth of goatskin from which dangled his supernatural armoury of leather-encased charms and amulets. He laid no claim, despite his official recognition as District Head, to any territorial jurisdiction outside the steep, narrow valley of his priestly kingdom; a realm half shrouded, even at high noon, by the shadow of the towering slopes that bounded it on either side, and always murmurous with the music of fast-running waters from the cascading courses of a score of mountain streams.

The truth was that neither Panti Yoro (such, meaning "Chief of Yoro", was his title) nor the people whose heavenly water rights he guarded were interested in the well intentioned endeavours of Residents and District Officers to reinforce local authority in the area; they were nothing more than a loose confederation of small village communities, speaking the same language and inheriting the same customs, and associating with one another only in those pursuits, such as the dry season hunting expeditions and the performance of harvest rituals, that demanded communal cooperation. Government in its distant secretariats might, if it had ever heard of the place, put its finger on the map—a little uncertainly, albeit; for in these peripheral districts triangulation might serve as a signpost, but topography was a will-o'-the-wisp —and exclaim "here (or hereabouts) resides the District Head of Yoro"; but in fact it was the old men of the villages who were the only locally recognized executive and judicial tribunals, and custom was the only valid sanction.

The warrant of the greybeards was never challenged; but, in effect, they were no more than trustees and spokesmen for a more powerful and more ancient authority, the spirits of the ancestors, and their decrees and edicts translated the age-old traditions of the tribe. Untutored as they might be in the arts of civilization, the Mumuye were not a people without discipline, and, as generally in primitive societies, their laws and usages were more scrupulously observed than the legal and moral codes of many more sophisticated communities. For the life of the pagan in Nigeria, far from being a life of careless insouciance, was one of continuous submission to a supernatural rule that commanded his actions from cradle to grave. For the supreme adventures of birth, marriage and death, as well as for the initiation of the young men, for the sowing and the harvesting, for hunting and for war, there were obligatory observances and rituals. Among many pagan peoples there was a belief in the existence of a Supreme Being; but this remote deity was too distant and too imperfectly conceived to be the ruler of an earthly kingdom. Inhabiting the country of the ancestral shades was a company of lesser dignity, the demigods and fetishes, fickle in temper, unpredictable in mood, jealous of their tutelary rights and, more often than not, malevolent in disposition; and it was with the will, if it could be ascertained, of such as these that there was a meticulous compliance, lest neglect should provoke anger and calamity befall. In his supernatural beliefs the pagan was an imaginative child frightened by stories of the bogey-man. But he believed that the bogeyman could be diverted from his vengeful or malicious purposes by gifts and flattery. Hence propitiation was the stained altar of the primitive cult.

Remembering the Mumuye I have sometimes wondered what thoughts their scarred, impassive faces did not reveal. That they could be cheerful as well as quarrelsome in their cups there was plenty of evidence; but, apart from drinking and love-making and the occasional pursuit of wild animals, what pleasures did they enjoy that could load the scales of fortune on the side of happiness? They had everything they wanted for the satisfaction of their daily needs, for there was little they required that they could not grow, make or gather. Every family had in their fields and their stock the means to replenish larder and wardrobe; hoes, weapons, pottery, baskets and musical instruments were all the work of local craftsmen; building materials were liberally provided by Nature. Calabashes served as jars and drinking vessels, and were also used to make a distinctive wind instrument associated with one of the Mumuye cults and employed principally for the disciplining of the women, who fled in fear from the eerie notes. Money they had not, and did not need except for the appeasement of tax-gatherers; and a sufficiency for this purpose could be "bought" by selling ground nuts at the depot of a local trading firm. As they knew nothing of nearly everything that money could buy they were not conscious of poverty. In the context of their surroundings and their material necessities they were neither rich nor poor.

In the domains of human rights and spiritual reward the assessment is less simple. They were free, if freedom means the right and means to work without a master; but they were chained to their superstitions and in bondage to supernatural forces, and their thoughts must often have been darkened by the shadow of unholy dread. I do not know whether in any redeeming adventure of the spirit their minds were unbarred and illuminated; but who is to say that, in the fervour of some ritual potation, there could not have come a sudden godlike moment, a Bacchic revelation of the divine essence and ordering of created things? There are many doors to Truth; and to possess the keys of understanding is not the undivided prerogative of the prophets and the sages.

CHAPTER VIII

THE RIVER

FINALLY there was the river.

I am not thinking now of any one of the multifarious concourse of minor streams that, according to their several moods and phases, trickled, cascaded and meandered through or flooded the topographical wildernesses of the large Nigeria-in-one-sheet map issued by the Survey Department; those streams that in our daily travelling we waded through, swam or crossed precariously with the aid of our steel bath-ferry. I am thinking of the Niger and the Benue; the great waterways whose wide immense-vista'd valleys received the tribute of a thousand affluents from Senegambia to Chad; the progenitors of the Delta; the veritable father and mother of the Oil Rivers of philatelic memory.

The Muri Division, nearly twice the size of Wales, was cut in two by the Benue, which flowed through it for a distance of about a hundred miles, and it sometimes saved time and labour to use the river as a highroad. I was always glad of an excuse to do so; for such a journey opened up yet another of Africa's adventurous wonderlands. Our first experiment was on my posting to the Muri Division, when during the dry season we travelled from Yola, capital of the Adamawa Province, to the riverside town of Lau, the nearest point by road to Divisional headquarters at Jalingo.

We left Yola early one morning in the Resident's poling barge, a flat-bottomed punt-shaped craft six or seven feet in beam and something less than thirty in length. An improvised awning of mats gave welcome if inadequate shelter to two deck-chairs placed for my wife and myself in the bows; our loads were stacked amidships; and the servants and a Government messenger disposed themselves aft. The crew, eight in number, were divided into bow and stern parties : each of them wielded a pole cut from a branch of the raphia palm, and kept his paddle for occasional use in deeper water. There was a "captain"—he wore no badge of rank and was distinguishable from his colleagues only by being more talkative—who was responsible for deciding the course.

During the few weeks of full flood, when the stream was a noble highway spanning half a mile and more from bank to bank, the stocks of trade-goods for the riverside canteens—soap, salt, cheap ironmongery and enamelware, printed cottons to tempt the eyes of African ladies—were brought up river in the white man's "fire canoes"; and in exchange were carried down the season's accumulation of ground-nuts or hides from the interior. But now, in the cloudless, hazy, blue and golden days, when the waters had receded and the river bed become a network of narrowing channels winding their tortuous ways among smooth yellow sands, the long clumsy-looking canoes of the Yoruba or Hausa river traders still carried up and down the roots, the nuts and the dried fish of native commerce. At this time, too, the deeper reaches were populous with fisherfolk. They dragged the seine or cast their circular lassoo-like nets, and smoked their catch beside the blackened mat-walled tents they built upon the higher sandbanks. Navigation at this time of year demanded nice judgement when, as often happened, the stream divided to embrace a sand-bank between two channels of apparently equal width but, as we soon discovered if the captain had made an unlucky guess, by no means equal depth.

The crew began their task in workman-like fashion, bringing their poles down vigorously in unison for a sustained spurt, and then after a brief pause repeating the manoeuvre, so that, with the added propulsion of the current, we went ahead in famous style. But as the voyage progressed the bursts of energy grew shorter and the rest intervals longer. The poling was accompanied at first by a kind of river-chanty laced with jocular interjections and companionable laughter; but as physical output declined so did the flow of quips and snatches, and presently there were prolonged periods of inactivity and profound quiet, with nothing but a desultory splash to interrupt the sibilant rustling of the water beneath us.

It was then that we realized how deep could be the surrounding silence. The African bush in the day-time is not often noisy, and it is not until the approach of darkness that Nature seems to speak with all her voices. Then, the occasional chirruping of a cicada is replaced by a continuous stream of stridulent vibrations, drowning the minute inquisitive whine of the ubiquitous mosquito, and broken into only by the bray of bull-frogs in their marshy hiding places, the eerie whoop of a venturesome hyena, or the restless muttering of distant drums. But even during the day there is evidence from time to time of life and movement. The long-drawn-out plaint—staccato, accelerando, diminuendo, in a descending scale—of the Senegal *coucal* ("idle fellow" the Hausas call him), that sounds almost like a burst of sardonic human laughter. The "drumming" or creaking of the bush-lark —more like a distant policeman's rattle than the motions of a bird —as the creature vibrates its wings in soaring flight. The sudden churring of a startled francolin as it takes to the wing. The chattering conversation of a flock of guinea-fowl – a medley of cries half way between cheeping and clucking—as they feed upon the ground. All these, with the grace notes of the wind among the leaves and the fragile patter of the rain in season are like the tuning up of separate instruments in an orchestra that never performs a symphony. On the wide reaches of a great river there is nothing of this. Except when the rain falls there are seldom any instruments to listen to, for the wind has no branches to play upon, and the birds of the sand-banks, though numerous and of great variety, are not of sylvan breed, and have little to say to us or to one another.

As the sun climbs higher towards its zenith, and colour ebbs from the burning sky, this world of silence and scarcely perceptible movement that we have entered becomes more jealous and possessive. An hour ago we could make out the misty foot-hills that lie on either side of the far-spreading valley; but now they are lost in the lethean dust of the noonday haze; and the trees of the river plain are lost, and the cattle that were browsing in the marshy vistas; and it is as if they had never been, and we were floating on a mirage, suspended in a strange dream dimension belonging neither to time nor to space. The water is glazed, invisible, without ripple or tremor, and the bushes along the bank ahead are shapeless and unreal—islands of phantasy in a waveless ocean that has no end and no beginning.

But the sand-banks that float past, and the birds that populate them—swiftly running sandpipers, plovers with legs like tiny pairs of stilts, a solitary heron, the sacred ibis, a distant colony of pink-backed pelicans—all these are surely real, and drowsily I turn my head to watch the movements of a giant stork, the saddle-bill, with his black, white and pillar-box red markings. On the wing a miracle of grace, but here, as he paces the margin of the stream with slow pedantic steps and forward-inclined carriage, absurdly suggesting a schoolmaster invigilating at an end-of-term examination, or perhaps, with his generous waistline and respectable black coat tails, some prosperous but not too worldly character of fiction. Give him a pair of spectacles and he might be Mr. Pickwick.

Over there are other storks, seemingly immobile, a regular multitude. No eccentricity of individuals in that assembly. Nothing Dickensian. Nothing particularly human; unless one thought of a battalion of soldiers riveted at attention. And why, in any case, should there be anything human? Or again, why not? Didn't the birds, all creatures, inherit their farthing measure of God-stuff? "O ye Whales and all that move in the Waters. . . . O all ye Fowls of the Air. . . . O all ye Beasts and Cattle. . . ." St. Francis of Assisi. What would *he* have made of all this? St. Francis in Africa. "Good morning Brother Stork, are you enjoying Brother Sun? Do you like standing with one leg poised in the air, or have you just forgotten to put it down?"

Is that a log of wood I see there? No, it has its mouth open; must be a crocodile. What was that silly story they told us at Zungeru? Mouth open to catch flies—shuts mouth and dives into water—flies inside, can't escape—opens mouth and little fish swim in and gobble up flies—big fish swim in and gobble up little fish—crocodile closes mouth and gobbles up big fish—sagacious animal—remarkable ingenuity—surprising—very. Yes, of course, Brother Jingle, I mean Mr Crocodile, I mean. . . .

A gentle concussion as our bows come to rest on the firm sand of the river bed is sufficient to shake me out of my reverie. The captain has misjudged the depth of the shallow channel, or possibly he too has been day dreaming. The crew springs to life and, to the manifest indignation and alarm of a pair of Egyptian plovers—pretty little birds with dovelike colouring—who are busy with the instruction of a newly hatched chick in its first ground exercises, jumps overboard to steady the craft as it begins to swing broadside on to the current, at the same time pushing with concerted effort in the direction of deeper water. The Egyptian plovers' chick is pushed unceremoniously by its mother into a hastily scooped out hollow in the sand and temporarily buried, while the male parent attempts to divert attention by running up and down angrily with wings aflutter at a distance of some yards from his mate. But they are in no danger, and meanwhile the exertions of the crew are successful in getting us off the rocks without the necessity to lighten ship further by the removal of cargo, so progress is quickly resumed.

The current now carries us close inshore, and our attention is attracted by a continuous, excited twittering, resembling the sound of scores of miniature referee's whistles, which seems to come from the sheer face of the river bank in front of us. This, we now see, is undermined for a distance of a hundred yards or more along its upper length with a honeycomb of small cavities, as if it had sustained a closely-aimed and accurate bombardment of cannon balls; and gliding and darting to and fro like demented swallows are the noisy architects of these nesting chambers—hundreds upon hundreds of carmine bee-eaters, which, being insect eaters and no fishermen, have no scruples whatever about advertising their presence.

And so the lazy hours went by, and the long day, in which the illustrated book of Nature was never shut, drew at last to a close. A little before sunset we chose for a camping place a sandbank not far from a fisherman's tent, and our supper was an epicure's dish of freshly caught Nile perch, purchased just in time to preserve it from a smoky destiny.

My last memory of that first day on the Benue is of lying on a narrow canvas bed looking up at the stars and listening to the eternal music of the water-spirits as, veiled in a mystery of silver, they sped with chuckling choruses through the reeds by the river bank, or wandered with whispered harmonies through secret channels in the sand. No far from us were the fading embers of our camp fire and, beyond, the dark, motionless shapes of the sleeping servants and canoemen. We felt the peace of night upon us, and very soon the stars and the music of the river and the glow of the dying fire were gathered up and mingled with the stuff of dreams.

CHAPTER IX

CYPRUS (1)

IN 1935 I was offered and accepted a transfer to the administrative establishment of Cyprus.

It was too attractive a prospect to reject. An end to the inevitable separations that a married expatriate in Nigeria must face :
a good climate in which my wife and I with our daughter, now
aged four, would be able to live a normal family life. These were
the strong inducements that, when copies of a telegram from the
Secretary of State inviting applications for two vacant posts of
Commissioner in the Island had been circulated, decided me to
send my name forward. Candidates had to be not less than
thirty-five years of age and to be energetic, good at languages
and likely to be successful in dealing with the problems of a
politically minded community. I had the necessary seniority, had
passed my examinations in Hausa without discredit, and had
plenty of energy. I was not so sure of my qualifications for
success among a politically minded community—whatever that
might turn out to be. In any case I felt fairly sure that there
would be many applications from interested officers with better
claims to consideration than mine, and having taken what I
regarded as a pretty long shot in the dark I put the matter to the
back of my mind.

And then the unexpected had happened, and I was not quite
as prepared for it as I suppose I should have been. Of course I
would accept : my wife and I had talked things over very fully
before I had taken the initial step. But we should take away with
us more than a few nostalgic memories. One could not live, for
more than ten years in my own case, in such intimate contact
with a country and its people as we had done and send down no
roots. The Call of Africa. Her rugged and reluctant beauty that,
once revealed, was so impossible to forget. Her tremendous

horizons, her far-ranging escarpments, her solitary hills. Her rains and thunder : white, sunlit clouds piling up into the lofts of the sky above the darkness of a gathering storm. The babel of her market places, the voices of her creatures, the rumour of her drums. Her great rivers. Her silences. Such memories came crowding into my mind as I sat turning over in my fingers the note I had received from my Resident conveying the Secretary of State's communication. A piece of paper that, had I known it, was the first part of a travel document that was to take me round the world.

We embarked at Tilbury in December and reached Port Said on Christmas Day. The next morning, from the heaving deck of the Khedivial Mail Line's steamer *Fouadieh* we had our first sight of the Island. "Black Cyprus", as Flecker called it in his poem about the old ships : to the indignation of certain sensitive Cypriot souls who suspected an allusion to racial influences. But the Troodos massif—a sable cloud on the horizon beneath a lowering sky—suggested a more reasonable explanation of what might have been in the poet's mind. By mid-afternoon we had reached Famagusta, the weather had improved and the sun was shining with mellow warmth on Venetian ramparts and Latin cathedral towers. We travelled by a narrow-track railway to Nicosia, drawn by a small but purposeful locomotive, with whose speed and zeal the coaches rocked and rattled in sympathy as we made our way across a purple plain past plantations of olive trees and compact little villages whose mud-plastered and whitewashed houses glowed rosily in the setting sun. Then it grew dark, and when we stepped down onto the low platform at our journey's end the night was a canopy of stars.

"You will remain here temporarily," they told me next morning at the Secretariat, "until His Excellency has confirmed your posting." What they meant was that they were going to keep an eye on me until they had found out what kind of a fish they had landed. It was reasonable enough. After all, ten years experience in the practical application of the principles of indirect rule among the Moslems and the pagans of Nigeria was no guarantee that I should be able to communicate successfully with Greek Orthodox and Moslem Turkish Cypriots, to say nothing of a sprinkling of Armenians, Maronites, and Roman Catholics. Having survived scrutiny, I was despatched after two weeks to Larnaca and, as Commissioner, took over the District to which that town gave its name.

It was not a time of happy augury in international affairs. Hitler was building up his new army and Mussolini was continuing his invasion of Abyssinia while the nations loosed off successive volleys of sanctions that were always aimed short of the mark. The skies of world peace, such as it was, were growing darker and before long the ploughshares would be beaten into swords.

But for a time the danger receded, and meanwhile I found that my daily work provided ample exercise for my physical energies and plenty of bread and butter, as well as some rare delicacies, for the mind. One fundamental difference between Nigeria and Cyprus of which I became aware during my earliest days in the island, was that whereas in Africa Nature was a Sovereign Lady in Cyprus she was, if not subject to, at least in rigid treaty relationship with the Rule of Man. It was a subtle alliance. One looked for the first time northwards from Nicosia to the far-extending, many-pinnacled range of the Kyrenia mountains, fancifully perceiving among their steep, crenellated summits the outlines of some giant's castle in a fairy story. One looked again, this time with the aid of a pair of field-glasses, and lo! they *were* giants' castles. Or, at least, some of them were; for if the Crusaders, who built them on the tops of these precipitous slopes, were not giants in physical stature they must have been giants in ingenuity; and, like Bunyan's Pilgrim, they fought with giants. South of Nicosia, in the Larnaca District, was another eminence, whose peak, more suitable, one might have thought, for an eagle's eyrie than for human building enterprise, had been strangely transformed also, and this time more directly, in the service of religion—the celebrated monastry of Stavrovouni, the mountain of the Cross, founded by the piety of the Empress St. Helena. And not far away, among the foothills of the mountain-mass that dominates the south-western part of the island, were rich patterns of yellow, red, brown and purple, looking, as *The Handbook of Cyprus* colourfully described them, like oriental

D

carpets laid out on the hillsides—ancient spoil from the excavations of Roman copper-mining camps.

Spreading over the Messaoria—the central plain between the mountains—was no untamed savannah but, in the growing season, a sea of barley whose distant shores were groves of planted olives; and in winter the snows of Mount Olympus ascended to the sky above vistas of orange gardens. The lower slopes of the hills were covered, tier upon tier, with regiments of vines, and where the ground was too steep or too stony for viticulture were forests of grafted carobs, whose individual ownership enormously complicated the business of land registration. Higher still were apples (introduced possibly by Aphrodite as a memorial to her first initiate), walnuts in their green cases, fine red cherries and mulberry trees, which supported a traditional industry of the village women and yielded their end-product in the form of handkerchiefs, often dyed in gay colours, on the shop counters of the arts and crafts dealers. Even in the highest realms, in what was left of the forests after successive denudations to meet the shipbuilding demands of the island's conquerors, Nature was not left undisturbed to regenerate her solitudes; for a jealous Conservator was at constant war with that voracious creature, found everywhere in Cyprus—the Nubian or Syrian goat.

All these scenes and transformations were wholly understandable. Inscribe a circle on the pavement of a London thoroughfare and it will soon have been trodden upon by feet from half the nations of the world. Until the maritime discoveries of Portugal and Spain the Mediterranean was the thoroughfare of the great powers, and Cyprus had been trodden by alien and conquering feet since Man first learnt to sail the seas. Settled by Aegeans and sung by Homer, the island, at different stages of history, was tributary to Egypt, Assyria and Persia. Parts of it were colonized by the Phoenicians. It formed part of the empire of Alexander the Great, and after that was ruled for more than two centuries by the sceptre of the Ptolemies. It was in turn a Province of Rome and of Byzantium, and during the Roman period was given by Anthony to Cleopatra. It was invaded by Haroun al Raschid and conquered by Coeur de Lion, who afterwards sold it to the Knights Templars for 100,000 bezants—a sum worth a little less than the same number of sovereigns. It was subsequently, for three centuries, a Latin kingdom under the Lusignan dynasty, and towards the end of that period the port of Famagusta was under the sovereignty of the Genoese Republic. Cyprus then became a military outpost of a not, in those days of Ottoman militancy, very serene Venice, and finally for another three hundred years a dependency of the Sublime Porte until (after suitable arrangements with the Sultan) it was brought under British administration as part of Disraeli's achievement of "peace with honour" in 1878. Small wonder if by then Nature had learned to be submissive to the moods and necessities of the island's changing masters.

I cannot speak authoritatively about Aphrodite and the apples. If she had any say in the matter, the daughters of the island were not slow, according to certain chroniclers, to respond to her suggestions. "The women," wrote a sixteenth-century Venetian geographer, quoted in Cobham's *Excerpta Cypria,* "are very lustful, and so we read in Justin that Cypriot girls, before they marry, are wont to lend themselves to the unholy pleasures of foreigners who touch there in ships." And in the same volume is an Italian sonnet of slightly earlier date, which declares that the ladies of Cyprus sought no great profit from their favours. It could be that the reputation of these damsels has suffered undeservedly from legendary associations coupled with the popular notion of the foam-born divinity as a votaress of exclusively carnal delights.

As to that I prefer the interpretation of Botticelli, who chose to illustrate a different facet of the precious stone of love. The calm and wistful goddess of his creation—that lady with the gentle eyes—is no unchaste voluptuary. She it could have been who garlanded the glades with asphodel, who carpeted the plains of spring with white and mauve anemones and decked the mountain paths with tender sprays of cyclamen. Not far from Paphos are the Venus Rocks—scarred sentinels that guard a curving strand beneath the white-cliffed cape of Zephyros, God of the south wind, who guided her across the waters in her fluted coracle of shell. A tiny haven where the incoming waves dissolve into a lake of crested ripples and floating flakes of foam, bubbling through innumerable pools and crannies until they reach the golden limits of their shoreward journey; there at last to vanish with a curtsey and a sigh. Surely a fitting landing place for this child of daybreak and the drifting winds.

In an island that had suffered so many conquests it was not surprising to find a diversity of race, language and religion. There was, in fact, no relict of the ruling classes of the Lusignan and Venetian periods: by far the largest part of the population was and always had been composed of Greek-speaking Cypriots; but the Turkish section accounted for about twenty per cent of a grand total, then rather less than half a million. Included in the mixture, and contributing in some degree to the political-mindedness of which I had been made cognizant, were the lesser minorities, among whom, were a small Italian community (but, as one of their ladies once said to me at a party, "of course, we are not proper Italians"), some Levantines and English settlers, and a few Syrians, most of whom were birds of passage. Nearly all these divisions and elements were represented in Larnaca.

This town of ancient origin had acquired importance in Turkish times as the home of the consular corps and the headquarters of the British Consul, and it still preserved a cherished, if somewhat faded, quasi-diplomatic tradition, upheld by a body of consuls and consular agents whose number seemed altogether disproportionate to the international stature of the island. In a community of such variously interwoven affiliations and in which, moreover, so many prominent citizens managed to be related to one another, it was advisable that I should lose no time in finding out, not only who was who, but who depended upon whom.

Shortly after taking up my duties I sat down with my wife to prepare from the signatures in our visitors' book a list of those to be invited to a house-warming cocktail party. Names like those of Themistocles, the advocate, Dervish, the Judge, and Hamid, the Inspector of Police, were easy to classify; though one felt it would have been more in keeping with classical tradition if a certain Agamemnon, in the absence of any military command, had turned out to be the Chief of Police instead of a leading grocer. De Jongh was a dentist (of Dutch extraction), and Feinstein, a Jew from Palestine, came occasionally to supervise the management of a factory that performed the complementary function of producing false teeth. Mantovani ran a tourist agency and was the Consul for Italy: he was a friendly companionable soul, whose professional interests and peace-loving nature must have been sadly disturbed by the widening breach with the country of his ancestors. Lapierre, as might have been conjectured, was Consul for France. But names could sometimes disguise more than they revealed. That of Vondiziano was prominent in the English consular annals, but Greek was the mother tongue of its holder, who was now Consul for Portugal. "Bottomley" and "Greenwood" sounded solidly English, but the respective families had been resident in the Levant for several generations.

All these people were to become our good friends, from whom we received many kindnesses and much hospitality. One of the first to make our acquaintance was the obscurely named Vondiziano: he came to the house to give me practice with my Greek conversation, which, though it had progressed beyond the "Can you direct me to the post office?" stage, could certainly not as yet equip me to dissect the niceties of urban or rural politics. He was a serious, rather sad-faced little man, whose care-scarred countenance was more eloquent than his habitual composure and his occasional laconic utterances. I did not know a great deal about his affairs, but had been given to understand by those who recommended his services that his family had seen better days, and that the modest fee he was prevailed upon to accept would be welcome.

To tell the truth, he was not a very methodical instructor. He would sit upright in the hard-backed chair of his choice, swinging in his hand the reading glasses that he would adjust whenever I preferred some written exercise, and would correct my stumbling sentences and reply with painstaking accuracy to my questions about grammar and construction; but he seldom took any tutorial initiative, and left it very much to me to make the running.

One day, in search of a topic, I asked him about his consular duties: as there was only one Portuguese national in the island they could scarcely have been onerous. He told me that he had once had some trouble with sardines.

"Sardines?"

"Sardines."

"Ah, yes. Sardines."

"I received a consignment," he continued, "arranged by the Portuguese Government. They hoped I could interest importers here."

"And were you successful?"

He shrugged his shoulders and pursed his lips. "Nobody wanted them," he replied. "People said they were too expensive. I did my best. I did not know anything about sardines."

"What did you do with them, then?"

"They remained in my office for a long time. A very long time. A very long time. In the end. . . ." He relapsed into a mournful silence.

"You had to throw them away?" I prompted.

"It was difficult. There were many boxes. I do not understand how such things should be stored. It became embarrassing. One day I hired a boat: they went into the sea. It was early in the morning," he added, as if to forestall any accusation of unconsular conduct.

He may not have taught me very much Greek, but I learnt a little about human dignity in the face of adversity.

The cosmopolitan atmosphere of the town did not extend into the villages, where the pattern of rural life was uniform and changed little. There was at that time no enmity between the Greek and the Turkish elements. The two divisions lived side by side, sometimes in different villages, sometimes in the same village together; but always in separate communities, and there was hardly ever any intermarriage. The Turkish system of village administration under a Mukhtar, or headman, assisted by Elders, had been retained; and the men all adopted the Turkish style of dress, consisting of wide-sleeved shirts, open at the neck, with or without an unbuttoned waistcoat, baggy trousers and high heavy-soled boots, the Moslems being distinguishable by the addition of a turban.

This attire suggested a womanlike preoccupation with agricultural tasks, even during the long hours that were often spent in gossip and coffee drinking at the coffee shop while the women were busy at their domestic duties, or in undertaking such lighter labours in the fields as they could be left to get on with. I remember once noticing at a certain mountain village, through which I happened to be passing, a score of able-bodied males thus pleasantly relaxing while their women folk, each carrying on her shoulder a large stone required for some local building project, advanced arduously in single file up the steeply climbing street.

The Cyprus coffee shop took the place of the tap-room of the old-fashioned English country inn; and it was there, in the absence of any more formal meeting place, that I would usually be greeted by the Mukhtar on my arrival to transact public business when I went on my rounds of the District. Distances were short, and roads were good; most of the villages were not more than an hour's drive by car from headquarters; so I was able to visit them fairly frequently.

There was always a good attendance on these occasions and the whole adult male population turned out, if not to take a declamatory part in the proceedings, at least to see fair play. I would take a seat somewhere near the entrance, with the Mukhtar, a business-like figure wearing a black coat with his badge of office displayed in the lapel, on my right, and the District Inspector, my Cypriot assistant, on my left. The villagers gathered round us, some standing, and an inner ring straddling their locally carpentered, rush-seated chairs, placed back foremost to provide an arm—or elbow-support, and with chins resting appraisingly on the backs of interlocked fingers. The proprietor, distinguishable by his rolled up shirt sleeves and white apron, stood behind his counter at the back of the room, ready to serve the thick, black, treacly coffee that was sold for half a piastre (two-thirds of a penny) a cup. The scene was set for democracy to take the stage.

In spirit rather than by the letter. I had not been chosen by an Assembly and they were powerless to remove me if they wanted to. I was in fact a Tyrant, and for all they knew I might have been wise, benevolent, ambitious, venal, corrupt, or merely stupid. But they were ready to accept my rule and to give me an attentive hearing, believing, or at least hoping, having given voice to their apprehensions and their needs, that I might possess some power to protect them from the thumbscrews of usurious money-lenders, or to help them to scrape together the pathetically small sums they required to finance some scheme for the irrigation of their thirsty fields.

For rain in Cyprus never seemed to be sufficient, and though Earth possessed gifts in abundance, she bestowed them too often with a grudging hand. Indebtedness rode on the shoulders of the peasant like an Old Man of the Sea. He was always in debt—for seed, for provisions, to provide a daughter's dowry—and the opportunist merchant, or, as often as not, the village grocer, who was ready enough to supply credit at a price, regulated his rates of interest by the prospects of the harvest, adjusting them steeply upwards in times of threatened drought. During my years in Cyprus the energies of Government were bent, and the sheaves of reports, memoranda and draft legislation bore witness, to the attempted solution of the twin problems of debt settlement and agricultural credit.

Trespass and damage by goats formed another topic that was very likely to be raised on these rural occasions. Goats kept by the small holder as a side-venture assisted him to eke out his slender resources; but the utility of these animals was matched by their destructiveness, and their depredations often led to bad blood and sometimes bodily harm resulting from disputes between the shepherds, under whose charge they were placed to tend with their flocks, and owners of property adjacent to the grazing areas. Tempers could be volatile, and during my first year in the Larnaca District "harm by knife" was responsible for nineteen cases of serious crime investigated by the police. Of these offences no less than fourteen were committed with a pocket-knife.

The conduct of proceedings at the coffee shop followed a familiar course, which seldom deviated. After extending a general greeting and asking a few questions about health and crops, I would leave it to the District Inspector and the Mukhtar to carry on the discussion, putting in a word from time to time when it seemed appropriate.

The people were quite happy with this procedure. In a Greek speaking village I could have managed unaided at a pinch, for although my grasp of idiom was, to say the least, uncertain my remarks seemed to be intelligible; but it was convenient, and less of an obstruction to the free flow of rhetoric, for the Mukhtar and any others who might seek a hearing, to put their case to a compatriot, who would be able, if necessary, to make clear to me the finer points of their argument. The discourse was often lengthy, and sometimes impassioned, but the majority were content to leave the debate to the protagonists and enact a chorus-like role with occasional nods of approbation or, if what was said was not to their liking, a disdainful sucking of the teeth. The general atmosphere was one of tolerance, and my own reception was always friendly. When it was all over I would shake hands all round and depart, slightly embarrassed by a presentation bunch of flowers.

Larnaca itself was a place where time was leisurely, as if brooding over the transformations wrought by a chain of centuries. For here the strands of history had no clearly seen beginning and emerged from the mists of prehistory and legend to run through the changing patterns of successive epochs. Here in ancient *Citium* Phoenician traders sorted out their merchandise from Asia and from Africa. Their silk and silver: their rubies, sapphires and pearls: their embroidered muslins: their spike-nard, their frankincense and myrrh: their ivory, their tortoise-shell and gold. One of these merchants of *Citium* gave something more to posterity than a contribution to the luxury of the pre-Christian West; for he was the father of Zeno, the founder of Stoicism who, honoured in stone, surveyed the contemporary scene philosophically from his pedestal in one of the public gardens of the Municipality.

Less well authenticated was the popular legend which identified the first Bishop of Kition (as the Greeks called it) with no less renowned a character than the resurrected Lazarus. On second interment the remains of the saint were, so it was said, deposited in (but subsequently removed from) a sarcophagus that

D*

was embedded in the Byzantine foundations of the existing church of St. Lazarus, a much venerated monument. From the supposed presence of this relict the town and District derived the name of Larnaca, which is the accusative form of the word *larnax,* a tomb.

Not content to leave a monopoly of saintly legend to Christian apologists, the Moslems pointed with religious pride to the last resting place of a certain Arab lady, Umm Haram, believed to have been an aunt of the Prophet. This distinguished visitor was killed by a fall from her mule at a spot where now stands a mosque enclosing her shrine—a sanctuary to which Moslems from every part of the island were accustomed to make an annual pilgrimage. Except during these pious interludes the mosque and its surroundings, situated at a little distance from the town, were a repository of profound quiet. A cloistered courtyard sheltered a few trees upon which one could imagine even the birds alighting reverentially and reducing their matutinal conversations to an occasional chirrup. Two or three clocks of patriarchal stature— great-grandfather clocks—whose indications had little correspondence either with one another or the hour of day, seemed with their solemn tick-tock to invite attention to the silence rather than to interrupt it. I paid more than one visit to this tranquil place, for even in those days, before the ears of millions had been assaulted by the technological triumphs of our present age, I held quietude to be precious. And here, one felt, was a spot where Time himself, grown weary of his everlasting vigil, might well forget to number the shadows as they crept across the sunlit paving stones.

In comparatively recent times the consular quarter had been at La Scala—the "stairs" or landing place, as the Venetians named the seaside portion of the town; and here, it seems, there must have been remarkable opportunities for combining trade with diplomacy. In another of Cobham's *Excerpta* an English visitor to the island in the early part of the eighteenth century describes the transactions of the British Consul and his Company,* who, it appears, were accustomed to advance money to the inhabitants "for getting in their several harvests, in which

* British Consuls at that time were appointed by the Levant Company.

otherwise they would be at great loss. In this," he adds, "both parties find their advantage, for the English do not advance their money under twenty per cent and receive the interest in silk, wine, cotton, corn and other products of the country, on all of which they set their own price." From the same source we learn that the French were "well aware of this lucrative manner of gaining the people's affections, and would be glad to supplant the English, but have not sufficient funds, most of them being only factors to merchants at Marseilles".

Perhaps, after all, the village grocer of my own day might have had something to learn of business acumen and the arts of money-lending from the practices of the past.

At the beginning of 1936, when I first went to Larnaca, only two of the Consuls, the representatives of Greece and Turkey, were *de carrière*. Shortly afterwards, and somewhat, I have little doubt, to the relief of his genial predecessor, a career Consul arrived from Italy: this was a calculated move in Mussolini's policy of defiance in the face of opposition to his Abyssinian ambitions. One morning, on my way to my office, I observed that the familiar flag at the Italian Consulate had been replaced by one of much more grandiose dimensions, which in the absence of sufficient breeze to display the full content of its imperious message was drooping listlessly from the sloping pole that protruded from the consular façade beneath the proud escutcheon of the House of Savoy. Thus pavilioned in patriotism the Consul may have derived some moral satisfaction to compensate for the inconvenience of having his office window obscured by an imperial vista of green, white and red bunting.

A few days later there appeared outside the house of the Greek Consul, who lived next door to his Italian colleague, a flag of even greater size. This monstrous emblem, which, suitably hoisted, could have been seen for miles and necessitated a specially constructed flagstaff, trailed almost to the ground, as if in a notional attempt to identify at least this fragment of Cyprus as part of the sacred soil of ancient Hellas. Such colourful symbolism may have fed the fancies of the Greek-speaking populace, but the Italian gesture excited little sympathy, for the Duce's supporters in the island could probably have been counted on the fingers of two hands, and the occasional appearances in newsreels at the cinema of Haile Selasse were invariably greeted with frenetic applause.

There were other causes and occasions, of which I shall have something to say, that excited impressive manifestations of popular feeling; but, as far as purely municipal affairs were concerned, there was little to punctuate the town's amiable, if rather sleepy, progress. Nobody ever hurried; and what could not be undertaken or decided today could be attended to tomorrow or the day after. Except for the straggling mule-carts and occasional ambulatory strings of camels, there was not much traffic in the streets. Very few persons owned private cars, and my own official journeys into the District were made in a taxi whose owner-driver charged the equivalent of fourpence a mile and did not mind how long he was kept waiting. When my wife and I went out to return social calls we were driven in an open four-wheeled carriage resembling the victoria that England once knew : it was drawn by a pair of small grey horses at a thoughtful pace of six miles an hour.

Not that Larnaca lacked civic enterprise. The Municipality— a steam-roller rather than a bulldozer—advanced with cautious but solid assurance, and if it sometimes seemed to be moving backwards that was all part of the process of consolidation. It had recently built a central market to accommodate the meat, fruit and fish stalls whose contribution to the congestion of the narrow, canvas-roofed alleys of the traditional shopping quarter was more picturesque than hygienic, and I suggested to the Mayor that the Municipal Council might care to consider taking in hand the renovation of the town water supply. This came from a chain of wells through an intricate underground distribution system constructed in the middle of the eighteenth century by the ruling Pasha as a pious act. There were no meters or gauges : in return for the prescribed fee a subscriber was entitled to a certain share of the available flow, described as a *sacorafi* and being the volume of water that would find its way through a circular aperture of regulation diameter (whose exact measurement I forget) bored in the main supply channel. This had long been regarded—by the suppliers if not by the consumers—as an eminently fair arrangement. When rainfall had been abundant and pressure was high the householders all benefited alike, and in times of drouth the trickle diminished according to its distance from the source; which was, after all, what one had to expect. As additional subscribers appeared it was an easy matter to bore more holes in the pipe, and the Municipal Council was assured of its just revenues with a minimum of trouble and expense.

With a growing population such a method of apportionment obviously could not continue indefinitely, and everybody agreed that it was now time that something was done. But the proposed undertaking presented certain unique difficulties, apart from the burden of capital cost; for it appeared that no plan of the system had ever been made, or if it had, it had long ago been mislaid, and nobody knew where to search for it. Nor had anybody except the official caretaker, a conscientious but ageing illiterate who was approaching superannuation, any precise notion of the whereabouts and alignment of the various distribution channels. This knowledge, depending as it did upon memory and occasional verification by experiment, was not easily communicable and, for all practical purposes, was a family secret, which, it was supposed, would be passed on by the caretaker on his retirement, assuming that, as was proper, the keys of office would be handed over from father to son.

Confronted with these perplexing difficulties the Municipality hesitated. It might after all be expedient to leave things as they were for the time being. Demand had not yet completely overrun supply. Who knew?—the missing plan, if it had existed, might yet come to light. Meanwhile a considerable expenditure, to say nothing of the technical complexities of metering and the recurrent cost of more complicated accounting, could be postponed. When I handed over to my successor, the project had got no further than the head-scratching stage.

We spent two years in Larnaca. We were happy there—my wife in her involvement in social and charitable activities, I with my administrative duties, which opened so many doors of understanding, and both of us in our first full enjoyment of family life and in the many kindnesses that we received from those around us.

Chapter X

CYPRUS (2)

THE Greek-speaking Cypriots, as I knew them, were a well-ordered and fair-minded community, able to sip most of the wine of life without being tempted to excess. But there was one stimulant which always proved exciting: its character and significance could be deduced from the size of the Greek Consul's flag.

The word *"Enosis"*, spelt with a capital, meant union with Greece; but I doubt whether this notion went all the way to convey the emotional content of the ideas for which the expression was convenient shorthand. Times change, and had the possibility of independence been anywhere upon the political horizon during the years between the wars other aspirations might have been voiced; but in those days the disintegration of the British Empire had not begun. What had not changed through the centuries, even under the most discouraging circumstances, were the consciousness and insistence upon by the Greek Cypriot people of their Hellenic origin; and that conception, that insistence, drew their inspiration from a vista that extended in space and time far beyond the shores of modern Greece. For Hellas, like Jewry through the ages, was a nation—a commonwealth of kinship—and not a country. It was with that nation that those who influenced Greek thought in Cyprus identified themselves; and in so doing they stepped outside the narrow confines of their island home to become citizens of a more heroic, more adventurous, more passionate world—a world of legend and epic, in which they became the companions of the Argonauts and fellow wanderers with Ulysses.

It would be going far too far to suggest that imaginative fires of this kind were perpetually smouldering in the Greek-Cypriot breast; though one could believe that they were ready laid and capable of being lit by those who were prepared to bring about a conflagration. What is indisputable was the close preservation by the Greek Cypriots of their racial identity. They were, moreover, responsive to the authority of those who claimed the privileges of ethnarchy.

The claimants were not far to seek. One could not move more than a mile or two in Cyprus without encountering the presence of the Orthodox Eastern Church. The village church dominated the humble one-storey dwellings of the peasantry, and the village priest was never far away. Bearded and inscrutable, he was a sombre and, as I thought, rather incongruous figure in his stove-pipe hat and wide-skirted ankle-length gown of ecclestiastical black; but he managed to clothe his doleful garments with a certain dignity, and whatever the power of his ministry to keep alight the candles of simple faith he certainly believed that to work was to pray. He was often himself of peasant birth, and it was no uncommon occurrence to find him with his habit tucked up and bundled over one arm while he harnessed a donkey, or busied himself with the manipulation of an olive-press. This distinctive familiar of the Cyprus scene was the visible sign of an institution that had always regarded itself as the leader of the Greek-speaking inhabitants.

The Church of Cyprus had a history which went back to apostolic times and contained some vivid political chapters. Christianity was introduced by Paul and Barnabas in A.D. 46 and spread rapidly. The independence of the Church was recognized in the fifth century by the Emperor Zeno, who conferred upon the Archbishop the exceptional privileges of signing his name in red ink, of wearing a cope of imperial purple and of carrying a sceptre in place of a pastoral staff. During the Lusignan and Venetian periods the Church was in eclipse, and its hierarchy were placed in subordination to the Latin Archbishop; but within about a century of the Turkish conquest they received recognition by the Porte as the guardians and representatives of the Greek populace. In this way they gradually established a political ascendency that threatened, if it did not altogether usurp the prerogatives of the Musellim, the Turkish administrator of the island; and in so doing they sowed the seeds of their own downfall. For the people grew weary of the arbitrary rule that was imposed on Greek and Turk alike. "The Archbishop of Nicosia", wrote Louis Lacroix in his *Isles de la Grèce,* "had annexed pretty well the whole administrative authority . . . and all the inhabitants looked upon him as the real Governor. The Turks were deeply hurt at seeing themselves fallen under the rule of those whom of old they had conquered." As for the Greeks, according to another visitor to the island they were extremely submissive and respectful towards their bishops. "In saluting them they bow low, take off their cap and hold it before them upside down. They scarcely dare speak in their presence."

A day of reckoning arrived in 1821, and was stained by bloody and barbarous excesses. In that year the outer walls of the Ottoman Empire were beginning to tremble under the impact of the revolt in Greece. Alarmed at the possibility of repercussions in Cyprus, the Porte gave orders for the Greek community there to be disarmed, and followed up this precaution with the despatch of a large body of troops from Syria and Palestine. At the same time, lest half-measures should leave any residue of risk, authority was given to the Musellim to "kill as many of the Christians as he thought worth killing." Urged and possibly threatened by local Turks, who were thirsting for an opportunity to pay off old scores, the Musellim lost no time in assuming the role of executioner. The Archbishop and Bishops were enticed to Nicosia by a subterfuge, and then, in front of the Governor's palace, the Bishops were beheaded and the Archbishop was ignominiously hanged from a tree.

This was a signal for a general unleashing of pent up Turkish fury. Leading Greeks, laity as well as clergy, who upon any pretext, however slender, could be marked for vengeance, were sought out and dragged from their hiding places to the capital. Upon these unfortunates the slaughterers levied their toll of hatred, and the streets of Nicosia were slippery with carnage. For thirty days the terror continued and "the Turks ceased not to massacre and often to hack off the limbs of living victims."

This holocaust dealt a crushing blow to the secular pretensions of the Church, but it was far from destroying its inherent vigour or its influence over Greek community. Its leaders remained ever watchful of opportunity, and during the British régime it was actively concerned in the *Enosis* agitation that led in 1931 to island-wide riots, beginning with the burning down of Government House in Nicosia. In consequence of the Church's complicity in this movement the hierarchy was temporarily dismembered by the deportation of two of the three Bishops, the Metropolitans of Kition and Kyrenia.

Firm and unequivocal measures were taken to prevent further disorders. The Legislative Council was abolished and power to legislate was vested in the Governor. Civil liberties were heavily restricted by a series of minatory enactments, which made it an offence to take part without a permit in any public assembly, procession or meeting of more than five persons and prohibited the ringing of church bells except for divine service, as well as the flying of other than British national flags except on consular premises. To round things off a press censorship was also imposed : this was lifted after the coronation of King George VI, but was replaced by a Press Law that provided stringent penalties for the publication of subversive matter. All these restrictions remained in force during my sojourn in the island, and although there were at times more than a few murmurings of dissatisfaction and a good deal of clandestine political activity there was no outbreak of disorder.

The operation of the press censorship added a tiresome and ungrateful task to my duties as Commissioner. All the island's principal newspapers were published in the capital; but Larnaca boasted a four-page weekly whose sole *raison d'être,* since it carried a minimum coverage of local events and scarcely any external news of any kind, seemed to be to give publicity in a leading article, which seldom occupied less than two columns, to the political philosophy of its owner-editor. He possessed an oratorical style which, had its vehicle been the platform rather than the pen, would have assured him of large audiences. He also displayed a masterly proficiency in the art of insinuation and the employment of veiled imagery, and it was his weekly exercise to find out how close he could safely steer his literary cockle-shell to the threatening blast of the magisterial wind.

For all that he gave me a good deal of trouble I liked the man and had sympathy for him. In appearance he was tall and spindly, with lank, dark hair accentuating the parchmentlike texture of his large and pallid features. An El Greco countenance. His manner when circumstances brought us face to face was withdrawn and inscrutable: one might have described him as saturnine had it not been for the vitality of his long thoughtful fingers and the hint of sleeping passion in his eyes. Whenever I saw him he was neatly dressed in a suit of inexpensive material that seemed to have little substance, and I used sometimes to wonder—a little impertinently perhaps, for I knew nothing of his circumstances except that he was employed in the office of a local advocate—whether his wardrobe could produce more adequate protection against the occasional chill of winter. I judged, however, that he enjoyed no ample benefice from Fortune, and that he was the kind of person who would have welcomed poverty if by privation he could have manifested his convictions.

His articles were invariably tendentious. Not very happy in my command of the blue pencil I started by deleting a word here and there, or perhaps striking out a sentence or a paragraph that seemed to me to transgress the limits of the permissible. He accepted these excisions without protest, but every week a borderline phrase, an implication, a suggestion, which I had unwisely allowed to pass in the last issue in the hope that he would mend his ways, was developed, magnified, enlarged upon, until it became impossible to do any satisfactory editing without mutilating the sense of the whole composition. At this point I did what I should have done earlier and invited him to come and see me.

"I can't pass this," I said. "You'll have to get on to another theme."

His expression was an accusation and a reproach. He pointed to the offending proof where it lay on my desk. "All this says . . ." he began.

"Yes, yes, " I interrupted somewhat brusquely, for I did not want to be drawn into an argument, "I know what it says. But the point is what the people who read it will think you want them to understand. I don't doubt," I continued, in an attempt to take the edge off my abruptness, "that you write like this in duty to your conscience. But I have my duty to do as well. Now please go back and write something else : that is if you wish me to pass it for publication."

In silence he took up the rejected sheet and withdrew. Shortly afterwards the publication of the newspaper was discontinued as an act of protest. My feelings were of relief; but I should have felt truly uncomfortable if I had not been certain that the production costs of the ill-fated periodical must have considerably exceeded its exiguous earnings.

It would have been a mistake to assume from such incidents, or indeed from any of the emotional eruptions of which Greek Cypriot sentiment in the mass had proved itself to be capable, that there existed in the island any innate hostility towards the British as a nation. The conflict, such as it was, concerned aspirations and policies : it was not between peoples and persons. In the Cyprus I remember the name of England was held in high esteem and Byron was a national hero by adoption : in fact there were Cypriots in Larnaca who proudly bore the name "Milordus", bestowed by parents in honour of the poet-champion. The exchange of Turkish for British rule in 1878 had been accepted happily enough, as, indeed, had the exchange of Venetian for Turkish domination been generally acceptable three hundred years earlier. The Church had hopes, no doubt, of being able to reascend the ladder from which it had been so violently cast down in 1821. British institutions and achievements were admired, and British officials, it was soon decided, were just and impartial, and unassailably honest.

In my day there was, moreover, a genuine attachment to the British Royal family, to which King George of Greece was related. This was demonstrated with simple sincerity after the death of King George V, when memorial services were attended by large and silent crowds in towns and villages, and many humble folk publicly kissed the portraits of the well-loved monarch as a last act of homage. There was consternation at the abdication of King Edward VIII, but the sentiment that rapidly gained ground was one of admiration for the "business-as-usual" methods of the British Government and people in facing a major constitutional crisis. The coronation of King George VI was marked by island-wide celebrations and spontaneous rejoicing.

Naval occasions, too, were always popular. A cruiser or a destroyer of the Mediterranean Fleet occasionally put in at Larnaca, and during these visits the drab exteriors of the dozen or so coffee shops that faced the roadstead were transformed overnight into a pageant of red ensigns—an emblem regarded as likely to convey a welcoming spirit to seafaring patrons, but, since it belonged to the free expanses of the ocean, to be less irritating to insular susceptibilities than the imperial aura of the Union Jack. Unaware of these subtleties, and impressed by such an apparently patriotic display, as also by the heartiness of the popular welcome that was always accorded to the liberty men, the passing visitor might well have concluded that the Cypriots were a people of undivided political attachment to the British connection.

The passing visitor had not seen the medal's other face. As the Navy sailed away the welcoming ensigns were hauled down. If the law had permitted it, they would have been replaced permanently, or at least until the next British naval visit, by the cross and stripes of Greece. Denied this privilege, the Greek Cypriots made the most of any legitimate opportunity to show their colours in other ways.

There was always some excitement during the annual pan-Cyprian sports meetings, at which competitors from all over the island met to match their prowess in the traditional Greek games; and at these gatherings the Police took precautions to contain possible "patriotic" demonstrations. The meetings were always attended by the Greek Consul, whose mere presence, notwithstanding the invariable correctness of his behaviour, was bound to add spice to an already stimulating dish. I made it my business to be present as well during at least part of the proceedings, in order to correct any impression that the Government regarded the games as a purely Greek exercise. My recognition of the occasion presented a slight problem to the organizers in the arrangement of seating, since although as Commissioner and representative of the Government I was entitled to precedence, it would never have done for them to relegate the Consul to a position of inferiority. The difficulty was overcome by placing the Consul and myself side by side in the two centre seats of a row of chairs arranged on a platform, and there we made our public appearance, seated like the Colossi of Memnon, without undue disturbance to the balance of political proprieties.

One day while I was in charge at Larnaca the island was visited by a distinguished Royal personage : none other than Prince Andrew of Greece, father of our own Prince Philip, and— what at that time and in that place was of particular moment— uncle of George II, King of the Hellenes. His Royal Highness, who was travelling privately as a guest on board the yacht of an Australian friend, had let it be known that he would like to go ashore in Cyprus, but desired that no formality or official ceremony should be observed. The Cyprus Government, for its part, was only too ready to respect the letter of these wishes, since the public response to such a visit, had it been advertised, might well not have stopped short at orderly demonstrations of enthusiasm.

Larnaca was to be the first port of call, and I was instructed by the Secretariat to wait upon the Prince as soon as the yacht arrived and on Government's behalf to place myself at his disposal in any matter in which I could be of service. In particular I was to suggest, should the Prince wish to see something of the island, that he should allow me to act as his guide.

The yacht made Larnaca at first light, and after an early breakfast I went down to the jetty and was rowed to the vessel where she lay at anchor not more than a cable's length away. I judged that even if the Prince was not ready to receive visitors there would be somebody on board to whom I could explain my purpose and arrange to return at an hour convenient to His Royal Highness.

At the yacht's side was an accommodation ladder, hospitably lowered, and this I ascended, expecting to find at least a deck-hand to whom I could give a message. But on deck there was nobody at all to be seen, nor were there any signs or sounds of human activity. I wondered what to do. There was nothing to take the place of a front door bell, and to announce my presence by shouted halloas was clearly out of the question. All I could do, I decided, was to wait. Somebody would be bound to come on deck before long.

Somebody did, or at least started to. Not far from where I was standing were the closed double doors of a companion-way, presumably leading to the cabin accommodation, and above these doors, in the open space of the hatch, there suddenly appeared a head. A moment's glance at the dignified and aristocratic features that were revealed was enough to assure me that here, indeed, was the distinguished passenger to whom I was to offer my services.

The unexpected sight of an unannounced stranger must have been something for which the Prince could scarcely have been prepared. There was a moment of silence, and then, as I began to move forward, hat in hand, to introduce myself, there came the words "It isn't me", and the head disappeared as suddenly as it had come into view.

My second attempt was made a little later in company with the Greek Consul. I realized that my earlier approach had been clumsy, and I was very conscious of lacking the kind of experience that might have assisted me in such a situation. But I soon realized that I had nothing to worry about. It was the first time that I had been presented to a Royal personage, and I had yet to appreciate that princes are remarkably well able to put two and two together, and know better than most people how to put others at their ease. Prince Andrew elected to remain on board during the morning and to accept my services as cicerone on an afternoon drive to Kyrenia on the northern coast.

The Geek Consul accompanied us on this excursion, but as my Commissioner's flag was flying from the bonnet of our car the Prince's presence passed unnoticed until our return in the evening, by which time rumours of the identity of our visitor had begun to circulate, and a large crowd had gathered round the entrance to the pier from which he would re-embark. It was not at all the kind of crowd that had filled the streets and thronged round the loud-speaker outside my office to listen to the King's broadcast on Coronation Day: its psychology was altogether different. *That* crowd had been good-humoured, leisurely, relaxed —an "English" crowd. *This* crowd was expectant, emotionally charged, dynamic—Greek. As we made our way towards the waiting launch it surged forward in a frenzy of excitement, cheering, waving and gesticulating in delighted recognition of one who, in his brief passage through their midst, personified for them the eternal verity of Hellas. And on every side arose impassioned cries of "Ζήτω! Ζήτω!" May he live! Hurrah! Hurrah!

No picture of these times would be complete without some reference to the sentiment of the Turkish Cypriots. As a minority, their principal concern was always to keep their heads above water among the powerful currents of the Hellenic tide. They regarded the British administration as a kind of lifebuoy, and before the dissolution of the Legislature they had usually been ready to lend their support to any Government-introduced measure that came before the Council. They were thinly represented among the literati and the professional classes generally; and this was, without doubt, another reason why they looked for support to British bureaucratic rule.

Notwithstanding the barbarities of the past, their relations with the Greek Cypriots, if somewhat aloof, were on the whole amicable, notably in the rural areas, where the village communities jogged along together happily enough, and any instances of minor friction there might have been were purely local and transitory. Some of the Turkish youngsters seemed to have lost faith in the island's prospects for their future advancement, and a few adventurous attempts were made to cross in small boats to Turkey, where the regime of Mustapha Kemal was greatly admired. But here it should be added that, in fact, many of the young Greek-speaking villagers were also anxious to leave the island in order to better their condition. A number of them obtained passports for travel to England, where some remained to serve in the restaurants of Soho and fashionable hotels.

But the pattern of these and other signs and tendencies, of dreams, aspirations and political discontents, was soon to be lost in the deepening shadow of approaching war.

CHAPTER XI

CYPRUS (3)

W E spent the first four months of 1938 on leave in England :
our last, as it was to turn out, until the summer of 1946.
On our return to Cyprus I was posted to the Secretariat as Chief
Assistant Secretary.

I could not have foreseen then that for the next fourteen years
I was to spend most of my time upon the highways rather than
the footpaths of administration; that my main preoccupations
over that period would be with the writing of minutes and
memoranda and the drafting of despatches, with meetings, interviews and the conduct of Government business in legislative
chambers, and not, as hitherto, with the more intimate aspects
of the rural or urban scene. It was not until I went to the Western
Pacific in 1952 as High Commissioner and became a kind of
District Officer *in excelsis,* with nobody but my staff—and they
in deferential accents—to say me nay, that I was able from time
to time to disengage myself from the main traffic of administrative
affairs in order to move about among the people and learn more
of their needs, their customs and their way of life.

Not that I had any reason to complain of this turn of fortune.
I had my share of ambition, and it was recognized throughout the Service that a secretariat officer who had displayed his
talents by the written and the spoken word, and been well
reported upon, might one day aspire to lay down his pen in order
to take proud possession of a set of Governor's plumes. In my
new guise I was to be required to act often in the office of
Colonial Secretary whenever its substantive holder was on leave
or administering the Government in the absence of the Governor
himself. As senior civil servant under the Governor, the Colonial
Secretary held a post of no little responsibility, and I considered

104

myself fortunate to have such an opportunity of gaining experience of this kind so early in my career.

I had a great deal to learn, but my Chief, later to become Sir
Andrew Wright, was a perceptive and conscientious instructor,
and under his watchful and friendly guidance I was able to avoid
some of the pitfalls it would have been all to easy for me to
tumble into. Among much else he impressed upon me the
importance of being succinct and clear on paper.

A good deal of legitimate fun has been poked at the occasional
pomposities of official English. In our attachment to clichés and
rather stilted phraseology we were no doubt sometimes led into
mild absurdities; but a well drafted despatch usually said what it
meant to say, and that precisely and without irrelevance. If
criticism was justified the most obvious target was not obscurity
but a somewhat precious style. In signed despatches it was formal,
cold and colourless, and yet correctly and conventionally
patterned—like the icing on a wedding cake. There was nevertheless something to be said in defence of these dubious embellish-
ments.

In the administration of Britain's Colonial Dependencies two
broad principles—one might call them conventions—were
recognized. That they were to some extent mutually contra-
dictory did not impair their validity : it was merely an instance
in the Colonial sphere of the British genius for reconciling the
apparently irreconcilable. One of these principles was that a
British Dependency was not governed by the Secretary of State
for the Colonies but by the Governor. He it was who, according
to his judgement and discretion, exercised in the fullest knowledge of local conditions and immediate circumstances, must take
the decision in any fateful issue on which he was empowered to
act. To suggest otherwise would be to strike at the foundations of
delegated authority and constitutional practice. This was the
Outpost-of-Empire or Man-on-the-Spot principle.

The second principle, with which the first might seem to be at
variance, was that the Secretary of State was ultimately responsible to the Cabinet, and hence to Parliament and the British
electorate, for the welfare, advancement and good government
of the Colonial peoples. To suggest otherwise would be to strike

at the foundations of parliamentary sovereignty and constitutional theory. This was the Downing Street or Question-in-Parliament principle.

The real authority and influence of a Colonial Governor, as distinct from the powers with which he might be invested by Letters Patent, Royal Instructions, Orders-in-Council, local statutes and Colonial Regulations, were dependent upon his personality and the degree of local confidence he could awaken and command. But in all that passed between Government House and the Colonial Office the operation of the convention that the Secretary of State, on the basis of Principle One, would never if he could avoid it issue a direct order to a Governor in opposition to the latter's advice, coupled with the convention, based on Principle Two, that if the Governor were to receive such an order he would never disobey it, was bound to find some reflection in the forms and phraseology of official correspondence.

In the spirit of the Man-on-the-Spot convention it was necessary to preserve the image of the Governor as one resolute of purpose and unswayed by political pressures, a rock among the shifting sands, a sheet-anchor in angry seas, a Solon in the giving of the law, a Solomon in the measurement of justice. A paragon, in fact, of proconsular virtue and magisterial correctitude. One who could be relied upon to do no angry action, even if in moments of provocation he should let slip a sinful word. Undeterred by circumstances and immune from the influence of vulgar emotions, he must never, so it was understood by those who committed his thoughts to paper, betray fear, anxiety, hesitation or ingnorance. But since, being human, he was in fact sometimes alarmed, anxious, undecided or without information, and also, being honest, desirous of telling the truth, it was important to devise and adhere to phrases that, while able to reveal something of his doubts or misgivings should convey no trace of defeatism, and be capable, if necessary, of standing up to the test of public scrutiny and criticism.

Thus, although the Governor must never confess to alarm he might sometimes view an event with "some concern", or even, in extreme cases with "dismay". A situation with which the Government was faced was never "alarming", though it might become "serious" or, if in fact critical or desperate (a word never to be employed) "grave". This was as far as it was permissible to go. In like manner "ignorance" was disguised as "uncertainty", though I doubt whether anyone ever failed to gather the true import of some such phrase as "I have at present no certain indication of his intentions", when substituted for "I really haven't the slightest idea what he is going to do".

It was however in the conflict, or, rather, in the endeavour to avoid conflict between the Man-on-the-Spot and the Downing Street conventions that official choice of words achieved its nicest refinements. Thus, for example, the Secretary of State, having decided to turn down some gubernatorial request involving, let us say, an authority to incur unbudgeted expenditure, would express himself as "reluctant", for this reason or that, to agree to whatever the proposal might be. Or he might press for some line of action to which the Governor had no intention, if he could help it, of committing himself. In that case the Governor would "find some difficulty", for one reason or another, in following the course suggested. It was a sparring contest without blows : the stage of blunt refusal or positive command was never reached : and if a genuine set-to seemed imminent the matter was either postponed, or some kind of compromise was arrived at, usually by means of demi-official correspondence.

Sir Richmond Palmer, who was Governor of Cyprus at the time of my arrival and remained there until 1939, was a man of steadfast convictions and bold action, to whom the idea of compromise was unattractive. He was firmly persuaded that the restoration of the civil liberties of which the population had been deprived after the 1931 disturbances would quickly pave the way for further *Enosis* demonstrations with attendant unrest and possible violence; and he was satisfied that the only way to prevent the political pot from boiling over was to strengthen the container and keep the lid rammed down. There were undoubtedly substantial grounds for his assessment of the probable consequences of a return to the previous constitution, and in his general policy he had the support of the Secretary of State. In March, 1937, Mr. Ormsby Gore (later to become Lord Harlech) had stated in reply to a question in the Commons that no alteration in the constitution of the Cyprus central Government was under consideration, and that it seemed clear that, having regard to local conditions, the sound line of advance lay in first and foremost encouraging the Islanders in the management of their local affairs in the districts.

The views of Mr. Ormsby Gore and those of the leaders of the "politically minded community" unfortunately did not coincide, and Sir Richmond Palmer, who was judged to be the stumbling block, was unpopular with many people in Cyprus.

In the Secretariat Sir Richmond was easy to work for, provided one understood his methods and the direction of his thoughts. Though capable of scholarly and encyclopaedic research into subjects that interested him, he never wasted words. He knew what he wanted and saw that it was done with a minimum of argument and discussion. His directives were seldom long enough to fill more than a single sheet of paper : which was fortunate, since his handwriting was almost indecipherable and nobody liked to send them back to him with a query. Often they would consist of no more than a single sentence : "We had better tell the Secretary of State what X (a notable malcontent suspected of subversive designs) is doing," or "Should we not try to get a better standard of accommodation in our hotels? Consult Commissioners." This was enough for us to work on. We knew the bent of his mind, the arguments he would want to put forward, the powers he would be prepared to take. In due course a despatch would be put up to him for signature, or draft legislation would be circulated for examination before discussion in Executive Council, and it was not often that we misread his intentions.

The Cyprus Secretariat was small but efficient. the Colonial Secretary and his four Assistants with about twelve clerks, complemented by a Treasurer and his staff and a small Legal Department. There was no Administrative Secretary, no Economic Secretary, no Development Secretary, no Establishment Section, none of the administrative specialists without whose services to a later generation the wheels of bureaucracy could not have been kept in motion. Still less at that time was it possible to foresee the setting up as part of the machinery of Colonial government of the numerous ministries, with their expensive but necessary personnel, which, in the days of Imperial twilight, would sing the swan-song of "colonialism". Undoubtedly before the last world war administration was more straightforward and less dictated by world events. Colonial constitutions were not being revised or rewritten every twelve months or so, and we should have regarded any prediction of sovereign independence within a generation as scarcely more than a chimera. There was little international curiosity about the affairs of dependent territories. For that matter, as far as the British Colonies were concerned, there was remarkably little national curiosity either.

It was the year before 1939. As the hopes of peace with Hitler's Germany drained away, we grew busy with the study of security documents and defence plans. The Law Officers laid aside other work and began to draft Defence Regulations. But these precautions were taken unobtrusively and, for the most part, in secret : on the other side of the closed doors business went on in its normal rather sleepy fashion, and there was nothing in the daily scene to suggest a mood of uneasiness or apprehension. Cyprus, after all, was quite a long way from central Europe—or so people thought. In the narrow streets of Nicosia pastry- and sweetmeat-vendors proffered their sugared plums and apricots with assortments of small cakes and spiced pastries displayed in protective glass-covered cases; the fruit-sellers trundled long barrows, laden in the winter season with toppling pyramids of oranges; in the Turkish Quarter old men sat at their doorsteps, each with his bubbling hookah : from the bazaar came a continuous clamour of hammers on metal in the Street of the Coppersmiths. Those who had pence and leisure sat outside the coffee shops and sipped their Cyprus brandy while they watched or gossiped. Outside the walls was the only symbol that could even remotely be associated with possible dangers to come—the Union Jack that flew from the flagstaff of the Wolseley Barracks. But those barracks, by their very name, seemed to be a link with the past rather than the present. They housed the modest establishment of the Cyprus permanent garrison. One Company of the Sherwood Foresters. That was all.

War, when at last it came, did not for some time bring any

outwardly visible changes; but there was a heartening response by all the people to the general call to arms. A recruiting officer arrived in Nicosia from Middle East Headquarters, and a Company of muleteers was enlisted, equipped and sent off for training in time to earn the proud distinction of being the first unit of Colonial troops to reach France. Later on, the Cyprus Regiment was raised and gave a good account of itself in Libya and other theatres. Everybody except the few quasi-Italians at Larnaca, who, faced with the prospect of detention should Italy become involved, were content to lie low, was stoutly for the Allied cause, and for the time being politics were at a discount.

Until the early summer of 1940, when Mussolini thrust his dagger into the back of a gravely wounded and, as he hoped, mortally smitten France, we in Cyprus still regarded ourselves as being beyond the range of probable attack. Thereafter, and increasingly with the invasion of the Balkans, the envelopment of Greece and the fall of Crete, the island was like a village at the foot of an erupting volcano, whose devastating flow creeps ever closer with its threat of seizure and destruction. During this uncertain phase defence measures were strengthened and intensified. The regular garrison was brought up to battalion strength and augmented by a Volunteer Force, raised for home defence, in which, with many other civil servants, I enrolled. The Attorney-General, now Sir Stafford Foster-Sutton, became Commanding Officer, and we were drilled twice a week by seasoned N.C.O.s of the Sherwood Foresters. In due course the Force was organized in subordinate units, and presumably on the strength of my military record, inadequate as I felt it to be, I was given a Company to command.

Even at this stage, or at least until the agony of Crete, it was difficult to believe as we marched up and down on parade, or dutifully went through the motions of loading and unloading our not very up-to-date rifles, that we might soon be called upon to fire in anger. When we had mastered our military A.B.C. I planned schemes and exercises for the Company in the open country that surrounded the approaches to the capital: it somewhat resembled, with its boldly coloured undulations and panoramic background of hills, the landscape targets of O.T.C.

days at Westminster, and was as good a training ground as one could wish to find.

I enjoyed these long hours in the open air, as, many years earlier, while at Woolwich, I had enjoyed my sketching and reconnoitring excursions into the neighbouring countryside. For all I knew, they might be the prelude to bloodshed and anguish, but my mind was not preoccupied with thoughts of that kind. My concern as an amateur soldier was with the subtleties of the terrain, the sweep of the contours, the field of fire from this position or that, the folds in the ground or the direction of a watercourse that might give cover to an advancing enemy or an offensive patrol, the situation of trees and buildings that might obscure vision and affect the value of a defensive post. For us all it was an exercise involving scoutcraft and cunning, a kind of game, resembling on a small scale the war games played by "red" and "blue" competitors and umpired with flags and whistles : a game to be played later on, perhaps, with sterner purpose when Fate would be the umpire and the forfeit death.

But there was a knowledge that I gained from these exploratory exercises that was something deeper than an appreciation of the military aspects of topography. As an artist discovers in some attractive subject, in its form and arrangement, in its colours, in its lights and shades, a vista of truth that inspires his treatment of the composition; so I found, if I did not consciously seek, in the way the land rose and fell upon the bosom of the plain, in the curves of the valleys, in the veins of the winding stream-beds, in the powerful sinews of the hills, some understanding of the anatomy and strength, the nakedness and beauty, of the earth beneath her mantle of green and gold.

After the invasion of Crete we began to take things very seriously. It seemed obvious that we were in the main line of German advance and could expect to be invaded at any moment. Arrangements were made rapidly by the Government for the evacuation of British residents and the wives and families of expatriate Government servants. My wife and daughter sailed early in June, 1941, with a ship-load of passengers for Port Said, whence I hoped they would find means to continue their journey to Southern Rhodesia, where we had friends. It was an anxious parting, but I was relieved by the knowledge that if it came to hostilities they would be distant from danger. I had no idea when we should meet again, and no great confidence that we ever should, though my mood was on the whole fatalistic rather than despondent. I think this state of mind was general : we in Cyprus had up to this moment remained in sheltered security while England stood up to the blows of her adversary. Now, it seemed, the time had come for us to step into the arena. The tempo of life had quickened; irrelevances were discarded; essential values were revealed at their true worth; the hour was suddenly adventurous.

The Cyprus Volunteer Force had been mobilized, and our military morale was given a further fillip with the arrival of an Australian mechanized cavalry regiment. Khaki was becoming a familiar colour in the streets, and cabaret proprietors, who had been on the point of closing down, stopped putting up their shutters and looked about in hope of profitable custom. Meanwhile we were buckling on our armour. My Company had been allotted the task of defending the western boundaries of Nicosia— a rather tough assignment, I felt, for a hundred riflemen and two temperamental Lewis guns with an exasperating proclivity for developing "stoppages". This was a perverse kind of occupational disease, concerning whose treatment and prevention the manual of operating instructions was ominously informative, and I had no great faith in our ability to effect a rapid cure in case of emergency. But I did not communicate these misgivings to the willing band for whose destinies I might soon find myself responsible. They were cheerful, they were tough, and I was quite sure that if it came to a show-down they would put up a game fight.

We spent our days energetically, digging fire-trenches and preparing machine-gun posts in case the Lewis guns should function. It was warm work in the blazing June sunshine. In front of our position was a threshing floor strewn with glowing piles of grain, which were being removed by their owner in leisurely journeys with a mule cart. There was a drift of irony in this peaceful process; but in some indefinable way the contrast with our own so differently directed labours was almost reassur-

1. Traditional Salute by followers of the Emir of Bida at the greater Moslem Festival

2. Pagan village in the Niger Province of Nigeri

3. Merchant adventurers of the Niger

4. The Venus Rocks near Paphos, Cyprus (author's daughter with companion)

5. The author as Colonial Secretary, Gibraltar

6. R.S.C. Nareau

7. Ellice Islands girls in dancing dress

8. The author as Speaker of the Mauritius Legislative Council

ing. As if Fate were dealing out two hands of cards, and was not yet certain which one to play.

The rest is anti-climax. I cannot go on to relate that, having steeled myself for the fray, I went out with high resolve to do battle with the King's enemies; for they failed to arrive. The alarm was a false one. We were not, after all, to be tried in the fire. Instead of sending his troops to Cyprus, Hitler turned upon Russia, and our hour of danger was past. Six months later I had been granted leave and was on my way to join my family in Southern Rhodesia.

With some assistance from the Royal Navy I reached Salisbury on Christmas Day, 1941. A few days later I was informed by telegram that I had been selected for appointment as Colonial Secretary of Barbados.

E

Chapter XII

BARBADOS

M Y first sight of Barbados was from the air. The green fields
of growing sugar cane, and the brown and gold of the trash
that looked like bracken on an English common on a day in
autumn, might almost have been part of an English landscape.

There was much else in Barbados that recalled England,
though relations with the mother country had not always been
harmonious.

"They [the Parliament of England] alledge that this island
was first settled and inhabited at the charges, and by the
esspecial order of the people of England, and therefore ought
to be subject to the same nation. It is certain, that we all of us
know very well, that wee, the present inhabitants of this island,
were and still be that people of England, who with great
danger to our persons, and with great charge and trouble,
have settled this island in its condition, and inhabited the
same, and shall wee therefore be subject to the will and command of those that stay at home? Shall we be bound to the
Government and Lordship of a Parliament in which we have
no representatives, or persons chosen by us, for there to pro-
pound and consent to what might be needful to us, as also to
oppose and dispute all what should tend to our disadvantage
and harme? In truth, this would be a slavery far exceeding
all that the English nation hath yet suffered. And we doubt
not but the courage which hath brought us thus far out of our
own country, to seek our beings and livelihoods in this wild
country, will maintain us in our freedoms; without which our
lives will be uncomfortable to us."

That extract comes from a Declaration published in 1651 by
Lord Willoughby, the Governor of Barbados, with the advice of

the Colonial Legislature. The immediate threat to comfort was the Navigation Act, approved by Oliver Cromwell as a challenge to the Dutch monopoly of the carrying trade : it prohibited the importation of goods into any English Colony unless they were carried in English ships or, if brought from Europe, in ships of the country in which the goods were produced. Barbadians felt indebted to the Netherlands for assistance in providing many of their essential requirements and were not prepared to deny to Dutch vessels or to those of any other nation the freedom of the island's harbours. The Declaration concludes defiantly :

"Wherefore, having rightly considered, we declare, that as we would not be wanting to use all honest means for the obtaining of a continuance of commerce, trade, and good correspondence with our country, soe wee will not alienate ourselves from those old heroick virtues of true English men, to prostitute our freedom and privileges, to which we are borne, to the will and opinion of any one; neither do we thinke our number so contemptible, nor our resolution so weake, to be forced or persuaded to so ignoble a submission, and we cannot think, that there are any amongst us, who are soe simple, and soe unworthily minded, that they would not rather chuse a noble death, than forsake their ould liberties and privileges."

But there were other and more serious causes of dispute with the Parliament of the Commonwealth. Lord Willoughby, who, for all his championship of democratic principles, was a staunch Royalist, had, as one of his first acts of government, consented to legislation which declared the right of King Charles the Second to the dominion of the island; whereupon the English Parliament declared the inhabitants of Barbados to be traitors to the Commonwealth, and in due course an expedition was despatched to enforce the submission of the rebels.

The expedition was rebuffed, first by the guns of Fort Charles, which flashed haughtily, but without inflicting much damage, at the ships of the passing squadron, and then by the defeat of an attempted landing in longboats. Forced eventually by superior numbers to capitulate, the resolute governor was nevertheless successful in obtaining a "Charter of Barbados"—a liberal instrument, one of whose articles provided that no taxes, customs, imposts, loans or excise should be laid, nor levy made on any of the inhabitants of the island without their consent in a General Assembly.

It would be difficult to find more convincing evidence than Lord Willoughby's Declaration of the independent and uncompromising spirit that possessed the islanders in those early days; but the challenging tones of that document would not have been far removed from the mood and temper, nor its arguments from the point of view, of the Barbadian "plantocracy" at any time during the following three centuries. For Barbados had never regarded herself as a dependency of England. In the minds of the white settlers and their descendants she always had been a fragment of England, a "little England", as she had sometimes been called, in her own right; and if with the emancipation of the African slave population the English image was transformed into something that could more properly be designated as Barbadian there was ample evidence, even in my day—in the Legislative Council and the House of Assembly, corresponding to Lords and Commons; in the entrenched parochialism of the system of local government; in place names such as Hastings, Worthing, Highgate, Oxford, Cambridge and Windsor; and, not least, in the dominating influence of cricket as a national sport—in all this there was continuing evidence of the island's English roots and affiliations.

In discovering these and other similarities it was easy to awaken the fancy that Time had sometimes absent-mindedly turned over his glass and left the sands to run the other way. There on a bold skyline, a lonely landmark from the past, was a windmill; and here, in busy Bridgetown, where Nelson's statue facing Trafalgar Square looked down towards the careenage, one might see a boat manned by Harbour Police dressed in the sailor jackets and straw hats of Nelson's day. Not far away was the harbour itself (this was before the construction of deep water berths in Carlisle Bay), a narrow waterway which sheltered the inter-island schooners on which most of the regional traffic depended. Barbados possessed, like London, a capacity for concealing in her bosom much of the evidence of her dependence upon maritime adventure, though the buildings of Bridgetown were not quite high enough to prevent the secret from leaking out, and like inverted pendulums the criss-crossing mast-heads of the tall ships sheered aloft to trace the dying motions of the ocean swell.

The House of Assembly, a recurring motif in the Barbadian tapestry, was still of all the island's institutions the most politically potent. When it saw reason to commend a governor's actions it would take its purse from its pocket with prerogative gesture and pour out a golden tribute of approbation. But if by the least act the holder of the King's Commission should happen, however unwittingly, to offend its dignity or trespass upon its privileges, a very different temper was at once displayed : a piece of cannon was wheeled into position, the weapon was primed and aimed, the charge was ignited, and with a flash, a rumble and a cloud of smoke a Resolution of displeasure went hurtling in the direction of the unfortunate transgressor.

Barbados is a small island, shaped like a shoulder of mutton, with a greatest length of only twenty one miles. It seemed an inadequate area to contain the 332 sugar estates and the 18,000 small holdings (most of them less than one acre in extent) whose output had to support a population of 200,000. Sugar was ruler of the economy, and I was impressed by the intensification of research and agricultural enterprise within such limited confines, as well as by the visible evidence of human domination over the terrain. In an earlier chapter I have remarked that in Nigeria Nature was sovereign, but in Cyprus she was closely bound to the rule of Man. In Barbados, as far as territorial occupancy was concerned, she was a vassal, claiming no prescriptive rights over the jealously cultivated acres of the plantations, the crowded gardens of the peasants, the floors and curtilages of the hard-working sugar factories, the teeming congeries of little wooden houses in their narrow ill-conditioned tenantries, the crooked alleys and congested streets of Bridgetown, or the sites of the "great houses" with their long verandahs or "galleries" and solidly furnished interiors, which, rising here and there from the broad sweep of the cane, testified to the leisure and comfort of the wealthy planter in more spacious days.

It was sugar, assisted for nearly two centuries by slavery, that had dictated the social order since Cromwellian days, and the earlier history of the period contains some distressing and occasionally shameful records. According to Schomburgk* a number of royalist conspirators were transported to Barbados in 1656 (to "barbadose" was the expression that came into use to describe this kind of punishment), and there, having been sold as slaves "for fifteen hundred and fifty pounds of sugar each, more or less, according to their working faculties", were made to suffer cruel indignities. Many of those implicated in the Monmouth rebellion were similarly treated. At the beginning of the eighteenth century the average price of a negro slave was £23 8s. Before 1805, when the relevant statute was repealed, the legal punishment for the murder of a slave was fixed at £15.

Of the total population at the time of my arrival about 10,000 would probably have claimed pure European descent, though by no means all those whose complexions revealed no obvious colour would have been able to produce family trees on which no alien shoot had been grafted. The original settlers had brought with them a number of white servants, and within fifty years the total of white inhabitants, including transportees and others who had arrived voluntarily under contract of service, amounted, with their families, to more than twenty thousand. In my time there was still a small section of "poor whites". This depressed and seldom noticed minority had retained their racial purity, though they had never been able to better their circumstances. They were employed in agricultural "gangs", or lived precariously as fishermen.

The non-white majority supplied the island's labour force, but included a fairly prosperous middle class and had given men of mark to the professions as well as to politics and commerce. White and coloured met and did business together in board rooms as a matter of routine, but the clubs and the drawing rooms of the exclusive caste were closed to all, whatever their complexions might suggest, who were known to be of mixed parentage.

Nevertheless, the citadels of privilege were already beginning to crumble. The white man was steward of a diminishing estate,

* *The History of Barbados* by Robert H. Schomburgk, 1848.

and those whom his ancestors had commanded, protected, punished or rewarded were listening to a new doctrine. Forthright in his championship of popular causes was W. Algernon Crawford, a Member of the House of Assembly, and editor of *The Barbados Observer,* a newspaper which, as it proclaimed in every issue, was "dedicated to the service of the PEOPLE, that no good cause shall lack a champion and that wrong will not thrive unopposed." It was this newspaper that, in its valedictory article upon my departure, had recorded such pronounced convictions about my attitude towards "the glorious British Empire". But although in his conclusions on this point Mr. Crawford was slightly adrift, and obviously had some doubts of my capacity to free myself completely from the corrupting influences of imperialism, it would be ungracious not to acknowledge the generous tribute to my services that he saw fit to publish.

The working classes as a whole, notwithstanding their poverty and the inadequacy and often insanitary condition of much of their housing, were cheerful by nature and schooled to adversity. They were kind and simple people, ready to smile at misfortune and to split their sides at a bawdy joke. They were sometimes accused by those in more comfortable circumstances of laziness and improvidence. It was certainly true that an increase in agricultural wage rates had on occasion resulted in a decrease of output by some who were content to go on earning the same money in return for shorter hours; but those who laboured in the fields were no doubt the best judges of the value to them of their leisure. They were devoted to their children, and although the majority dispensed with the marriage ceremony there were many faithful unions among those who did so, the status officially accorded to the female partner in such cases being that of "reputed wife". They were superstitious, though many of them were devout and regular church-goers, and at midnight on Christmas Eve all the churches in the island were thronged with the streams of worshippers before the bright altars.

Historically speaking, they were a disinherited community. It was not only the discipline of tribal life that had been taken from them : that, certainly, they had never known in Barbados, for their people came from fifty different countries and the traffic lasted for two centuries. Nor had they any common language other than the English they learned from their masters. Something else, it sometimes seemed to me, had gone out of them. Something of the vigour and purpose of the husbandman whose stake in the soil was to the African another name for freedom. It was the ambition of nearly all these humble folk to own a little land, were it no more for each than a few square yards on which to build a cabin, but an ambition that few were able to attain.

But this was not the whole picture. A strong local patriotism had grown up, which held together and anchored their affections to their small island even when, as sometimes happened, they left that little country of slender promise to seek their fortunes on the mainland. Barbados was their home: they were Barbadians. And to proclaim oneself a "Bajan", as they called it, was to assert superiority over Trinidadians, Jamaicans, Dominicans, St. Lucians, Antiguans, Kittivonians and all the rest. Barbados was a mistress, a mother, to whom they would all give service; and in this the whole community was at one. This universal loyalty was the lodestone of an interracial understanding. In the Barbados Volunteer Force, a body raised, like the Cyprus Volunteer Force, for home defence in emergency, and in the civil defence services that were organized to deal with air attack, white and coloured were comrades in arms and service and bent their energies to the common cause. Threatened danger had emphasized this patriotic unity, but that threat was not the only occasion for its display. On the cricket field all awareness of colour disappeared when Barbados was upholding her honour against a visiting team. And in the House of Assembly, in which there were more coloured members than white, there was only one voice when it came to what was regarded as a national issue. Then, as the spirit of Macaulay might have written, all were for the island and none was for the race. In Cyprus the Greek-speaking community had looked beyond their shores to discover themselves as children of Hellas. In Barbados, in any question of nationhood, what lay beyond the coastline had become irrelevant: the people were Barbadians. It was this kind of insistence upon insular identity and interest, which in the Caribbean was by no means confined to Barbados, that was later to destroy all hopes for the success of a broadly based Federation of the British Caribbean territories.

Such was the scene into which, carried by the recently established service of British West Indies Airways, we descended in April 1942. As a newcomer, I obviously had much to learn; but the first lesson was that in matters of administrative procedure one had, in Barbados, to do as Barbados did. Many forms and practices—in particular that of seeking prior sanction by Resolution of the House of Assembly for any item of expenditure, however urgent, that could not have been anticipated—were embalmed in tradition whose rigidities were seldom compatible with the need for swift and decisive action.

Of serious consequence, at least in its implications, was the inability of the Governor to be confident of adequate support in the Legislature for measures that needed their consent. There was no official majority, and the Government's only spokesmen and representatives were the Attorney-General in the House of Assembly and myself in the Legislative Council. But it was the House of Assembly that held the purse strings, and the Attorney-General, as an elected member, claimed the right to oppose Government policy if he considered that it would not be in the best interests of his constituents. It was a paradoxical situation and the successful working of the system was greatly dependent upon general good will and the personal influence of the Governor himself. It spoke much for the persuasive perseverance of Sir Grattan Bushe, who was Governor of Barbados throughout my sojourn in the island, that he was able to cut his way through these constitutional entanglements, and that in addition to widening the franchise and raising the professional standards of the Public Service he succeeded in preparing the way for the system of Ministerial responsibility that was subsequently introduced.

At the time of my arrival there was much preoccupation with defence measures, for with recent successful attacks on merchant shipping in the Caribbean the stern realities of war had crossed the Atlantic. "If," proclaimed an advertisement prominently displayed in a shop window, "if you would learn about this new war that has come to the Americas, read *Time*." I did not find it necessary to follow this advice and I doubt whether general demand for the publication was brisk. Barbados had, in fact, done a great deal to conserve and increase natural resources and organize manpower. Planters had turned over part of their sugar lands for the cultivation of sweet potatoes and other substitutes for the imported rice (normally the stable diet for much of the population) whose supply might be restricted; the Barbados Volunteer Force, already mobilized, was in active training; a Volunteer Brigade was being formed to act as an auxiliary Force in support of the Police and the Fire Brigade, and the civil defence organizers were staging realistic "incidents" in which the "injured" lay about in uncomfortable postures awaiting attention by the first-aiders of the local branch of the St. John Ambulance. This body, under the inspiriting generalship of Lady Bushe, did fine work in caring for survivors from vessels sunk by the U-boats, which had begun to operate with diabolical success.

War measures apart, it was for the British West Indies as a whole a time of stocktaking, reassessment and impending change. With few exceptions the islands were in a state of chronic poverty caused by over-population, under-employment and the ravages of recurrent plant disease. In a full-scale effort to revive the economy and restore the fortunes of the area the Development and Welfare Organization in the West Indies—known locally as "the Circus"—had been set up by the United Kingdom Government to provide grants and loans for expanded medical and health services, better equipped hospitals, more schools and increased and more diversified agricultural production and research. Experts, engaged in every kind of statistical investigation and scientific experiment from demography to soil chemistry, were as busy as bees in blossom time, and the offices of the advisers and planners, who had their headquarters in Bridgetown, were hives of constructive activity under the energetic direction of Sir Frank Stockdale, the Comptroller. For all that the buzz of investigation was sometimes a little confusing, it was a bold enterprise, which contributed in its results to the raising of living standards; but Barbados, ever cautious, was at times uneasy about accepting capital benefits that could be expected to impose increased recurrent burdens on the exchequer, and there were those who were suspicious lest the gift-horse should in some way turn out to be a wooden one.

Much of my time was devoted to the preparation and delivery of speeches. Indeed, it was by this medium that most of my contacts with the people were made, for there was little scope among a populace consisting to a large extent of agricultural workers living on other people's land for the rural excursions and let's-sit-down-in-the-shade-and-talk-about-it type of discussion with village communities that I had enjoyed in Nigeria and, to a more limited extent, in Cyprus. But to numerous assemblies of persons, and, indeed, through the wide publicity that I was always given in the press, to the whole island I seemed always to be addressing myself, not because I enjoyed talking, but because it seemed to be expected of me. As Government spokesman in the Legislative Council it fell to me to take charge of Government Bills of whatever kind—a duty that compelled me to devote study to a large number of subjects about which I was surprised to find I had been so ignorant; but, apart from this purely official task, I was always being called upon to attend, and usually to speak at, one public function or another.

I was invited to sports meetings and cycle-track races and, after appropriate congratulations, presented trophies to perspiring runners or exhausted bicyclists. I was present at school speech-days and handed prizes to children who, according to their dispositions, were cheerful, cheeky or shy, or merely exuded a conscious virtue. Wondering what a wolf would feel like in sheep's clothing, but feeling on the whole more sheepish than wolfish, I mounted the solid pulpit of the James Street Methodist church and addressed an annual missionary meeting. At the conclusion of what must have seemed a very amateur performance the choir sang an anthem, and two ladies executed a duet entitled "They shall hunger no more". During the temporary absence from the island of the Governor I inspected the Volunteer Brigade and commended their energies, pinned medals upon the breasts of policemen who had done the State some service, and congratulated them, shook hands with footballers in approved fashion (but a very few remarks sufficed for this occasion, for the crowd was waiting for the game to begin and the referee was beginning to look impatient), and addressed the two Chambers of the Legislature at its formal opening. "Words, words, words." If all my words had carried wings the skies of Barbados would have been dark with them.

I have never been one of those for whom a few notes will serve to turn on a tap of eloquence, and I used to dictate my speeches at length and read them through until I could repeat them nearly enough from memory; though in the hope of avoiding the impression of a set piece I would make last-minute interpolations if anything happened while I was waiting to speak that seemed suitable for comment, and I could think of anything apt to include before I found myself on my feet. By this, as I like to think, fairly innocent stratagem I may have acquired some undeserved credit as an extempore speaker, but the observant could scarcely have failed to notice the sheets of paper that I always had ready in my hand in case memory should fail. My conscience tells me that there may have been a touch of vanity about it all; but at least I did not fall so low as to adopt the device revealed to me by my oculist concerning one of his patients (whom, very properly, he did not name), a Member of Council who had asked for reading glasses with special lenses to enable him to peruse a document held at arm's length beneath the level of the table when standing up to speak in the Chamber. As far as my own speeches in Council were concerned, or at least such parts of them as contained any indication of Government policy, I never hesitated to refresh my memory openly, for I knew that my every observation would be taken down in writing and not only could, but certainly would, provided any political end might thereby be served, be used in evidence against me.

But the task which brought me closest to an understanding of the lives of simple folk was the chairmanship of a Committee appointed by the Governor to investigate the housing problems of the island. There was much to be remedied. The Barbadian's home, like the Englishman's, was his castle; but for the manual labourer and the petty craftsman it was a humble and usually sorry piece of construction, taking the form of a small two-roomed cabin with perhaps a lean-to shed, which served as a kitchen, though as often as not the cooking was done in the open air. Bathrooms were non-existent and "sanitation" consisted of an open-pit closet, shared in many cases with a neighbour. Houses were frequently in bad repair, and some were patched and frail like a worn-out dress. The whole problem was aggravated by serious overcrowding in the Capital, where many came to seek the better opportunities that few discovered. The occupants nevertheless made the best of their conditions, and even in the meanest alleys of Bridgetown housewives were proud and tidy, yards were kept clear of litter, floors were swept and scrubbed, and a few pieces of cheap glass and china were ranged neatly on a shelf in the living room; a slip of curtain veiled the paneless windows, and illustrations cut out of newspapers decorated the walls. Our report put forward various proposals for slum clearance and subsidization with assistance from Colonial Development and Welfare funds, though we could not hope to eradicate the whole of the evil, due as it was to poverty and general economic depression.

Associated with me as a member of our Committee was a man for whom I formed a great respect and admiration. A lawyer, a Member of the House of Assembly and of the Executive Committee (the advisory body which was consulted by the Governor on policy matters), he was already a commanding figure in public life and was to win his way to further distinction by his quiet perseverance and his simple honesty of purpose. This was Grantley Adams, who became Prime Minister of the short-lived West Indian Federation. His power to persuade and, if necessary, to compel lay, I think, in his modesty and his patience. Although he was neither a fanatic nor a fire eater, he was a man of deep convictions and dedicated aims.

Together with other members of the Committee we spent a good many hours visiting and inspecting the dwellings of the poor. Some of these wretched abodes scarcely afforded protection from wind and rain, and their termite-infested timbers were rotten and ready to collapse and crumble on the imposition of any unusual strain. One day we were examining the condition of these so-called houses in an area of Bridgetown known, history possibly but more probably Heaven only knew why, as Golden

Square, which was one of the worst slums in the island. In order to test the integrity of a board that we suspected of having been eaten almost through by the voracious insects, somebody took a penknife from his pocket and applied the point of the blade with gentle pressure to the doubtful area: it yielded like a bar of saturated soap. I saw Grantley Adams watching this experiment with an expression on his face that was more eloquent than any words he could have found, and I knew that in this silent, sympathetic observer the poor possessed an advocate and a friend who would never fail them.

There were many others whose faces I can see in the mirrors of the past, and some of them are framed in the background of the Legislative Council chamber. The Council itself had preserved through many changes the authoritative influence derived from its historic status; and though, as a second Chamber, its powers were limited, it performed its reviewing functions with watchful diligence. Debates never, in my recollection, became heated, and what was described in the minutes as "applause" was no more than a discreet tapping of pencil-ends on the long table from both sides of which members rose to speak. Dr. John Hutson, the President, was knighted while I was in the Colony, but everybody went on calling him Dr. John, as they had done for all the long years during which he had won the affections of the whole community, white and coloured, by his dedicated services to the sick and suffering. His small but commanding figure and his manifest impartiality, coupled with the benign wisdom of years, brought a becoming dignity to the Council and added lustre to a venerable institution, whose existence, in the form of a Senate, was continued in the post-independence Constitution of the island.

In a less elevated sphere was Sergeant Proverbs.

He combined the functions of caretaker, orderly and messenger-in-chief at the Public Buildings, where the Secretariat was housed. Six feet two in his size eleven regulation boots, with his grizzled hair, his shining spectacles and a countenance that was more often benevolent than stern, he looked, despite his dark blue trousers, white patrol jacket and red stripes, more like a village schoolmaster, or even a lay preacher, than the still active member of the Barbados Police Force, albeit approaching superannuation, that, in fact, he was. He used to open and tidy my office before my arrival in the morning, bring me a cup of tea when I needed a stimulant, and put up the shutters after we had all gone home; so his day was a long one. He was always there to ensure that visitors were conducted with proper ceremony or to challenge anyone whom he might suspect of having no legitimate errand, and I am certain that during official hours he regarded me as being under his personal surveillance and protection.

One day I left the office after a midday sandwich to clear my thoughts with a stroll to the quay for a sight of the restless masts and the silver piles of freshly caught flying fish that were unloaded there. I must have been unusually preoccupied with whatever had been engaging my mind, for as I emerged from the precincts of the Public Building to cross the road I narrowly escaped collision with a taxi. On my return, Sergeant Proverbs, who had evidently observed the incident from a window, met me with a look of scarcely veiled reproof.

"Better be careful, chile; dey no-good drivers be comin' roun' dat corner fast, fast. Warn't no mo'n de bredt o' my li'l finger 'tween yo' an' dat taxicab."

I will not be certain that he called me "child". Indeed, if I adhere to the strict letter of the truth I may have to confess that he did not address those words to me at all. Not with his lips. But what was written in the quasi-paternal solicitude of his countenance I have faithfully reported.

There was Mary, the fruit-seller.

"Good morning, kind gentleman," she greeted me one day. "Please buy a lovely pear."

I had noticed her once or twice on my daily comings and goings as she squatted close to the entrance to the Public Buildings behind her capacious basket of oranges, bananas and avocado pears. She was no longer young, but in spite of her shuffling, slightly limping gait, her shabby dress and her untidy lock of hair straggling over one eye she preserved more than a shred of dignity and was raggedly handsome in a down-at-heel, defiant sort of way. She had eyes that might once have been roguish and had certainly looked upon the world with knowledge, perhaps even with vision enough in adversity to glimpse, if only for a moment, the precious jewel in the toad's head.

I bought a pear for the sake of comradeship, although I had a tree of them in my garden, and after that I became a fairly regular customer. Sometimes she would produce a musk melon— a rare delicacy imported from Dominica—or proffer in her cupped hands some Julie mangoes, judged in Barbados to be the best-flavoured species of that popular fruit. There was a period of two or three weeks during which I missed her from her accustomed post, and then I found her again waiting for me with an empty basket and a look in her eyes I had not seen before. She had been ill, she told me, but, thanks God, she was better now. She owed rent and her landlord had threatened to turn her out if she didn't pay him something to go on with. She had no money to satisfy him or to replenish her supplies. Would I, God bless me, help her with a loan of five dollars until she found her feet again?

I produced the money, and by agreement it was repaid in convenient instalments in the form of small additions to my periodical purchases. She was still plying her not very lucrative trade when I left the island. I doubt whether she is still in the land of the living. If she is, I hope she has found solace in old age and kept her memories bright. I think she would have done.

Especially I remember Sir Grattan Bushe, under whom it was a privilege to serve. He knew how to encourage, and how to correct with words that carried no sting but left one reflecting upon the ease of error and the need for vigilance. As former Legal Adviser to the Colonial Office he brought a shrewd judgement and the discipline of legal precision to the service of an original and fertile mind. Fools were suffered, if not gladly, at least with patience, but knavery, if he detected it, could expect short shrift. Despite personal tragedy—his son had been killed in action—he preserved a buoyancy of spirit and a twinkling sense of humour—very real but not always apparent—which caused him, I believe, to be something of an enigma to the Barbadians, who were not quite sure what to make of him.

It would not have been difficult for fancy to cast him in some mythical role. As Puck he would have imagined no great mischief, but he would have taken delight in anticipating the space

men by putting a girdle round the earth in forty minutes, and as
Ariel he would have been ready "to fly, to swim, to dive into the
fire, to ride upon the curl'd clouds." But probably, despite a
deficiency of inches, it would have been in the armour of Don
Quixote that he would have been most faithful to his task. He
was, in fact, an entirely human figure: gentle, forbearing, yet
like a tiger to spring upon any lurking evil of injustice or abuse.
A little man with a gigantic shadow.

Chapter XIII

GIBRALTAR

GIBRALTAR is a name to call the memory to attention. For those who now mournfully survey the fading afterglow of Empire it could be written in a list that would include Trafalgar, Jutland and El Alamein and, by a romantic stretch of the imagination, the Road to Mandalay and the White Cliffs of Dover. But for many people throughout earlier centuries it had comparable associations. Once it was the Key of Spain, and in the time of the Western Caliphate it was the Mount of Conquest. "The Mountain of Tarik", once wrote a poet of Granada, "is like a beacon spreading its rays over the sea and rising far above the neighbouring mountains. One would say that its face almost reaches the sky and that its eyes are watching the stars in the celestial tracts." In passing it might be observed that, making all allowance for poetic licence, one would be remarkably wide of the truth in saying anything of the kind : Gibraltar's highest altitude—1,396 feet above sea level—is much less than that of the neighbouring heights of Spain and, across the straits, the 3,000 feet summit of Mount Abyla, the other Pillar of Hercules, puts the pretensions of the Rock to shame.

But if this eulogy has allowed imagination to slip the leash, we are brought back to earth by the no less enthusiastic but more realistic references in the narrative of Ibn Batuta, the famous fourteenth century traveller of the Moslem world. For him Gibraltar was "an obstacle stuck in the throat of the unbeliever", and his account goes on to mention the "fortifications, walls, towers, gates, arsenals, mosques, stores and granaries." Evidently a place where the Moors had decided to trust in God and keep their powder dry.

I found Gibraltar, when, translated from Barbados, I arrived there in December, 1944, to assume duty as Colonial Secretary, full of relics of the past and reminders of the present. The massive walls, gates and bastions situated along the seaward boundary of the town, and the open-mouthed galleries high up on the North Front gave colour to legends of blood, thunder and cannon balls. Other, more ancient, fortifications were no less ingeniously planned. The ruins of Moorish Castle, whose construction is reputed to have been begun in A.D. 711, the year of Tarik's conquest, and the well-preserved remains of its ancillary wall, direct in its ascent of the Rock as a Roman road and as scornful of gradient as the funicular that has now been installed—these were testimony of successful resistance to early attempts to invade and capture the fortress.

Further South, beyond the Admiralty harbour, and cut off by a minor promontory from the metallic clamour of the dockyard, was the small harbour of Rosia, seldom frequented and at peace with its memories. Here it was that after Trafalgar the body of Nelson was carried ashore and up a winding stair from the quay with those of his men whose little page in history is written on the headstones of the Trafalgar cemetery, adjoining the Southport Gate. And in all parts of the town and in its surroundings were barracks where the sound of bugles from reveille to the last post, the roll of drums and sometimes the skirl of bagpipes kept unbroken the thin red line of military tradition through the complicated nexus of modern defence.

Cannon balls were now used for merely ornamental purposes, and blood was happily absent, but modern weapons provided plenty of thunder when the heavy guns mounted on top of the peninsula rattled windows and occasionally shattered them during a practice shoot, or when, usually at night, house foundations shuddered in response to the explosions of depth charges dropped by patrolling vessels at the entrance to the harbour. Whether this activity was a routine exercise designed as a deterrent to potential attack, or indicated an actual encounter with the enemy I never discovered, for the Navy told no tales.

Not to be outdone by the Senior Service the Royal Engineers operated their own explosive devices within the Rock itself, whence muffled detonations at any time of day indicated the progress of some new tunnelling scheme. This traditional occupation, begun during the time of General Eliott, had in the course of a century and a half created a system of transverse and longitudinal galleries and excavated chambers, which now accommodated storage depots, as well as power and other installations which would enable a heavily besieged garrison to maintain itself in a state of troglodytic defence.

The plan of Gibraltar at sea level covers only two and a quarter square miles, but this measurement gives no indication at all of the almost endless succession of vistas or the numerous transformations of the same scene presented from different altitudes and points of view. Armed with the necessary passes one could wander for many miles, climbing or maintaining an even course around the Rock at different levels without ever covering the same ground twice. One morning shortly after my arrival I ascended one of the roads that had not been placed out of bounds to the public and paused at a point about half way from the top to survey the scene. Although it was midwinter the sun was warm, and the slopes that were not too steep to retain a covering of soil were patterned with white narcissi. The view was superb. The sun that had enticed the white flowers into blossom had not been strong enough to melt the snow from the surrounding heights of Andalusia curving southwards to overlook the little whitewashed walls and house fronts of Algeciras. Far below were the town, the harbour and the dockyard—a lilliputian scene in its own dimension of space. Across the blue waters of the straits was snow again, upon the lofty summits of the Moroccan Atlas. It seemed strange that from a fortress bristling with barbed wire, and concealing a machine gun or an observation post in almost every crevice, one was able, looking out across that narrow seaway to a coast whose outline had been familiar to mariners since the dawn of history, to forget momentarily the very existence of the war with all its instancy.

The main problem with which Gibraltar was faced when I arrived there was, however, no longer one of defence but of resettlement. After Dunkirk the greater part of the civilian population had been evacuated, a small contingent to Madeira, but the large majority, some sixteen thousand in number, first to London and then, when the V-bombs made life there too hazardous to be comfortable, to camps in Northern Ireland. After the D-day landings the Rock was no longer within a danger zone, and the all clear was given for repatriation.

This was by no means a simple operation. Only those engaged in essential services had remained in the Colony, and these were few in number. The normal employment of the Gibraltarians was mainly in Government and commercial offices, since they preferred white collar jobs to manual pursuits. The labour force, skilled and unskilled, including all the workers in the dockyard as well as most of the domestic servants, resided in Spain and were admitted daily through the security gates at the Gibraltar end of the neutral ground. This meant that civilian social services were reduced during the evacuation to something like a care and maintenance basis and Government staff was minimal : now all the belts and fly-wheels of the administration would have to be set in motion and new machinery be installed in order to meet the pressures that would be exerted.

My energetic predecessor, Miles Clifford, presented me with a deskful of working plans and a sheaf of blueprints, the fruits of a concentrated study of the whole complex of repatriation and rehabilitation which must have occasioned much burning of the midnight oil. As a first step a resettlement board had been set up and a system of priorities for the return of the population had been approved. One of the problems with which the Government was immediately faced was to provide education for the children as they arrived. A Director of Education had been appointed and was hard at work, and schools were being reopened, but they were still short of staff, and volunteers came from the Services to teach in their spare time. The boys and girls enjoyed having a geography lesson from a sergeant who had fought on two continents, or being taught arithmetic by an airman in the intervals between operational patrols. The R.A.F. were particularly popular with the young folk. Just before Christmas they decided to have a children's party, and in order to collect their guests airmen in uniform went up and down the streets, stopping the boys and girls they met with the question "Would you like to come to our party?"

But what was to prove to be by far the most intractable of the problems before us was the need to provide adequate housing for the returning citizens. To the simple question, why could not they reoccupy the accommodation they had vacated?, there were several not so simple replies.

One of these, of course, had to do with the military presence. Gibraltar had always been a fortress first and a colony afterwards, and the very expression "Colonial Government", which was used to distinguish the civilian side of the administration, seemed to suggest that *the* Government was a preponderantly military affair, or at least a double-barrelled piece with a military finger on the trigger. In days before the development of nuclear weapons had reshaped the whole stategy of global defence it was axiomatic that Service necessities must be paramount, and the first of these was for room to accommodate a greatly increased garrison with all its extensive armoury, technical equipment and ancillary services.

In the matter of living accommodation the Navy was able to consume most of its own smoke. The appropriations of the R.A.F., extensive as they had been, were confined to the level tract adjoining the North Front. The surrender of this area, which had formerly contained a race course and sports grounds, as well as the kennels of the celebrated Royal Calpe Hunt, dealt a serious blow to public amenities, but it involved no loss of civilian housing. The Army, which with sundry excavated areas disposed of considerably more of the Rock than met the eye, had managed to house a good deal of its augmented rank and file within its own bailiwicks, but some overspill was inevitable and this, together with the loss of properties destroyed by Vichy bombers in retaliation for British action against the French fleet at Oran, considerably narrowed down the resources available for civilian rehousing.

The root cause of the problem, however, was not to be found in Gibraltar at all, but in the Spanish frontier town of La Linea, where, before the evacuation, many Gibraltarians, for lack of an abode on the Rock, had obtained a lodging, and whence they used to walk every day to work. Upon their departure the Spaniards, who had an overcrowding problem of their own and, like Nature, abhorred a vacuum, were quick to overrun the vacated accommodation. The prospect of reclaiming any of it in the absence of secure titles, to say nothing of international difficulties, was slender in the extreme.

Also to be taken into account was the natural increase in population among the evacuated families.

It was hoped that, as part of a long term solution, the Army would be able to vacate their barracks and other property in the town area and concentrate in another part of the Rock, thus enabling replanning for civilian needs to be undertaken on a comprehensive scale. A Town Planner had been engaged as a first step in laying the stones of a new Gibraltar, but there had been little time for his ideas to get beyond the paper stage. In any case the military plan was hanging fire and, even when sanctioned, could offer no early relief for the congestion to be expected.

In order to meet the situation a start had been made with the erection of Nissen huts adapted to the needs of family life, as well as on the repair of the bomb damaged property and its conversion into family flats—tasks on which labour was working overtime under the stimulus of our efficient and active little Commissioner of Works, John Coelho, who did the work of half a dozen men and seemed to have the gift of being in twenty places at the same time.

"Impossible", he would exclaim when I suggested to him still further schemes for producing ten units of accommodation where only five had stood before. "Impossible", he would repeat, and then almost immediately, as professional caution gave way to native enthusiasm, "How soon do you want me to have them ready?"

While these preparations were in train pressure from the Gibraltarians awaiting return continually increased. Although glad enough at first to escape from the perils of the metropolis they had found the winter climate of their new temporary home too rigorous for their liking. Ships filled with repatriates were arriving at frequent intervals, but this human stream was accompanied by strings of petitions from those claiming a higher place in the queue. The doors of friends and relatives were hospitably opened, but there was a practical limit to the utility of such expedients. Even before the war overcrowding had been a chronic threat to health, and a day now came when the doctors hoisted a red flag and declared that if it were permitted to increase there would be serious risk of an epidemic. Our temporary housing projects could not keep pace with the demand and it was essential, without further delay to start building in a big way wherever suitable sites could be found.

An extensive project for the construction of large blocks of flats was approved by the Governor with the advice of the Executive Council and the blessing of the Secretary of State. The services of a firm of architects were engaged, and the search for sites began. This was not an easy quest, for with the competing demands of the Services every unoccupied parcel of land that was not so steep as to make it impossible to stand upright was as jealously watched and guarded as if it had been a claim on a gold reef. After diligent reconnaissance we discovered what appeared to be a promising area, the architects produced their preliminary designs, the City Council said they could supply water and electricity, the health authorities studied drainage and were content, and the Army had calculated that when the flats were built their roofs and chimneys would be in no danger of being blown off by defensive artillery fire from superior heights. We did not expect the Navy to be greatly interested in these land operations, but decided that, to be on the safe side, we had better put them in the picture. I showed them our plans and described the general lay-out.

"This will be all right with your people?" I asked hopefully.

"No," said the Navy.

"Why not?" I enquired.

A hairy nautical finger hovered over one of the plans.

"Because," the Navy replied, "just here"—the finger descended purposefully on the centre of a projected building—"just here there's a magazine with some fairly sensitive stuff in it. According to Admiralty Regulations there has to be a building-free safety zone of at least *that* circumference." A trimly manicured finger nail described on the drawing board a circle that demolished two of our most carefully selected sites as effectively as if an explosion had actually occurred.

"Well," I said, "that's a pity. But, of course, if you say so. . . ." Then, after a moment's reflection, "We shall have to remove the children without delay."

"Children, what children?" asked the Navy.

It was my turn to do some pointing. Extending a little finger in order to direct attention to an oblique but nevertheless inescapable consequence of what I had just been told, I put it down in a sector of the danger zone.

"Just *here*," I explained, "there are two tenements and a building we are using as a school. I don't know about the tenants. I suppose if one lives in Gibraltar there are bound to be residential hazards. But if, now that you've warned us, anything happened to those children while they were at school we should have a pretty serious charge to answer. I shall have to let the Governor know about this and advise him to have the school closed at once. We shall scarcely be popular with the parents. I hope you'll help us to explain."

This left the Navy in a thoughtful mood. Having reported to the Governor I consulted with the Town Planner and went with a revised site plan to see the Army in the person of the Deputy Fortress Commander.

"It seems," I said, pointing to the plan, "that we shall have to substitute these two new sites for part of the area we intended to use." And I explained the Naval objections to the previous proposal. "Can you give me the green light for this?"

The Army rose from its chair, unlocked a wall cabinet that concealed a large-scale military map of the Fortress from unauthorized eyes and indicated the area in which I was now interested.

"I'm afraid there's a difficulty. You see, just here we have a magazine with a good deal of heavy ammunition. War Office Regulations. . . ."

Here was an impasse which only the Governor could break through. Whitehall, if appealed to might, be able to find a way round the Naval difficulties, but if military and civilian interests conflicted the Governor, who was ultimately responsible for both, would have to come down on one side or the other. In this case either housing needs were an irresistible force or ammunition was an immovable object.

In the event he was saved from this dilemma. Following my representations a telegram had been despatched to the Secretary of State in which the assistance of the Admiralty was invoked. The Navy effected a tactical disengagement whereby the danger to the school was removed. At last we were able to go ahead.

Whilst engaged in these preliminaries I was assailed from an unexpected quarter. I had not been very long in Gibraltar when I received a visit from a prominent lawyer who had just returned to the Colony.

"Now don't," he said as he shook hands and accepted the chair I offered him, "now don't run away with the idea that I'm a pain in the neck." And he went on to impress upon me the need for urgency in dealing with the repatriation problem.

I suspected that his real purpose was to assure me that any action he might deem necessary in the execution of his professional purpose would be taken with the best possible personal good will, and I became sure of this when a little later I received a second visit at which, with apologetic cordiality, he presented me with notice of an intended action against me for the unlawful detention in Northern Ireland of those Gibraltarians who were still unable to return. This raised nice questions of responsibility, but as the case was never brought to Court I do not know what view would have been taken by the Bench of my alleged iniquities. Before I left the Rock I had the satisfaction of seeing the new blocks of flats beginning to rise from the ground; but it was not until 1951, four years after my departure, that the Colony was able to welcome back the last of its exiled children.

Although during my two and a half years on the Rock the problems of resettlement and rehousing were my principal concern, there was scarcely any aspect of the daily life of the Colony that could fail to excite one's interest and attention. Interspersed in the Gibraltar mosaic there were many unusual, sometimes quaint and often amusing pieces. One might well, for instance, wonder, if unaware that the building had originally been the property of the Franciscan Order, why the official residence of the Governor should be known as "The Convent". Another historic site was the "Governor's Cow Meadow". The natural facilities of Gibraltar could scarcely be adapted for dairying; the cow meadow had been relinquished to assist the demand for building sites; one cow only remained on the Rock and this was owned by the Admiral.

The day after my arrival I was invited to lunch by the Governor, Lieutenant-General Sir Ralph Eastwood. As soon as we were seated my curiosity was aroused by the sight of a small velvet cushion, placed on the table in front of his Excellency, on which were reposing three or four keys of solid construction and massive proportions. These, as I afterwards discovered, were none other than the famous keys of the Fortress which, during the Great Siege, were carried by General Eliott on his swordbelt, and which tradition required should always be in the possession of the Governor.

Once a week there was an impressive ceremony* when, at sunset, the keys were handed by the Governor or his representative to a military escort in order that, as in the days of the siege, the Waterport Gate might be locked against intruders. After the sounding of Retreat the escort, bearing the keys, was marched to the gate where suddenly from the shadows a sentry with bayoneted rifle sprang forward with the challenge.

"Halt; Who goes there?"

"The Keys."

"Whose Keys?"

"King George's Keys," came the proud reply, and the sentry drew back.

"Pass, King George's Keys. All's well."

Hardly less surprising than to find a cow as part of the Admiral's domestic equipment was the discovery that the celebrated Barbary apes were entrusted to the custody of the Brigadier commanding the Artillery. The roving and acquisitive habits of these sagacious creatures had become an embarrassment, and there was a well authenticated story that a certain Governor had entered his dressing-room one morning to discover one of

* Similar to the ancient Ceremony of the Keys performed at the Tower of London.

them trying on a selection of military head-dresses. After this grave breach of discipline the apes were permanently confined to barracks in a specially constructed wire enclosure and supplied with regular rations under the supervision of an officer of the Royal Regiment.

The old superstition that British sovereignty over the Rock would continue only so long as the apes remained there is well known, and Sir Winston Churchill during a visit to Gibraltar had given instructions that the strength of the pack, which was becoming depleted by accident and natural wastage, should not be allowed to fall below twenty-four. New recruits were obtained with the assistance of British Consular officers in the neighbourhood, who enlisted the good offices of Spanish authorities in Morocco to maintain the establishment. These strictly informal transactions were not the subject of any pecuniary arrangement, but it was customary for a complimentary case of whisky, a sufficiently prized commodity, to be delivered to the obliging Spaniards, who evidently felt that a bottle in the hand was better than a fortress in a fable.

Before I landed on the Rock I wondered a little apprehensively how I should get on with a military Governor, and whether I should find myself engaged in wordy battles with red-tabbed brigadiers and gold-braided commodores in defence of the rights of the civilian population, who would rely on me as their advocate. In fact this was never a problem. I must admit that the military employment of the written word was often terse and unequivocal to the point of abruptness. Their letters read rather like operation orders, and their reference numbers were never quotable in a single breath. For their part, it is possible that they regarded some of my communications, which it was often necessary to phrase cautiously, as examples of bureaucratic subtlety. But we did not spend too much time writing letters. Some humorist once remarked facetiously that if you wanted to get anything done in Gibraltar you had to drink gin with the Navy, beer with the Army and brandy with the R.A.F. The suggestion, if a little crude, was not to be disdained. At all events we all got on very well together. The two Governors under whom I served, General Eastwood and General Anderson were both, in their different ways, men of great charm and sympathetic understanding, and I count it a privilege to have been their lieutenant in that little world, where the discipline of their experience and their soldierly compassion did so much to smooth away the rough edges of our daily perplexities.

I have touched, however lightly, upon most of the aspects of Gibraltar that came within my purview, but something remains to be said of the Gibraltarians themselves. They were a cheerful, industrious, lively-witted community of very mixed descent. After the British occupation many immigrants came from Genoa and other parts of Italy, and there was a large Jewish influx from North Africa and elsewhere, with an occasional Cockney streak introduced when some susceptible member of the garrison had fallen for one of the daughters of the Rock. Of the former Spanish occupants there were no direct descendants, for upon the arrival of the British the small existing population had departed, bag and baggage, for the Spanish hinterland; but love laughs at fortresses as well as locksmiths, and Gibraltarian cradles were often rocked by Spanish hands, even as Spanish was still the language of the domestic hearth. This notwithstanding, there was no sense of affinity with Spain. The Gibraltarian regarded himself as a cut above the Andalusian (who, it must be confessed, reciprocated the sentiment) and was sturdily proud of his British citizenship. Events have since demonstrated the firm attachment of those upon the Rock to Britain.

Chapter XIV

NORTHERN RHODESIA

THE tide in the affairs of men, which, taken at the flood, leads on to fortune, was flowing fast for me when in 1947 I was appointed as Chief Secretary to the Government of what was then Northern Rhodesia. There was a period during which it grew sluggish, but in the end it carried me to open waters.

I was happy to be back in Africa after a twelve years' absence, interrupted only by a brief stay in Southern Rhodesia on the way from Cyprus to Barbados. But owing to the nature of my duties and responsibilities it was not for me at all the same Africa to which I returned. Gone were the days of long treks on horseback from village to village through the bush, with a train of carriers and sometimes a chiefly cavalcade in flowing robes to escort us to the music of pipe and drum; gone the arcadian choruses that greeted us on pagan hillsides; gone the peaceful hours when we glided down the stream of a great river with the silence broken only by the splash of paddles. Such scenes survived only as memories, as did the meetings with village heads and elders, when I would discuss the state of the crops or the prospects of the harvest, the incidence of sickness, the opening of a new market or the building of a village school, at the same time listening to complaints, receiving petitions and settling disputes with the aid of the Emir's representative.

In Northern Rhodesia duties of this kind were the task of the District Commissioners, responsible to the Provincial Commissioners, who received their instructions from Government through the Secretary for Native Affairs, and as Chief Secretary I was outside the picture. But as "chief of staff" to the Governor, with the duty to act for him during his absences from the territory, it was incumbent upon me, if not to have a finger in every pie at least to know something about its ingredients.

I made the most, therefore, of whatever opportunities occurred for going on tour, for I did not believe that a Chief Secretary could do his job properly, either as adviser to the Governor or as "head of the civil service", unless he had seen all he could of the country and its people and made personal contacts with as many members as possible of the administrative and professional staff. During our five years in the Protectorate my wife and I covered many thousands of miles by car on visits to the townships and the *bomas,* as the Government stations were called.

It was not like the old days in Nigeria, and we did not get nearly such an intimate picture of African life in the villages; but it was at least more revealing than travelling by air, and as the population was sparse and centres were far apart a rapid form of surface transport was essential. Roads were by no means universally good, and there were only a few score miles of tarred surface. In the dry season the red dust not only made its way into the interior of one's car, but even penetrated to the contents of suitcases carried in the boot, while during the rains the roads often became treacherous quagmires through which progress could be made only by driving in the ruts formed by previous traffic. These ruts sometimes became so deep that vehicles with inadequate clearance were marooned on the narrow surface between them with impotent wheels suspended in space. We never travelled during the rainy season without chains, a pick and a shovel, and a supply of sacks. It was also advisable when making a journey by unfrequented routes to carry at least a tin of meat, a packet of biscuits and a supply of drinking water, for if a breakdown occurred assistance might be a long time coming.

Even if I had had the time to make my journeys in more leisurely fashion I would not have found much to remind me of Nigerian days. In Nigeria, for all its tribal diversity, there had been extensive Emirates, with roots and recorded histories extending back for centuries, each displaying its characteristic culture and a way of life based on long established traditions and institutions. Northern Rhodesia presented a different pattern. The whole country was a heritage of the scramble for Africa—a sphere of influence recognized internationally as British when in 1890 it was included in the Charter of the British South Africa

Company. Before then it had been over the centuries a kind of many-men's land, an area of aggressive invasion by migratory tribes, and for many years before the British presence had suffered from the ravages of Arab marauders who, in nefarious alliance with chiefly authority, had traded guns for ivory and slaves. At the time of which I write native society was fragmentary and backward; there were no large African cities, and the population in the tribal areas lived in small villages under the local authority of petty chiefs.

Only in Barotseland was there a sizeable, cohesive and comparatively highly organized African kingdom. There the Paramount Chief was an autocrat of the old school, commanding the deep respect and loyalty of his people—a personage of no mean status who, on ceremonial occasions, appeared proudly in a picturesque and handsome, if slightly tarnished, uniform of ambassadorial type, which had been presented to the then ruling chief by Queen Victoria. He was attended by an august body of courtiers including a Prime Minister who, whenever I saw him, was dressed in a grey frock-coat—a garment which he must have found inconvenient when in the kneeling posture which custom required him to maintain in the presence of his royal master.

To turn to the European scene was to discover a composite picture. The chief source of the country's prosperity was the mining industry, whose output was steadily increasing, and the wealth thus generated and reflected in the territorial revenue had speeded the growth of the white population, which was estimated in 1949 to have reached a total of some 36,000. This number included, besides those working in the mines, many settlers who were producing maize and tobacco. The miners were a shifting population with no permanent roots in the country, but they were a politically significant section. In their employment with the mining companies Africans were excluded from a large number of jobs, and this constituted a colour bar that was an obstacle to satisfactory race relations. The white farmers were in the main liberally disposed towards the Africans, upon whose labour they depended, though among farmers of Afrikaner stock there were those whose sentiments towards the native people were influenced by a strong master-and-servant complex.

These Afrikaners, notwithstanding their unrelaxed attitude towards the "black man", were a hard-working, self-reliant and God-fearing community with all the qualities of stubborn endurance that had enabled their ancestors to break a trail into the hinterland, and as pioneers in a new country they were a solid and stable element. Some of them had penetrated to areas that were far from the main centres of population and were thrown very much upon their resources. I recall a story that was told me about a small boy who belonged to one of these Afrikaner families. He had left home for the first time to go to school and was being questioned by his teacher about his life on his parents' farm.

"What do you do when you want a doctor, Johnny?" he was asked.

Johnny was puzzled by this. "What's a doctor?" he enquired.

"Why, surely you know what a doctor is? Who do you ask to come and help you when you're sick?"

The small boy pondered for a moment and then his face lightened. "Jesus," he replied simply.

With the recent opening of new mines and the general increase of prosperity immigrants from the South were being attracted in increasing numbers. Economically the country was surging forward and among the white community there was a feeling that political progress was not keeping pace. Substantial constitutional advances had in fact been made over the years, and there was already a Legislative Council with an unofficial majority. But the balance of power was held by those unofficial members who had been nominated by the Governor to represent African or other special interests. With their support the Government could enforce the passage in Council of any measure, even if it were unanimously opposed by the elected unofficial members. This position was not to the liking of the elected unofficials who were vehement in their protest against what they described as "Colonial Office Rule", and in the hope of compelling further constitutional concessions those of them who had been appointed members of the Executive Council had resigned from that body.

This was how matters stood when I first arrived in the territory. It was a difficult situation for the Government and for

F

myself personally, since I was very soon called upon to act as Governor during the interval between the departure of Sir John Waddington, the retiring Governor, and the arrival of his successor, Sir Gilbert Rennie. The difficulty was due to the lack of any adequate means of consultation with the elected unofficials. I found myself, in my acting and temporary capacity, unable to agree to certain proposals for devolution of responsibility for the preparation of the annual estimates for the coming year, and became the target for a good deal of hostile criticism during the session of the Legislative Council at which the estimates had to be passed.

I did not, however, regard the episode as indicative of any personal antagonism, but rather as a symptom of the general post-war political restlessness, and, looking back, I feel sure that the unofficials believed that the interregnum following Sir John Waddington's departure would be a propitious opportunity to emphasize their demands. This they did in no uncertain fashion towards the end of the session when a demand for the grant of responsible government was made in forthright terms by the Senior Unofficial Member and nominated member representing African interests, Sir Stewart Gore-Browne. Concrete proposals, he declared, existed on the unofficial side for the ending of the present impasse, and these should be forwarded, with a view to discussion, to the Secretary of State. He could not think that I, or the new Governor when he came, or the Secretary of State when he heard of the proposals, would be so ill advised as to force them [the unofficials] to adopt the only alternative open to them. That alternative would be to use such powers as they already possessed to paralyse, or partially paralyse, the Government.

In due course the Secretary of State paid a visit to the Territory. Responsible government was not granted, and the Government was not paralysed, though there were occasions when it might have been described as hamstrung. Despite temporary interruptions in the normal consultative processes there was in fact a good deal of informal discussion, which sometimes took place at what was known as a "Hubert meeting" of the Legislative Council—a procedure instituted by a former Governor, Sir Hubert Young, whereby all the members of the Council met informally and in private to talk over policy matters and enable the views of the unofficials to be ascertained by the Government on proposals which would require the approval of the Council in a formal sitting before they could be put into effect. Another measure, which was subsequently established, was a system whereby unofficial members accepted a quasi-ministerial responsibility for certain subjects such as agriculture, health and local government. This innovation went some way to meet unofficial aspirations.

The politically dominant figure in the Northern Rhodesia that I knew was, and had been for some time, that of Roy Welensky, known now to the world as Sir Roy Welensky, who succeeded Lord Malvern as Prime Minister of the fated Federation of Rhodesia and Nyasaland. Although, as an official, I was part of the system against which he had raised his standard, and notwithstanding the disagreement which had marked the beginning of our relations, I came to regard him as a colleague rather than as an adversary, and I believe the feeling was mutual.

I well recall my first meeting with him, which took place a few days after my arrival. I noticed that despite his heavy build he still moved with the light step of a boxer, but the challenging tilt of his chin kept company with brown eyes whose glance was kindly as well as shrewd. I had the impression nevertheless that it must have taken an opponent of no little courage to stand up to him in the ring in the days when he was heavy-weight champion of the Rhodesias. We got on well together. He understood the rules and conventions by which I was circumscribed and respected my adherence to them. For my part I admired the tenacity of purpose and the perseverance that had enabled him, with no advantages of wealth, privilege or expensive education, to win his way to positions of responsibility and leadership, and make himself the master of his opportunities.

He was a quick thinker who could lay bare the bones of an argument while others were still dissecting the tissues, and in Council he could be a formidable antagonist—a vigorous fighter whose blows were hard and straight. But he seldom hit twice in the same place and his arguments were never laboured or prolonged. His private life was simple and unaffected. A devoted husband, an affectionate father and a genial host. He read extensively in the fields that interested him and his crowded bookshelves contained volumes of poetry as well as works on gardening, for he was a man who loved flowers.

Welensky played a prominent part in the arguments and discussions which led to the eventual creation of the Rhodesia and Nyasaland Federation. The concept of the closer association of Northern and Southern Rhodesia and Nyasaland was not new. For years there had been a spread of political opinion favouring the complete amalgamation of the two Rhodesias, and in 1938 a Royal Commission under the chairmanship of Lord Bledisloe had examined the pros and cons of amalgamation or federation of the three territories. Although the Commission concluded that amalgamation rather than federation should be the ultimate objective, they drew attention to the unanimity of native opposition to amalgamation that existed in the Northern territories. In Northern Rhodesia the African at that time, or at all events the politically conscious element who could sway public opinion, looked upon Southern Rhodesia as a white man's country in which Europeans owned the best land, and whose native policies, if extended to the North, would become a threat to their own land ownership, freedom of movement and tribal life.

This attitude was well known to the Northern Rhodesia unofficial members, who realized that as a declared political objective amalgamation would be a non-starter. As for responsible government I do not believe that, despite the panache with which the claim for this advance had been produced, there could have been many of its advocates who felt any confidence that, with the Africans still as politically immature as they were, the Secretary of State would be prepared to consider such a proposal. The aim of closer association in a form that would be generally acceptable was not however abandoned, and in the early part of 1951 I was entrusted by Sir Gilbert Rennie with the leadership of the Northern Rhodesian delegation to a conference of officials from the three territories and of the Colonial and Commonwealth Relations Offices, which was held in London to examine the possibilities.

The conference took place in the Commonwealth Relations

Office in the premises which, not long before, had housed the Colonial Office. The heavily balustraded marble staircase and the long spacious corridors preserved an atmosphere of proconsular dignity and imperial solidity which even so late as 1951, when the foundations of Empire were already beginning to quiver, did not seem outdated. For me the familiar building was a repository of many memories. Not far from the entrance hall was the room where, more with hope than with confidence, I had presented myself for scrutiny and questioning after my application to enter the Colonial Service, and upstairs was the handsome and imposing chamber in which I was first summoned on my appointment to Gibraltar to the august presence of the Secretary of State; and now I was to take part in discussions which might lead to fateful decisions for a sizeable slice of British Africa.

Those taking part in the conference formed an imposing phalanx of civil servants, including two Assistant Under-Secretaries of State as well as legal and constitutional advisers, making, with secretaries, a total of thirty persons. The Chair was taken by G. H. Baxter, Assistant Under-Secretary of State in the Commonwealth Relations Office, whose patience, tact and good humour were able, despite occasional divergencies of view, to secure a unanimous report.

His counterpart from the Colonial Office was Andrew (later Sir Andrew) Cohen, who became Governor of Uganda and, like Baxter, died prematurely. Cohen had a great deal to do with our affairs in Northern Rhodesia. A restless personality with a brilliant mind. In his room at the Colonial Office he had the disconcerting habit of rising from his chair during a discussion and pacing about the room while he carried on his argument, so that one was compelled, if one remained seated, to keep turning one's head or twisting one's body uncomfortably in order to keep him in view, or, if he showed no disposition to resume his seat, to rise oneself and adjust one's position continuously in sympathetic response to his peripatetic progress. One could not help thinking that to a deaf onlooker the scene might well have suggested the movements of two improbably attired footballers dodging each other in slow time.

Whatever may be said—and a good deal has been—of this

unhappy chapter in the history of changing Africa, there were obvious economic and administrative advantages to be gained from a closer linkage of the three territories, particularly in the field of transport and communications and the utilization of resources. Northern Rhodesian copper production required Southern Rhodesian coal, and the Rhodesia Railways, which were a common life-line, had to meet competing demands for locomotives and rolling stock. Trunk roads and air services were interdependent, and all three territories shared a common port in Beira. Northern Rhodesia had most of its economic eggs in the copper basket, but with Southern Rhodesian chrome, asbestos and tobacco and Nyasaland tea, a slump in the price of one commodity could be cushioned by a sustained market in others. There were also in our estimation social benefits to be derived from the quickening and expansion of a centrally planned economy, since greater prosperity would enable improved educational and health services to be provided.

In framing our recommendations we were by no means unmindful of latent African suspicions, but we hoped that these might be overcome by our plan for a federal constitution which would leave as territorial responsibilities all those services, such as agriculture, forestry, fisheries and veterinary services, as well as provincial and native administration, which closely touched the African's daily life and general welfare. In this way his gardens, his traditional rights, his customary practices and his tribal allegiances would be free from interference by an alien hand and continue to be the direct concern of Administrative Officers and other servants of Government whom he already knew and trusted.

As everyone knows, these paternalistic seeds fell on stony ground, and in the light of subsequent events it was evident that the extent and potency of African fears and suspicions had been underestimated. The reasons for the disappointment of the high hopes with which the federal constitution was formed are complex and have received close scrutiny, but since I left Northern Rhodesia in 1952, before a final decision was taken to proceed with the federal proposals, I cannot speak with personal experience of all that occurred.

It is, however, undoubtedly the case that external events

played an important part in the history of that period, and that it would scarcely have been possible in 1953, when the enabling legislation came into force, still less in 1951, to foresee the emergence across the breadth of Africa of all the countries that with triumphant ceremony and flags of many colours marched proudly forward to independence within the next few years. Small wonder that, with the general loosening of Imperial ties, the Africans of Northern Rhodesia and Nyasaland should have become excited by the possibility of achieving their own independence and that they should aspire to the freedom of the black North as opposed to the feared domination of the white South.

Despite administrative pressures and political preoccupations, I was able during my time in Northern Rhodesia to appreciate and enjoy much that Nature had contributed to a fascinating terrain. The crowning spectacle was, of course, the Victoria Falls, in times of flood sending up in a white cloud "the smoke that thunders", and in the dry season descending here and there in a diaphanous stream, as of sunlit bridal veils falling down and down into the chasm of green waters below. But there were other revelations, subtle and illuminating. The long straight roads extending for mile upon mile through closely wooded country with few open vistas to vary the scene were sometimes monotonous and uninspiring, but in the dry season, when the sunlight filtering through twisted branches was drowsy and mellow, and the dead grass was a golden sea stilled in a moment of fury, the bush became a place of beauty.

In 1952 I received my long hoped for and final promotion. It had been decided that the responsibilities of the Governor of Fiji, which had hitherto included the administration of the territories of the Western Pacific High Commission, should be divided. In future the British Solomon Islands Protectorate, the Gilbert and Ellice Islands Colony* and the British side of the

---

* Colonies are territories that have been annexed to the Crown. Their peoples have the status of British subjects. Protectorates have not been so annexed and their peoples are not British subjects but British protected persons. The same principles of government apply to both Colonies and Protectorates, and the distinction, which normally derived from the degree of sophistication of the peoples concerned, is now of historical rather than constitutional interest.

administration of the Anglo-French Condominium of the New Hebrides would be under the jurisdiction of an independent High Commissioner with the status of Governor. For appointment to this newly created post I had the good fortune to be selected.

Part Two

High Commission

"Whosoever will be chief among you, let him be your servant."

The quotation, from *St. Matthew, xx 27*, is the inscription on the memorial in the cloisters of Westminster Abbey to all who served the Crown in the Commonwealth Territories.

CHAPTER XV

QUEEN'S COMMISSION

THE doors of opportunity had been opened for me : I should now be called upon to justify, if I could, my right of entry. I was not ignorant of the role in which I should be cast. Indeed, I cannot think of any profession or walk of life able to offer to those who followed it a more complete training for the exercise of high responsibility than that afforded to a member of the Colonial Administrative Service in the performance of his normal duties.

Those which had fallen to me had been many and diverse. In Nigeria I had watched over and, as far as I was able, assisted the affairs of Moslem Emirates of medieval pattern as well as those of untutored pagan societies; in Cyprus, working in harmony with Greek and Turk, I had been actively engaged in the Government's preparations for island defence in the expectation of invasion; in Barbados, in the upper chamber of the Legislature, I had been responsible for all Government business; in Gibraltar I had grappled with the problem of the resettlement and housing of returning evacuees, and engaged in friendly skirmishes with the Army and the Navy in furtherance of civilian rights; and in Northern Rhodesia I had played my part in the evolution of constitutional half-way houses, which, in the post-war Colonial era, were soon to lead to such fundamental changes.

In the course of these activities, pursued for rather more than a quarter of a century, half of which time had been spent in a District and the remainder in senior Secretariat posts, I had necessarily made a great many human contacts : native chiefs and dignitaries of high degree; political leaders and politicians from right, left and centre; missionaries and ecclesiastics of all denominations; representatives of industry and commerce; Foreign Consuls; visitors such as admirals, generals, cabinet ministers, elder statesmen and, in Cyprus, the representatives of

Egyptian State services with whom it had been my task to negotiate the terms of agreements to be entered into for shipping and air connections. On one occasion I had even entertained royalty. In Legislative Councils I had made enough speeches to fill at least a volume of the local *Hansard,* and what I had said had been criticized, censured or even praised by the press according to the complexion and temper of editorial judgement. It had been quite a demanding apprenticeship.

If I did not know the ropes I had no excuse for my ignorance : I had served under eleven different Governors in five territories and myself temporarily administered the Governments of two of them. But to act as Governor was one thing; to hold the substantive appointment was another. One might say that in the one case, apart from matters of routine, I had only the duty of ensuring that approved policy was carried out, whereas in the other I might decide that it was right to change existing or introduce new policy, subject always to limitations of finance and, where constitutionally required, to the sanction of the Secretary of State. That was true as far as it went, but it was not just a question of a wider scope for initiative : in a certain sense I should become a lonely figure. As Chief Secretary, although by rank senior to my colleagues, I had always regarded myself as part of a team; and although while acting as Governor I, of course, fully accepted my constitutional responsibilities, I still found it difficult to regard myself as being more than *primus inter pares.* Now I must rise from the round table and take my seat at the head of one of different shape.

On the morning of the 15th February, 1952, at precisely eleven o'clock, there came from the loud-speakers of the *Cape Town Castle,* due shortly to sail from Cape Town harbour, the sound of a minute gun fired six thousand miles away. And at that exact moment, looking from the vessel's decks across the tall buildings of Adderley Street, I saw a flash and a puff of white smoke from the saluting battery on the slopes of Table Mountain. Thus, through the succeeding minutes did a much-loved monarch receive a last tribute of cannon, spoken in unison by field-pieces in the heart of London and the guns of Table Bay.

This sorrowful event could, it seemed to me, be seen by the

British people as the closing of an epic chapter in the troubled history of our times. "The King is dead. Long live the King!" Yes, but this time it was the Queen. He who had stood at the head of the nation during the years of trial had been succeeded by one whose name recalled the fame of an earlier heroic age.

For a better appreciation of the situation of the Western Pacific High Commission territories I found it necessary to brush up my geography. I had been informed that the duties of my new post would require me to travel by sea over great distances; but as my family and I were good sailors this necessity caused me no concern, though the relevance of the warning quickly became apparent when, with the aid of a large folding map of the Pacific, I was able to discover the precise extent of the area in which I should have administrative responsibility. The largest islands were those of the British Solomons, lying to the North-East of Australia and forming part of a long chain of islands, spread out like beads on a chaplet, across the eastern approaches of the Coral Sea. At the southern end of this chain, whose average distance from the Queensland coast was about a thousand miles, lay the Y-shaped archipelago of the New Hebrides. Farther to the East, in the neighbourhood of the equator almost due North of Fiji, I found the Gilbert and Ellice groups, small specks in a wilderness of waters. Farther East still, beyond the international date line, were the Phoenix group and, finally, the Northern and Southern Line Islands situated between Hawaii and Tahiti.

The distance from one end to the other of the High Commission limits was over 3,000 miles. An aircraft making a complete circuit of the territories by the shortest route would, assuming the practicability of such an improbable excursion, have to travel well over 8,000 miles and enclose an area two and a half times the size of Canada, nearly all of which was sea. Distances were indeed great, especially for small vessels with a maximum speed of seven knots, but almost the entire population, about 200,000 in all, inhabited the islands to the West of the international date line. Communities were concentrated for the most part in groups reasonably accessible from my headquarters in Guadalcanal, and though I travelled thousands of miles during my years of office

I did not spend so long at sea as to make me distinguishable by a nautical gait.

As soon as we arrived in London I called at the Colonial Office, whose headquarters were temporarily accommodated in Church House in the expectation that new premises would eventually be built on the old site of the Westminster Hospital opposite the Abbey. This project was soon abandoned with the accelerated change in status of so many of the dependent territories, though I doubt whether, even at that time, it was conjectured that before many years had passed the identity of the Office would have completely disappeared and that its remaining functions would be performed, first by the Commonwealth Relations Office and the Ministry of Overseas Development and later on, with the elimination of those entities in successive rounds of Departmental musical chairs, within the extending embrace of the re-named Foreign and Commonwealth Office.

The preliminary briefing at the Colonial Office of Governors and other senior officials who were about to take up their appointments was an important process in the system of Colonial administration, and the maintenance of close and friendly liaison between such officers and the heads of the "geographical departments" kept the official machine well oiled and free from bureaucratic grit. The Office itself was a repository of precedent and a storehouse of experience gathered from all quarters of the globe and every variety of climate from the deserts of Southern Arabia and the jungle of Malaya to the ice of Antarctica, and where local expertise was lacking its assistance could procure expert professional skill to deal with every aspect of development. Whether the problem was one of town-planning or of wild life preservation, of well drilling or of flood control; whether it was proposed to build bridges, dams, ships or harbours, or to undertake hydro-electric power schemes; whether it was decided to collect vital statistics or to study the behaviour of volcanoes; in all these and scores of other such cases if guidance was sought the Colonial Office was never at a loss.

The officers in charge of the geographical departments had intimate knowledge, often reinforced by personal visits and sometimes by periods of secondment overseas, of the territories with which they were concerned, and while not themselves, as civil servants, responsible for the good administration of those territories—for that responsibility rested in the first place with the Governor—they were called upon to advise the Secretary of State on policy recommendations which required his approval. The value of the liaison between the Office and the Dependencies went far beyond anything that could have been achieved by purely official relationships, and correspondence was frequently conducted by what was known as the demi-official letter.

This was a personal document which, although it often dealt with matters that might in due course require formal endorsement, was a convenient kite flying device, carrying no commitment. It enabled a Governor to take the temperature of Colonial Office opinion on a possibly controversial subject before finally adopting a line of policy, or to enter a little special pleading which might be out of place in formal correspondence. It was useful too, as I have already suggested, when some divergence of view might have developed about a matter which had already been the subject of official exchanges; for whereas the warmth or urgency of feeling permissible in a formal despatch must always be contained within phraseology appropriate to one who subscribed himself as "your most obedient humble servant" a demi-official letter might within decent limits be used to let off steam. But essentially this kind of letter was an informal communication between colleagues who had usually hob-nobbed together at some time or other. Occasionally, when the procedure was adopted in correspondence between different Administrations by writers who were not known to one another, such letters might begin with the words "Dear Department" or "Dear Secretariat", but these impersonal approaches seemed to me to be lacking in intimate appeal.

With the friendly and able assistance of all at Church House who were concerned with the affairs of the Western Pacific the scattered archipelagos and lonely islands that I had identified on my map became, from being mere names, a living world of ocean-bound communities distinguished, sometimes sharply, one from the other by race, language, culture and local environment, but each revealing some feature that contributed essentially to an oceanic pattern of life. Information which immediately affected my own plans was that there had recently been a hurricane in the Solomons and that, though, happily, there had been no loss of life, a wharf erected by the United States Forces during military operations on Guadalcanal had succumbed to weakened timbers and fallen into the sea. The work of providing houses and offices for my headquarters staff at Honiara, the Capital of the Protectorate, had in consequence to be delayed while fresh berthing accommodation was improvised, and my office would have to remain at Suva until such time as essential buildings at Honiara were ready.

This was disappointing; but as a "grand tour" of the territories would in any case be necessary as soon after my arrival as could be arranged, I decided to make my commission as far as possible a roving one until I could establish my permanent headquarters.

One of the gaps in my knowledge that I took steps to repair had disclosed my ignorance of the origin and *raison d'être* of the British presence in the area over which I should have jurisdiction.

The existence of islands in both the Solomons and the New Hebrides was first made known to the countries of Europe by Spanish explorers in the era of geographical discoveries that began with the Portuguese voyages down the West coast of Africa during the fifteenth century. At the close of that century the new world of the Americas lay revealed and the sea route to India had been navigated, but no-one had as yet unlocked the secret of the Southern ocean. To Alvaro de Mendana, nephew of the Viceroy of Peru, was entrusted the command of an expedition that reached the Solomons in 1568. Further exploration of the Pacific, including the historic voyages of Captain Cook, was continued by many navigators, mainly British and French, for more than two hundred years.

To the age of exploration succeeded an age of exploitation during which, by nefarious systems of "recruitment", Pacific islanders were carried off in the nineteenth century by "blackbirders" to work, and often to die, in the guano islands of the South American coast or on the plantations of Hawaii, Fiji and Queensland. The conscience of that world that had won its long battle against the slave trade was shocked by the shameful methods sometimes employed by notorious traffickers who, when compulsion could not be used with impunity, did not scruple to disguise themselves as missionaries in order to entice their victims on board the "thief ships", as they were called by the natives. It was in revenge for the kidnapping of five men from the Santa Cruz group of the Solomons that Bishop Patteson of the Melanesian Mission was clubbed to death in 1871, his life being taken by those for whom, as his memorial affirms, he would gladly have given it.

Another nineteenth-century intrusion was the arrival of the beachcomber. Not all of them were deserving of the suspicion with which as a class they have been regarded. They included, no doubt, many of the waifs and strays of society, among them remittance men for whom the springs of charity had run dry, lost legionaries of Fortune seeking asylum or adventure in an oceanic Never Land where salvation and damnation might be as close to each other as the two sides of a coin. Some of them settled down respectably and became influential citizens whose descendants took pride in their European ancestry. Others were unprincipled or desperate men to whom a region not yet subject to the laws of any civilized State offered a safe refuge from the consequence of their crimes or follies.

In order to protect the lives, property and interests of British subjects and island peoples alike, a series of Acts of Parliament and Orders in Council relating to the Pacific Ocean was passed into law from the year 1872 onwards. The original intention of those enactments was to prevent and punish "criminal outrages upon natives of islands in the Pacific Ocean, not being in Her Majesty's dominions nor within the jurisdiction of any civilised power", and also to provide for the good government of Her Majesty's subjects within such islands. There was at that time no intention to create any title or claim to British sovereignty over the islands—indeed, such a construction of the law was expressly repudiated—or to derogate from the rights of the tribes or people inhabiting them. The measures were designed above all to ensure that Her Majesty's subjects and others should not escape the consequences of their misdeeds if they chose to live in a no-man's land. To give operative effect to the legislation a High Commissioner was appointed in 1877, who, from the nature of his office was both a policeman and a judge: roles which, in terms of ultimate responsibility, he still continued to exercise. As a policeman his beat was an extensive one—the Pacific Ocean—and his symbol of authority was a vessel flying the white ensign, known to past generations of islanders as a "manawa".

By the end of the century the continuing operations of "recruiters" and the reprisals they provoked, which in the Solomons were resulting in a mounting tide of savagery, made it necessary to establish closer administrative control, and Protectorates were declared both over the Solomons and the groups that now compose the Gilbert and Ellice Islands Colony. In the New Hebrides, where Anglo-French co-operation had been exercised since 1887 through a Joint Naval Commission, a Condominium was established in 1906.

*   *   *

Before leaving England I had the honour of being received by the Queen in order to "kiss hands" upon my appointment. The formal act of homage is now omitted from the ceremony, which in my case consisted of a private audience with Her Majesty lasting for about twenty minutes. It was the first time that I had seen the Queen otherwise than in photographs or at a distance. I became deeply conscious of her graciousness and her loveliness, and when I made my final bow I knew what impulse had moved Sir Walter Raleigh to take his cloak from his shoulders and lay it on the ground for his Sovereign to walk upon.

We reached Suva by sea on July 3rd. A. F. R. Stoddart, the acting Governor, had invited us to stay with him for the days immediately following our arrival and had courteously made available the drawing-room of Government House for the swearing-in ceremony. In the palatial guest suite allotted to us I put on for the first time my white tropical Governor's uniform with its gold-braided gorgets and shoulder cords, packed before departure with all possible precautions against creasing in a case upon which I had kept a vigilant eye throughout our twelve thousand mile journey. My wife fastened for me the hooks of my tight high-fitting collar and made sure that my buttons were straight, my medals properly aligned and my sword-knot hanging correctly. I buttoned my white gloves and took up my helmet with its red and white plumes.

At the agreed time we entered the drawing-room and I took my place at a table facing the assembly. The Queen's Commission was then read. While I listened I reflected on the customary form of words in which the Queen commanded "all Our officers, civil and military, and all other Our loyal subjects in the said Western Pacific Islands, to be aiding and assisting to you, the said Robert Christopher Stafford Stanley, Esquire, as High Commissioner".

We all rose as the Chief Justice, solemn and impressive in his scarlet robes, handed me the Bible and I took the prescribed oaths. H. C. A. Bryant, First Assistant Secretary in the Western Pacific Secretariat, who for a few days had enjoyed a brief interlude of high office as acting High Commissioner, then made a speech of welcome to which, obedient to the directions contained in the programme of arrangements prepared by the Secretariat, I did my best "to reply suitably".

This concluded the formal part of the ceremony. We mingled with the guests and refreshments were served. The proceedings followed the pattern of similar ceremonies which I had attended earlier in my service and indeed been responsible for arranging. But this time I was not a spectator, but the central figure. I knew that for the next three years, for better or for worse, the fortunes of many communities I had yet to meet would be in my keeping. I was not afraid of responsibility, but I knew that I needed wisdom, and I knew that wisdom was not necessarily the gift of experience, far less of good intentions, alone. But where was wisdom to be found? Perhaps, if I sought it with faith and understanding, in the Islands of Solomon?

CHAPTER XVI

WATERS OF THE MOON

THE Pacific, ocean of many moods and not a few surprises, was formed, as one theory has suggested, when, in a tremendous convulsion of Nature before the continents were fashioned, a portion of the globe broke away to become the moon, leaving a vast cavity to receive the waters that overflowed the surface of the earth. A bold conception; but one to stir, once in a while, some lunatic fancy, as when, far from land on a day of azure skies and little wind, one watched from the deck of one of our small ships the long patient rhythm of the swell, extending everywhere to the horizon, and imagined the rocking of what had once been the moon's cradle. Or when, on a night of halcyon calm, the sea was like a dark lake, and the scarcely rippling waters were able to capture a tremulous likeness of their lost child.

Ocean of many moods. It has been noticed by travellers that the Pacific does not always maintain the reputation that its name suggests. Phases of lake-like calm are indeed rare except in reef-protected lagoons or the neighbourhood of closely sheltering islands, though I have met with them very occasionally in the open sea when, so imperceptible has been the swell, that the reflection of the clouds upon the surface was clear and unbroken. But "calm" is a relative expression, measurable by standards that may well vary according to the size and character of the vessel in which the observer is embarked. It would take little more than a capful of wind to ensure a lively interlude for one of the sixty-five-feet craft of the High Commission fleet, and though the waves were seldom more than mildly boisterous the test of a smooth passage in one of these vessels was whether, when the ship rolled, an unlocked drawer below a bunk in fore and aft alignment would stay in position and not slide out onto the floor of the cabin.

I never encountered the Pacific in the majesty of storm, though a hurricane, such as the one that delayed the building programme at Honiara, did occasionally descend upon the islands. The area of these disturbances was fairly well defined, and synoptic weather forecasts enabled shipping to receive reasonable warning of their approach. But it nevertheless behoved a navigator to keep his weather eye lifting, for storm conditions could build up quickly, and Nature did not always stick to the rules.

The surprises of the Pacific were sometimes associated with the volcanic activity that was endemic over a wide area and often took the form of submarine manifestations. In the surroundings of the Solomons and the New Hebrides there were submarine volcanoes which erupted at intervals to produce islands of cinders : these, however, usually subsided below the surface before they had cooled off sufficiently to provide a tenable *locus standi* for anybody proposing to lay claim to them.

Other evidence of this kind of liveliness presented itself one day when we were on a journey to the New Hebrides. The blue of the ocean became suddenly affected by a strange distemper in the form of brownish-yellow patches of colour, reminding me of the weed I had seen floating in the Sargasso Sea on a voyage made in childhood to the West Indies. Other more extensive areas of discolouration soon came into view, and we were not long in discovering that they were caused by accumulations of pumice, evidently thrown up from the depths. In a little while the water everywhere as far as our horizon had been covered, so that we might have been sailing through a sea of mustard. It was not until we had gone on for some miles that the aggregation began to break up and the sea became blue again. Some specimens, retrieved in a bucket, were as large as cricket balls, but most of the pumice, which easily crumbles, had disintegrated into a powder. I learned afterwards that it had drifted for scores of miles and formed such thick deposits on the beaches of some of the islands that the people of the coastal villages had been unable to launch their canoes.

Submarine eruptions, though no doubt alarming to any navigator in the vicinity, might well, one would hope, give sufficient warning of aproaching catastrophe in the form of submerged alarums or surface agitation to enable him to steer his vessel away from danger. A wholly different and ever present hazard, which had been responsible for a distressing record of shipwreck, was caused by the industry of the minute marine organisms, curiously named "flower animals" (alias *anthozoa*) but more generally known in their skeletal form as coral, which, if their ocean drift is arrested on any rocky coastal shelf, make use of it as a foundation for building operations destined, in due time, to reach the light of day. In this way, along the shores of the islands or in the adjoining waters the coral appeared as reefs, of which the Great Barrier Reef is an outstanding example. Elsewhere it grew up upon the summits of submerged mountains to form atolls, each consisting of a central lagoon encircled by small islets. Such were the islands of the Gilbert and Ellice Islands Colony. Reefs were well charted, but some of the charts were more than a little out of date, and the coral kept growing, so that after the lapse of twenty years or so a passage through a reef or a channel across a lagoon that had been deep enough for certain vessels might well have come to conceal an unsuspected peril.

I received literally striking proof of this on one occasion during a visit to the Western District of the Solomons. The boatswain, a Solomon Islander, in charge of the vessel, which was a smallish one drawing less than six feet, decided to take a short cut across a lagoon instead of keeping to the deep water outside it. Suddenly I felt a scraping of the keel, in itself an unpleasant sensation, and in a moment the ship heeled over alarmingly to one side, compelling us to cling for dear life to the nearest stable object to avoid the risk of tumbling overboard. For a few anxious seconds disaster seemed imminent, but the boatswain had taken the measure of the situation with a rapid glance and instead of immediately stopping his engines left them at full speed ahead, with the result that we ploughed our way through the obstruction and were almost at once riding free. Subsequent examination revealed no worse damage than a scraped keel; but I think we were probably luckier than we deserved to be.

Vulcan, the master builder, and Coral, the apprentice, with her myriads of flower creatures : these two had been the designers and architects of Pacific islands great and small. An incongruous association, one might think, resulting certainly in vastly differing examples of craftsmanship. For where in the larger islands the giant's work was manifest were sombre tracts of forest, covered often in the awakening light of morning by tenuous veils and threads of mist ascending to reveal a lost valley or a white waterfall. And higher still, summits clearly outlined in the sunlight, or shadowed perhaps by clouds gathered, island by island, above the long procession of the disappearing hills. But within latitudes close to the equator the eastward limits of the Solomons were the limits of all but a few of the great islands. Beyond, for many hundreds of miles, the hand of Vulcan had been sparing in its gestures, and it was Coral whose intricate shapes and patterns had made room for man amid the ocean solitudes. Here were no lofty landmarks to guide the approaching navigator : only fringes of palm trees rooted mysteriously in the waves and discoverable, if visibility was good, within something less than an hour's steaming distance by a vessel of our island fleet. But I was told that the Polynesians, for whom the sea holds no terrors, and who were accustomed (until restrained in the interests of their own safety by cautious administrators) to make long journeys between islands in their outrigger canoes, had an infallible guide to direction, if the elements were co-operative, in the reflections upon the clouds, visible for many miles, of the green lagoon waters of the atolls of their destination.

The sea had from time immemorial been the highway through and among the islands. In the Solomons, where, in my time, there was no internal air service and few roads, it provided a route that was almost everywhere the only alternative to a tedious and probably circuitous journey along bush tracks that might well be little more than narrow tunnels through tracts of dense tropical forest. Jungle was, as it had always been, a barrier to intercourse, and before the days of the Protectorate the co-existence of different communities on the same island did not lead to any kind of unification. The sparsely scattered villages were inhabited by small tribes or kinship groups isolated by custom and even by language from neighbours who might live no more than a score of miles away. When a journey was undertaken it was by water. The vessels were war canoes and the object of the expedition was the hunting of heads.

Head hunting, along with more commendable pursuits, long ago receded into the background of history; but canoes like those used in such excursions were, in my day, and as far as I know still are, to be found, and sometimes provided us with a ceremonial escort through the narrow channels that led like rivers through the enclosing jungle of some of the lesser islands. They were long slender craft with tall elaborately carved prows decorated with cowrie shells and inlaid with patterns of mother-of-pearl. They were sometimes manned by as many as twenty-four paddlers who, at the rate of perhaps sixty strokes a minute, forced them through the water with the precision if not quite with the speed of a university eight, creating an impression of dynamic purpose as they drummed rhythmically with their paddles on the sides of their canoe at the end of each stroke. Every few seconds one of the crew would lay down his paddle and raising a conch shell to his lips would sound a series of resonant blasts to mark the time and urge the others to fresh exertions. I once asked a Melanesian who was accompanying me whether there was a local name for a performance of this kind. "Oh yes," he replied, "we call 'em 'regatta'."

Every coastal village in the Solomons had its complement of smaller canoes, used for fishing or going to market, and there were many vessels, some schooner rigged, including powered craft, owned by missionaries, planters and traders. Sometimes, at night, looking seaward through the forest towards some quiet haven, one might glimpse a light appearing and disappearing between the trees like a firefly. This would be a lantern hoisted to the masthead of a cutter lying at anchor and rocked gently by the last impulse of the swell. Such craft were owned by members of the small Chinese community, traders who were content to visit areas remote from the highways of commerce and seldom or never frequented by those in a bigger way of business, for whom the profit on two or three bags of copra from a distant village was scarcely worth the time and cost of collection. For the Chinese who carried on a two-way trade by paying for his purchases in kind—with lengths of coloured cloth (known as "calicos" and worn like kilts), with sugar, salt and, surprisingly, canned fish, with axes, knives, soap, matches, cigarettes and plug tobacco, and occasionally banjos and mouth-organs—for the Chinese, for whom many mickles made a muckle, and whose long suit was patience, the enterprise was worth while; and for the Protectorate it helped to swell the export of copra on which prosperity depended.

Not least in the tally of the island shipping were the Government owned vessels. There were about a dozen of these, and although two or three of them, allocated to the Gilbert and Ellice Islands, were under the immediate administrative control of the Resident Commissioner of the Colony, I had as High Commissioner an overall responsibility for the distribution and utilization of the fleet.

I found in this aspect of my duties a certain private satisfaction. One of my boyhood ambitions had been to go to sea, and when my parents began to speak of the Navy as a possible career I responded eagerly. Entry into the Senior Service was at that time through Osborne and Dartmouth, but I got no further than the first step, which was an interview with an Admiralty Selection Board. I like to think that my inability to pass muster was due to no more than an unfortunate mistake in naming as Calcutta, on a wall map of India from which place names had been inconsiderately omitted, a large dot which, in fact, marked the situation of Madras; but whether it was my display of ignorance in this particular or what was regarded as a general lack of gumption that had been my undoing I was never to know. It was, however comforting to reflect, after forty years, that although I had failed to qualify for service under the white ensign, the blue ensign was a flag our little ships might proudly fly.

The *Nareau*, in which I made most of my longest journeys, had been designed and built for use by the Resident Commissioner of the Gilbert and Ellice Islands, to whom she was normally available. She was eighty-five feet in length and regarded as the pride of the fleet. Aware, as I had been, of her dimensions before I left England I had more than once speculated on the possible behaviour of a craft of that size in rough weather, and it was in one of the lesser London thoroughfares after a briefing visit to the Colonial Office that, with my thoughts running in this direction, I halted to judge my distance from a lamp-standard and then began to check my estimate by pacing. On the whole an unsuitable place for such an experiment. There was, in fact, never any doubt about the *Nareau's* seaworthiness. She was not a beautiful ship, being somewhat short and squat for her size, and always seemed to me to be somewhat over-weighted at the stern—an eccentricity which, while no doubt contributing to her stability, created an impression of sluggish-ness. But if she could take no prizes for yacht-like elegance or grace of line she knew a thing or two about the treacherous embraces of winds and currents. It might be less than kind, but it would not be unfair to say that when assailed by the elements she did not so much ride the waves as wallow among them. In an ocean world of moods and uncertainties her watchword was not "style" but "stamina". In the course of her service she had encountered a hurricane on her way to Australia for a refit, and I was told that although her hold and engine room had been partly flooded her behaviour by the best nautical standards had been impeccable. I doubt whether she would have succumbed to anything short of a tidal wave.

As in all our vessels space was at a premium, and certainly none had been wasted. Somehow or other room had been pro-vided for a ship's company of fourteen, six "first class" passengers and about forty tons of cargo. The principal passenger cabin, which was of reasonable size, gave access to a small private deck over the stern, usually, owing to the low freeboard, awash when we were at sea. There were cabins for the captain, mate and engineer : the rest of the crew had quarters in the forward part of the hull. They must have found it a tight squeeze; but as all of them were Gilbertese or Ellice Islanders and well accustomed to living close to the wind and the waves they usually slept happily and more comfortably on deck. Under favourable conditions the *Nareau* could steam at about seven knots. (The engines were diesel, but in nautical phrase we always steamed and never motored).

The complete absence in the Gilbert and Ellice groups of

coastal features or objects other than palm trees identifiable at a distance called for navigating skills which none of those Islanders yet possessed, and officers for the ships that would be employed there were usually recruited from Australia or New Zealand; but in the partly sheltered waters of the Solomons, where a ship was seldom for long out of sight of land, our vessels were captained by Melanesians with the rank of boatswain. They could set a course and read a compass with accuracy, but their mathematics were virtually non-existent. What they possessed in special measure was an intimate knowledge of the island waterways and, notwithstanding the near disaster in which I had been involved by the unsuspected growth of coral—a quite exceptional instance of miscalculation —the positions of the reefs. Even in the dark they seemed able to find their way with uncanny precision.

I recall in particular a certain night passage among some small islands forming part of the Ngela group, where before the war the capital of the Protectorate was situated. The moon was nearly at the full, the channels were well defined and free from obstruction and the shore line clearly visible on either side; but after emerging into the open sea a change of course would be necessary, and hidden reefs might present a danger if this were attempted too soon. The boatswain upon whom our safe passage depended was a pilot of long experience in whom I had full confidence, but when we were well clear of the land and on our final course I did put a question to him.

"How could you be sure when it would be safe to turn?" I asked.

"I wait." he replied, "until I feel the wind on my left cheek. Then I know all clear."

Chapter XVII

MARCHING RULE

A GOOD many years have already elapsed since I left the Pacific, and I can no longer write in the present tense about the way of life in the islands I knew. Since my departure history has marched in quick time. The Gilbert and Ellice Islands Colony was detached from the jurisdiction of the High Commissioner at the beginning of 1972 and now has its own Governor, and in the Solomons independence is in sight. When I assumed my responsibilities in 1952 none of the territories had fully recovered from the disruptive effects of hostilities, and the tide of fortune was slow to advance.

But it was in the Solomons that the havoc of war had been most devastating. Much valuable property had been destroyed, the coconut plantations, which were the foundation of the economy, had become derelict, and most of the threads of external commerce were severed or frayed almost to breaking point. It was not, however, only material that had suffered: there was an additional dimension to the problem of recovery. The minds of the people—of many of them—had become disturbed and excited.

What had occurred was the birth and growth during the immediate post-war years of a quasi-nationalistic movement, known as Marching Rule, which became opposed to the Government and demanded that the people should be permitted to run their own affairs without interference. It originated in the large island of Malaita, which contained roughly half of the Protectorate's 100,000 inhabitants, and soon spread to other parts of the group. The movement, which is easier to describe than to explain, was essentially an expression of native discontents awakened by the war-time spectacle of the white man's power and the prodigality of his material resources, particularly those which a generous Uncle Sam had lavished upon the United States Forces in order to ensure both their fighting efficiency and their bodily comfort.

The G.I. with his bonhomie and easy comradeship, ready to pay generously from his wad of dollar bills for some trifle of native craftsmanship or a small act of service had become, not only a very human friend, but the hero of a campaign of supermen, during which, as one commentor (Mr. C. H. Allen, formerly an Administrative Officer in the Protectorate and later to become Governor of the Seychelles, to whose account of these events I am indebted) has pointed out, the people of the islands had an unrivalled grand-stand view of some of the greatest battles of the war. There was evidently—so argued the bewildered islanders among themselves—some key to the white man's material paradise. The Americans possessed it, but if the Government or the missionaries had it they had never disclosed it or passed it on. Self help became the order of the day.

That was one part of the picture : there were others. G. K. Chesterton asserted that the finest line in English literature is "Over the hills and far away"—"the dumb refrain of all English poets". I would hesitate to discuss what might be described as poetry among the Melanesians, but I would suggest that if part at least of the essential stuff of poetry emanates from that kind of dumb refrain—a seeking for the distant land of the heart's desire—then there could have been many in the islands who, if "over the seas" were substituted for "over the hills", might in their thoughts have been close to the mood of all English poets—indeed, of all poets. For if one lives on a small island surrounded by a great ocean it is over the horizon that lies the promised land from which, though it may be unattainable, who knows?, one day a ship of fortune may come home. The so-called cargo cults of the Pacific have been associated with the expected arrival of mythical ships laden with good things. This myth found its way into the preaching of the leaders of Marching Rule (this name is generally accepted as being an anglicised corruption of a native word meaning "brotherhood"). To bring things up to date the ships would be Liberty ships and the crews and cargoes would be American.

Another distinctive feature of the movement was its insistence on rigid adherence to native custom. Scribes were set to work and laboriously produced a written code of traditional practice relating to childbirth, puberty, courtship, marriage, death and burial, as well as correct behaviour on all occasions, including rules for the avoidance of indecent conduct. This was the law and must be obeyed.

It might be thought that Marching Rule illogically, or at least inconsistently, combined a desire for the benefits of civilization with obscurantist devotion to superstitious credences. But if one believes that the good things of life, including material blessings, are the reward of virtue, and that virtue consists in following the ways of one's ancestors, there is nothing illogical in propitiating the ancestral spirits in order to obtain food, axes and "calicos", or even jeeps, refrigerators and Coca-cola.

Marching Rule was remarkable, in yet another way, for the high standard of its organization—the appointment of heads of areas and sub-areas—and for its discipline, enforced, by police squads of young men known as "duties", who were armed with truncheons and drilled on military lines.

The movement was not at first directed overtly against the Government. It advocated laudable policies of improved agriculture and better housing. The people of the interior were cajoled or coerced into leaving their lofty hill retreats and building villages for themselves along the coast. At a later stage, when non-cooperation with and opposition to the Government had become manifest, these villages were fortified by stockades and guarded by watch towers.

An edict went out that none of the young men was to leave home for customary employment on the coconut plantations unless paid four times the usual wage. This created a serious threat to the economy of the whole group, since Malaita, where intransigence was most deeply rooted, was the most heavily populated island in the Protectorate and a traditional source of labour, the absence of which would make it impossible to maintain the output of copra or to ensure the success of any plan for general development in which the cooperation of the people was essential.

After some vicissitudes, including the arrest and subsequent release on promise of good behaviour of its leaders, the movement had eventually resolved itself into a loose confederation which called itself the Malaita Federal Council. At the same time there had been a not very successful attempt on the part of the Government to set up a District Council for Malaita as an officially authorized instrument of local government. This attracted a few loyalists, but the bulk of the people under their Federal Council leaders stood aloof, and it was clear that the island was divided, and for the most part still uncooperative.

That was the situation as I found it when I visited the Protectorate for the first time during my preliminary grand tour of the three territories. To H. G. Gregory-Smith, the last officer to be appointed to the post of Resident Commissioner, which became redundant after my arrival, had fallen the demanding task of maintaining watch over the growth of the movement and keeping it, as far as possible, within bounds. In spite of setbacks I believed that the moment was not unpropitious for renewed attempts at conciliation.

After six years the driving forces of Marching Rule had lost much of their impetus. The arrival date of the promised cargoes was still unannounced and the credibility of the prophets had been shaken. A false step might add fresh fuel to dying embers, but cautious diplomacy could perhaps dispel bitterness from the ashes. I had, moreover, the advantage, which offers itself once and once only to any newly appointed administrator, of being able to wipe the slate clean. It was, of course, my duty to ensure the maintenance of law and order, but I was convinced that nothing was to be gained by a repetition of the warnings, police patrols, arrests and punishments that, however necessary at the time they were resorted to, had left a problem still to be resolved. I bore no personal responsibility for past policies and was not bound to adhere to them. I had as yet done nothing to justify confidence, and might well be regarded with suspicion, but I had not burned my boats.

There was a double task to be accomplished: to secure the confidence of all the people in the good will and ability of the Government to assist their legitimate aspirations, and to devise means whereby the potentially valuable ingredients of Marching Rule—its capacity for organization, its discipline, and the incentives to material progress that it had created—could be made use of for constructive ends. After consultation with Val Andersen, who was the Administrative Officer in charge of the Malaita District, and whose experience, patience and wise advice were of the greatest value, I took the first step in the policy of conciliation I had decided to pursue. It was essential to uphold those who had stood by the Government and joined the officially sponsored Council, and it was to them that our first approaches were made.

Preliminary soundings, made in the course of conversation with one or two of them during my first visit to the island, were not exactly encouraging.

"What," I had asked, "are we to do about these Federal Council people?"

The reply was short and simple—the equivalent in "pidgin" of an injunction to make things uncomfortable for the offenders.

"Hot 'em," they said.

Later at Auki, the capital of Malaita, I tried again with better results. On this occasion I met the whole of the official Council, and after thanking them for their loyal support urged the importance of all the people of Malaita working together when there was so much to be done that called for combined effort. I then asked them whether, if the Government could persuade the Federal Council leaders to co-operate, they would be ready, as I was, to forget the past and work with the former opposition for the common cause. The reply was favourable: the next step was to talk to the Federal Council, who responded to my invitation to meet for a general discussion.

The outcome of this getting together was, in the end, successful. The meeting was held in a small leaf-thatched building on the Government station at Auki. I sat with Andersen and Philip Richardson, the acting Resident Commissioner (I had not yet formally assumed the duties of that office) facing the members of the Council who were waiting, silent, unsmiling and ready, as it seemed to me, to be thoroughly uncompromising. After expressing my hopes of obtaining their cooperation in enabling me to accomplish my task, which was nothing more nor less than to learn about the problems of the people and do what I could to help them, I invited them to tell me what it was they wanted that they had not got. Andersen translated my remarks into "pidgin", which he spoke fluently with a wealth of picturesque idiom that was sometimes more graphic than refined.

Their spokesman was a little man with a large mop of hair and a quiet voice, who spoke good English. His name was Salana Ga'a and he had formerly been a member of the staff of the South Seas Evangelical Mission, a non-denominational body which had several stations in the island. His main request was that the people of Malaita should be allowed to elect a "big man", whose authority Government should recognize, to look after their affairs.

Andersen had warned me that this request would be urged, and I was ready for it. I think Salana's idea, or at least that of some of his more revolutionary-minded followers, was that there should be some kind of President of Malaita, who, once appointed, would be able to declare the island's independence of the rest of the Protectorate and carry on without interference by the Government. For some reason, possibly—though this is a matter for conjecture—not unconnected with confused interpretations of overheard American comment on the British colonial system, it was the Government that was regarded as the villain of the piece. The High Commissioner, however, was distinguishable from the Government. He was, they may well have argued, the servant and official messenger of the Queen of England, with whom nobody had any quarrel. If I could ensure that loyalties were firmly nailed in that direction I might be able to carry on on a personal basis without bringing the Government too much into the picture.

I said that before the appointment of a "big man" could be considered it was necessary to remove the divisions of the people. I was prepared, if they agreed, to make a fresh start and provide for the setting up of a Council which would represent all the people of the island, in place of the Federal Council and the existing District Council, and to such a Council the tax payable

G

to Government would be refunded to be spent in ways acceptable to them. The Council could elect one of its members as a "big man", whom I would recognize as its President, with due status and authority, provided that he was ready to promise publicly to do three things: to accept the authority of the High Commissioner as the Queen's representative, to work with the District Commissioner for the welfare of the people, and to obey the laws of the Protectorate.

After a good deal of head scratching and confabulation Salana Ga'a agreed with a suggestion that he and his friends should return to their villages and talk over my proposals with the people before making up their minds, and a few weeks later, after I had returned to Suva, I received a telegram to inform me that they had proved acceptable.

When with my wife and daughter I arrived at Auki on 26th January, 1953, for the formal inauguration of the new Council the general atmosphere was very different from what it had been on the occasion of our earlier visits to Malaita. I recalled how at Malu'u, the sub-District headquarters where my discouraging first contact with the loyalists had been made, we had been led past a line of armed police posted as a security measure at intervals of a few yards along the whole length of a path leading from the landing place to the Government office and flagstaff on the farther side of a coconut plantation. With not a soul in sight except the police and our official party these measures seemed slightly elaborate. I could not help feeling that the risk of becoming the target of a poisoned arrow loosed by a concealed dissident, or of an ambush by would-be assassins armed with clubs, was minimal. But it would have been unfortunate if I, not to mention my family, had been eliminated so soon after our arrival. I subsequently learned that there had been vague rumours of the possibility of an incident, and the District Officer in charge of the station had been quite right to take all reasonable precautions.

Now, at Auki, it was another story. From all parts of the lagoon onto which the Government station fronted, as well as from the channels leading through the outer reef barrier to the sea, continuous processions of canoes large and small from villages up and down the coast converged towards the stone jetty at which our ship was moored. Although it was not long after daylight a crowd of several hundred persons had already assembled on the shore to watch us land, and along the roads and tracks leading into the station from the jungle on the landward side came many small parties of men, women, and children, who smiled and waved their hands in response to our own greetings. It was a heart-warming experience.

On the 28th of January the official ceremony took place on the football field that was used for public gatherings. This not very level piece of ground was partly enclosed by shaded slopes, which provided a natural amphitheatre for a crowd of at least four thousand spectators who had come from all parts of the island. I had put on my uniform for the occasion and Salana Ga'a wore, in addition to his white skirt-like *sulu*, a waistcoat and peaked cap made entirely of shell money, one of the several kinds of primitive currency still used locally in some of the islands. It took the form of small tubular shaped pieces of polished shell, bored and threaded together like beads on to long strings, which could be sewn together to shape such garments, and had been presented to Salana by his supporters as a symbol of power and chiefly authority.

As I took up my position facing the Council the assembly rose to their feet at a signal and remained standing while a pastor of the South Seas Evangelical Mission asked for Divine blessing on the proceedings. Then came the Lord's Prayer repeated by the four thousand voices in a sonorous unison: the sound was like the long drawn out muttering of distant thunder. Again there was a signal, and as one man the crowd sank silently down while Salana Ga'a came forward to make his promises of allegiance and receive his letter of appointment. I realized during those moments, as never before, what discipline and sincerity had controlled the Marching Rule movement, and I prayed silently that those qualities might strengthen and inspire the Council and its helpers in their work. The ceremony concluded with the singing of "God Save the Queen" by a Malaitan choir.

The initial deliberations of the Council revealed some ideas of progress which tended to be more ambitious than realistic, among projects that were mooted being one for the purchase of a big ship to stimulate the commerce of the island and another for the opening of a gold mine; but it was not long before they learned to cut their coat according to the cloth that with Government aid they were able to provide.

In 1963 I received a copy of a booklet entitled *A brief History of the Malaita Council,* which contained a fairly comprehensive survey of resolutions approved, measures adopted and matters discussed during the first ten years of the Council's existence. These included: the introduction of a system of differential tax assessment to replace poll tax; the construction of staff houses, Court houses, market houses, school buildings, dispensaries and wharves, with financial provision where required; repairs to a leprosarium; the curing and preservation of fish and the establishment of fish ponds; trade unions; dog licensing; coconut stealing; "getting a trained lawyer"; recommendations regarding women's hairdressing styles; the prevention of sorcery; and the holding of elections to the Council by secret ballot as a more up-to-date way to hold elections than the "whispering election" previously used.

I conclude this chapter with a thought that assumes potency with the contemplation of the tragic record of brutal and cold-blooded assassination for political ends that during recent years has shocked the conscience of civilization: namely that in a part of the world which even in our fathers' days was often regarded as wrapped in veils of savage darkness a movement of widespread civil unrest and protest should have endured for six years without the loss of a single life.

Chapter XVIII

TO HONIARA

MARCHING RULE, because of its paralysing effect upon the economic recovery and social progress of the Solomons, was one of the most urgent matters to which, on my arrival in the Pacific, I had to give attention; but there were plenty of other problems, and among the highest priorities was the need to speed up the Protectorate building programme, delayed as it had been by the recent hurricane. I recall a remark by Philip Richardson during my first visit to Honiara. We had set out together to inspect the Government offices, workshops and institutions, and as we approached one of our first objectives he pointed to a ramshackle assemblage of shed-like buildings which appeared to be already in the early stages of disintegration.

"That, I regret to say," he observed, "is the hospital."

Provision for new buildings and additional equipment had already been approved; but, as with many other projects, the fruits of expectation were yet to be gathered. At the chambers of the Judicial Commissioner, where we had already called, and which, like so many of the temporary structures in Honiara, had been improvised from the abandoned remnants of military material, the floor had creaked and undulated beneath our modest weight as we walked over it. After this excursion we all got busy with the preparation of a comprehensive works plan to accelerate *inter alia* the transformation of the hospital and the upholding of Justice. A good deal of telegraphic correspondence with the Colonial Office became necessary, and a code name for the exercise was devised. We called it Operation Balbus.

In those days one did not have to look far, either in Guadalcanal, or indeed anywhere in the Western Pacific, to discover something rare and strange that was, directly or indirectly, part of the heritage of destruction. In the neighbourhood of Honiara the evidence of battle, murder and sudden death was only too apparent in the corroded cartridge cases, the rusted iron stakes and the twisted strands of barbed wire that lay scattered over the now deserted, but once bloodily contested, foothills behind the town. But the shards of war were everywhere, and there were not many islands whose beaches could not reveal the shell of a pontoon or a landing craft crumbling in the coral, or where the remains of a jeep, stripped of everything detachable, were not to be found overgrown by grass or festooned with vines and undergrowth in a patch of jungle.

Along the coast of Guadalcanal, between the capital and Cape Esperance at the north-eastern extremity of the island, lay the half-submerged and slowly disintegrating remains of five Japanese transport vessels, which had been driven to the beaches by American aerial bombardment; and one day I noticed something quite unusual was happening to one of these wrecks. There were green bushes sprouting from decks to which by freakish chance the winds and the birds must have carried soil and seed. As if Nature, in gentle mood, had commanded the creatures and the elements to cover up the scars of conflict; so that in years to come, when what remained of the old ships was as venerable as Flecker's old ships of Tyre, a man might watch, with imagination assisting vision but not in vain

> To see the mast burst open with a rose
> And the whole deck put on its leaves again.

With less indentifiably tragic associations were the peculiar difficulties created by the war for some of the Missionary Societies all of whom had remained valiantly at their posts. At one of their elementary schools, which they had had to close down and had only recently been re-opened, I was surprised, on being introduced to the pupils, to find among them several young men, including two or three who were already married and accommodated with their wives, who had returned to complete a long interrupted curriculum. Another bizarre consequence of the Japanese invasion was the existence in a semi-wild state on one or two of the islands of considerable numbers of cattle, which it had been impossible to evacuate from the hastily abandoned plantations where they had been kept in order to keep down the grass and undergrowth. These beasts had adapted themselves to life in the jungle, from which attempts were still being made to round them up.

It was not until the end of 1952 that I was able to transfer my headquarters permanently to Honiara. About the New Hebrides and the Gilbert and Ellice Islands, which I had already visited, I propose to write in later chapters. Their affairs were very little connected with those of the Solomons, and in both territories there was a Resident Commissioner to whom extensive powers were delegated. But with my arrival at Honiara I was enabled to combine the direct administration of the Protectorate with the exercise of my overall responsibility for affairs in the Western Pacific area, and as far as the normal run of affairs was concerned it was with the daily doings in the Solomons that I was most closely connected.

In all aspects of my task I was ably assisted by an experienced staff. My two senior lieutenants, Robert Minnitt and Alistair Macleod-Smith, respectively Chief Secretary and Financial Secretary to the High Commission were, like myself, newcomers to the islands and joined me while we were still based on Suva. Minnitt, who after service in Hong Kong had suffered the privations of a Japanese prisoners-of-war camp, was the kind of person whom everybody likes, considerate to his subordinates and a thoughtful and conscientious adviser upon whose judgement reliance could always be placed. Macleod-Smith, who had served in Nigeria and the West Indies and, since his retirement from the Colonial scene, has had a distinguished career in industry, was a man of no less valuable attainments which he combined with a restless zeal that often kept him at work, despite my remonstrances, until the small hours of the morning, and was never content to disengage himself from a problem until he had hammered out a solution. Minnitt and he worked extremely well together in a combination in which, to use military terms, strategic planning was admirably complemented by verve and audacity. I mentally assigned to them the roles of chief-of-staff and cavalry leader.

Philip Dalton, our Attorney-General, had been Solicitor-

General in Fiji—a useful background—and was transferred to us on promotion. My most vivid recollection of him is as captain of a toy balloon rugger team scoring a try at a Government House Christmas party; but he was a sound lawyer as well as a good mixer and a tower of strength both in Council and in chambers.

Macleod-Smith accompanied my family and myself when on the 18th of December, 1952, we left Suva for the last time. It had been arranged that in order to maintain continuity of correspondence Minnitt and Dalton should remain in Fiji until I had arrived at Honiara. Tom Russell, one of the Assistant Secretaries, now (1974) Chief Secretary to the High Commission, was also with us in the first party. Bryant had gone on leave and was shortly afterwards transferred to Nigeria.

We travelled in the *Kurimarau,* a vessel whose overall length of 120 feet placed her in a class above that of all the other Government craft. She had been built as an administrative and cargo vessel for the Unilevers combine, which owned many plantations in the area, and had been purchased after the war for use by the Protectorate Trade Scheme, an organization set up as an interim measure to handle the islands' interrupted export trade, still, at the time of my arrival, in the doldrums. She had, however, proved to be too large and expensive to operate to be economical and was eventually sold. But costly as she might be to run she was a most steady and comfortable ship, and ploughed her way through the heaviest seas with assurance and aplomb. I had first made her acquaintance in Fiji, when she came to my rescue by transporting me as far as the New Hebrides at the beginning of my first tour of the territories, the *Nareau,* which at the time was in dry dock at Suva and was to have carried me, having been delayed at the last minute by some malfunctioning of her internal arrangements. With me on board on that occasion were fifty head of Hereford cattle, with which it was hoped to establish the breed in the Solomons. They added interest to the voyage.

During her service in the Protectorate *Kurimarau* was commanded by Captain MacDonald, affectionately known as Captain Mac., a veteran navigator with an unrivalled knowledge of the island trade. With his wealth of marine lore, his nostalgic attachment to the scenes and surroundings he knew so well, and his hearty solicitude for his passengers, displayed in the abundance and variety of a table to which even the keenest of appetites sharpened by sea breezes could scarcely do justice, he could well have stepped out of a story by Joseph Conrad.

On the way to Guadalcanal we anchored off the small island of Anuda, known also as Cherry Island, which, except for one uninhabited islet, is the most easterly land in the Solomons. Anuda is not much more than two or three hundred yards across in any direction, and even its population of something less than two hundred persons must have found it a tight squeeze. We had hoped to go ashore, but the high surf on the only practicable landing place made this impossible without unjustifiable risk. But where a boat could not go in safety swimmers evidently could, for scarcely had our engines stopped when twenty or thirty Anudans, who had been standing on the beach, plunged into the breakers and had soon covered the quarter of a mile or so which, in such conditions, was the closest distance to which it was prudent for the *Kurimarau* to approach. On reaching the vessel they immediately clambered onto the lower deck where I had gone to welcome them, and in a very few minutes they were all over the ship.

One of them inspected the Chief Officer's cabin and appeared to be pleased with the effect produced by sprinkling the contents of a tin of talcum powder over his chest; another explored the bridge-house, where he was only just prevented from giving "full speed ahead" on the engine-room telegraph; and a third, attracted by my flag at the masthead, sprang nimbly into the rigging in order to examine it more closely. Yet another found his way into the bathroom and turned on the cold shower. I doubt whether the result was what he expected.

After we had presented the visitors with a tin of ship's biscuits and a case of canned meat I felt that the demands of hospitality were satisfied. Captain Mac assured me that the only way to make clear our intention to proceed would be to start the ship. It seemed a little discourteous, but as the islanders were apparently unable to take any other hints I consented, and they all dived cheerfully overboard as we began to gather way. The biscuits

G*

and the meat had been fastened to a raft of planks, and this was safely guided through the surf to the beach.

Four days later we arrived at Honiara. In spite of the general need for renovation the place had a cheerful and expectant air. It didn't seem to matter that the makeshift landing jetty, since replaced by harbour works with berthing accommodation for large ocean-going vessels, was full of cracks and crevices, or that the regrettable hospital and the creaking chambers of the Judicial Commissioner were by no means the only structures to be reaching the end of their short lives. Honiara was in fact facing fortune with a smiling face. The main street and only thoroughfare, Mendana Avenue, was lined on both sides with young flamboyant trees, there were bushes of hibiscus flowering in the little gardens of the clerks' quarters, and in the Chinese business and residential area, known as China Town, most of the stores, which depended mainly on Melanesian patronage, had been recently built and were gaily painted in bright hues, among which red and yellow seemed to be the most popular. The eastern end of Mendana Avenue crossed a river, the Matanikau, by a bridge of military pattern from whose untimbered iron deck a fairly frequently repeated sound like a sustained burst of musketry gave evidence of a lively movement of wheeled traffic. The populace was numerous, and if only cautiously excited—for the Melanesian was habitually reserved upon the surface—appeared to be taking an interest in all that was going on.

The pre-war capital, Tulagi, was a small island in the Ngela Group half way between Guadalcanal and Malaita. It was situated in a magnificent harbour, but there was no suitable and easily accessible hinterland for the development of natural resources, which it was hoped that the establishment of headquarters on the more promising terrain of Guadalcanal would encourage. The new Residency, which was to become Government House, had originally been built as a hospital for New Zealand Forces on a strip of land whose native name, Honiara, had been adopted for the new capital. The name was in fact an expression meaning "the place to which the winds come first." In Guadalcanal during the day-time all winds come from the sea, and the small area to which the description was originally confined juts out a little from the coast and therefore received their full blast. The name was chosen during the American and Allied campaign after consultation with the headman of the near-by village of Kakombona. That headman, when afterwards questioned about the matter, suggested, as the District Officer reported, that the name had subsequently acquired an additional significance, since it was applied to a place to which not only the wind but everything—ships, information, letters and so forth—came first before being distributed. Remarks that, whether or not innocent of any intention to be critical of administrative delays, were prefectly justifiable comment; though it could be argued that in a widely scattered area like the Solomons any channel of central administration would be almost bound to become something of a bottleneck.

The plan of the Residency, which was a single-storeyed building raised on concrete pillars and with a thatched roof and plaited grass wall panels decorated by Malaitan craftsmen, resembled the capital letter F. The long side ran roughly parallel with the shore line and was separated by only a few yards from the reef, which was silent, murmurous or noisy according to the state of the wind and the tide—sometimes soothing and sibilant, and sometimes thunderous, when a north-westerly squall sent the breakers crashing onto the beach outside our windows. A large tree, a favourite haunt of a kingfisher, overhung the water's edge in front of the verandah onto which our bedroom opened, and looking out across the sea one sometimes caught sight of a school of porpoises disporting themselves with acrobatic zest. The top of the F contained an L-shaped room, the principal reception room of the house, which was used during our tenancy for cocktail parties, dances, film shows, Scottish dancing, amateur theatricals, children's parties, and on one occasion, when untimely rain drove our garden party guests to take shelter, even as an improvised tea room. The bedroom accommodation included in the shorter wing a guest room which, because its door and windows were protected by mosquito gauze, was commonly known as the cage. This occasionally gave rise to misunderstanding, as when my daughter wrote to a friend: "We had the Bishop staying with us last week. We put him in the cage."

Under the previous regime the Resident Commissioner had used one of the rooms of the Residency as his office, but I did not myself find it easy to work amid such inevitable domestic distractions as the sound of eggs being beaten up in the kitchen, or the carpet being brushed in the room next door. The sight of my wife passing stealthily down the verandah alongside my windows in order not to divert my attention always made me remember something I wanted to speak to her about, and amid such interruptions, pleasant as they might be, it was difficult to conduct affairs of state with efficiency and despatch.

To overcome these difficulties I arranged for an office to be built at a slight distance from the house. It was so sited as to enable me when sitting at my desk to command a view of the sea and the coast curving beneath the lofty contours of the hills towards Cape Esperance: it would be pleasant, I thought, to be able to look up from my papers when I wanted to, and perhaps find inspiration in the serenity of these surroundings. My expectations were, however, thwarted within a few months by the rapid re-growth of trees which had been cut down to clear the line of vision, and as I was usually too busy to allow my attention to wander I decided to let Nature have her way.

In spite of limitations of space—the extent of the accommodation was scarcely up to Government House standards—we were able to do quite a lot of entertaining in a modest way. I knew from experience that Government House functions could be sticky, and we did our best to make them into happy social occasions. Garden parties, to which members of all communities were invited, were a convenient means of welcoming our Melanesian guests, who would have been embarrassed if included in cocktail or dinner parties of conventional type, which were alien to their way of life. Dinner parties were given from time to time for other guests, and on those occasions some formality in the arrangements for seating was unavoidable. People could be sensitive about seniority, and in a small community where it was not easy to ring the changes one table plan was often very like another. Speaking personally, although one appreciated the conversation of Mrs. A, Mrs. B, or Mrs. C, one or other of whom was pretty sure to be engaging some of one's attention at table, there were times when one would have found it agreeable to exchange amiable observations with Mrs. P, Mrs. Q, Mrs. R, or even Miss X, none of whom, owing to their husbands' or their own position in the table of precedence, one would be likely to find oneself sitting next to.

However, on Christmas Day protocol was brushed aside. Most people had their own parties, and we did our best to discover the "lonelies" in order to invite them to dinner. Seniority did not dictate the table plan, and we tried to work it out in such a way that everyone would find himself or herself with a congenial neighbour. After dinner there were games, sedentary at first to aid digestion but becoming more active and energetic as the evening advanced (Dalton was good at these), and the finale was usually a tug of war on the verandah. It was pleasant, as the classical phrase reminded us, to play the fool in season.

Chapter XIX

REINS OF GOVERNMENT

IF I were asked to suggest golden rules for administrators the list would probably boil down to little more than a few copybook maxims. In order to achieve the best in any walk of life it is necessary to be in love with one's job and to seek fulfilment in it. But every craft, every profession, has its apprentices, and particularly in the Colonial Service, with its infinite variety of scenes and situations, the path of understanding was a never-ending one.

As a Governor one's principal and sometimes most difficult responsibility lay in the making of decisions, not a few of which might be far reaching in their consequences. Any honest man can do what he knows to be right, whatever the obstacles to be overcome; but the dividing line between equity and expediency is sometimes blurred and not easy to distinguish. It is then that in any attempt to estimate the advantages of alternative courses of action disinterested advice is needful. And this indicates other qualities that a Governor should possess, for the worth of his decisions may well depend upon the judgement with which he has chosen his advisers and his skill in evaluating their opinions. The process, I used to think, recalling occasions when I had had to perform magisterial duties, was like deciding the weight to be attached to evidence considered as quality rather than quantity. Trustworthy advisers could undoubtedly be of great assistance, but responsibility for the final decision must always be one's own.

To turn from the principles to the machinery of administration in the colonial sphere was, as likely as not, to come upon a series of signposts each pointing in a different direction to the same indicated destination. The traditional form of colonial constitution—if so much diversity permits the expression—provided for a Legislative Council and an Executive Council, both normally composed of senior Government officials and some unofficial members, who might be nominated by the Governor or elected in proportions depending upon the degree of progress towards the accepted aim of responsible self-government—usually until post-war years a pretty long term objective.

In accordance with the Colonial Regulations the authorization of public expenditure required a vote or enactment of the Legislature, but its hold of the purse strings was controlled by the necessity for the covering approval of the Secretary of State and the release of funds by the Governor. And in any case, since a Legislative Council, at least during the early stages of its evolution, normally had an official majority, with dissenting unofficials, if any, in permanent opposition, it could scarcely in such circumstances be regarded as a democratic institution.

The Executive Council, composed of senior ex-officio members of the Legislative Council with, as a rule, unofficial members nominated by the Governor, was the nearest colonial approach to a Cabinet; but it was, in effect, an advisory, not a responsible, body. It met to discuss and advise the Governor on all matters other than those which he did not regard as being of sufficient importance to justify consultation. He was not, however, bound to accept the Council's advice if he did not agree with it, though in that case he was required to report his disagreement and the reasons for it to the Secretary of State.

In the Western Pacific territories at the time of my arrival, although some progress in local government was being made by District or Island Councils, there were no Legislative Councils or Executive Councils in existence. What did exist in the Solomons was an Advisory Council under the Presidency of the Resident Commissioner with provision for four official members ex-officio, five non-officials representing the European community and five natives of the Protectorate. All the non-official members were appointed by the Resident Commissioner.

The Council was by law required to meet at least once a year, but it was not so required to meet in public (although in fact it did so) or to publish the minutes of its proceedings. There were no matters about which it was obligatory for the Resident Commissioner to consult or even to inform the Council, and the extent to which he took members into his confidence or sought their advice was a matter for his discretion. Standing Orders did, however, permit any member to move a motion "tendering advice relating to public affairs or administration." A body so constituted and restricted in its powers and functions, though useful as a pressure gauge and a vent pipe for criticisms, was of doubtful value as an instrument of political precision.

The criticisms, emanating mainly from the planting and trading community, arose not only from the frustrations attributable to delays, but from an atmosphere of discontent originating in pre-war years and due principally to the remoteness of High Commission headquarters in Fiji, which, though exercising control over all the Protectorate's affairs, was felt on occasion to be lacking in sympathy with the islands' problems.

Such an attitude, to whatever extent justifiable, was certainly understandable, and my own appointment was, in fact, at least partly due to a good deal of intermittent pressure by the Europeans in the Solomons, who, with support by the Bishop of Melanesia, had petitioned before the war for the setting up of a Legislative Council. There would have been many difficulties, not least those caused by geography, in taking such a step, and in the judgement of the then High Commissioner it would have been premature; but I was told that the petitioners had been influenced by the belief that if a Legislative Council were created it would be a step towards providing the Protectorate with a Governor of its own, since they had observed that in almost all Colonial territories administered by a Governor a Legislative Council was part of the constitution. Except to the extent that my services had to be shared with the Gilbert and Ellice Islands and the New Hebrides it could therefore be argued that they had got what they wanted. I had, nevertheless, some sympathy with any who might feel that as far as any guarantee of Government action or even of public awareness was concerned their performance in Advisory Council was oratory in an empty forum, though for what I regarded as good reasons I believed that to bring a Legislative Council into being under local conditions as I found them would still be premature.

Apart from the physical difficulty of organizing electoral procedures in such a widespread area of poor communications—an obstacle which, though not necessarily insuperable, was still imposing—there would, in the first place, be the serious problem of finding a sufficient number of candidates for native membership. Native education had until recently been almost entirely in the hands of the Missions, who, not unreasonably from their point of view, had creamed off the most promising material in order to secure teachers and ordinands. It was no easy task for the Government to recruit staff for normal clerical duties, and to place upon Native members of a Council responsibilities for which they were inadequately equipped might well be to introduce a lack of balance into the proceedings of the Council which it would take a long time to correct. It may be that critics of today would consider my attitude to have been too paternalistic. I believe that even if a crystal ball had revealed to me what was to be the pace of progress I would still have hesitated to try to encourage those learning to swim by making them jump in at the deep end. In any case there was no Native demand at all for a Legislative Council.

The European community comprised only a small fraction of the population—well under 500 in an estimated total of about 100,000—and I was satisfied that even of this tiny minority there were very few, if any, for whom the absence of a Legislative Council was a burning question. It was, of course, indisputable that the value of their contributions to the fragile economy and, in the case of the Missions, to the social services of the islands was out of all proportion to their actual numbers. Without their endeavours, sustained over many years, it would have been impossible to avoid stagnation. They were deserving of sympathetic understanding and encouragement. It was a question of how to convince them of the Government's wish to give them just that.

With regard to their relations as individuals with the Government the simple fact of my headquarters being in the Protectorate, thus enabling anyone to get his business attended to within days rather than weeks, or even possibly, if he could call at the appropriate office, within hours, or to find me available for personal discussion when that would be helpful, should, I believed, go a long way to strengthen confidence. It remained to consider what procedures might be adopted in Advisory Council in order that in its corporate capacity it could be given a more important role in the conduct of public affairs.

I did not see the necessity for any constitutional change.

I have never had overmuch faith in the efficacy of legislation in itself as a means of ensuring orderly political progress in developing countries, or any confidence that constitutional instruments, however meticulously drafted, could work satisfactorily unless based on a substantial measure of general good will. During the years in which the transfer of power to dependent territories began to be accelerated the writing and re-writing of constitutions became a daily task. None of them lasted long, for when the golden gates of freedom were in sight half-way houses were not popular.

In the Solomons, at the time of which I write, Independence was not even a sail upon the horizon and, the Marching Rule problem once disposed of, I had no reason to doubt the existence of general good will. I nevertheless believed that until the possibilities of constitutional reform became more discernible, good will would go far to satisfy the needs of the day and that legalistic formalities could wait upon events.

I did, however, with the approval of all concerned, make two innovations. One was to set up a Standing Committee of the Advisory Council to meet fairly frequently under my chairmanship in order to discuss matters of public concern that I wished to place before them or they to raise with me. For practical reasons membership had to be restricted to Council members residing at Honiara, but others who might be visiting the capital could be co-opted as opportunity arose. Meetings were held in the privacy of my office, for part of their business would be the consideration of policy in embryo.

My other experiment was to introduce a procedure at formal meetings of the Council whereby, on a suitable motion, there should be a debate ranging over a wide general field of public affairs, during which any matters of special interest to members could be raised. The debate would offer opportunities for discussion comparable to those afforded in the House of Commons by motions for the adjournment, or, in certain Colonial legislatures, by a motion of thanks for the Governor's address. With the adoption of these two measures the Council, both in its critical and its advisory functions, ceased to be a rather blunt instrument and became much more a weapon of precision.

Each member carried an individual hall-mark of worth and originality. Distinguishable by his alert and rugged countenance was a Solomon Islander who, during the Japanese invasion of Guadalcanal, had resolved, as he afterwards declared, to "do something good for my King." Employed as an Army scout, he was captured while returning from a patrol, bound to a tree and threatened with death if he failed to disclose the whereabouts of American troops then in occupation of part of the island. He remained silent. He was bayoneted, first in each cheek, then in the neck and in the breast, and no word came from him. Left for dead by his tormentors, he somehow managed to free himself and drag his way to the American lines, where he insisted on making a report before having his wounds dressed. For this gallant conduct Sergeant-Major Vouza, as he then was, received the George Medal from his King and was also awarded the Silver Star for gallantry by the President of the United States.

Other Native members included, besides the recently converted Salana Ga'a, whom, in fulfilment of an undertaking given to him, I had appointed to represent Malaita, an active solidly built little man of quite exceptional ability, who was destined to become an important character in the history of the Protectorate. This was Silas Sitai, then Head Clerk and Administrative Assistant to the District Commissioner of the Eastern District. After education and training as a wireless operator in Fiji before the Japanese invasion, he volunteered on the outbreak of hostilities for service with the United States Forces as an interpreter; but this was unexciting work for a venturesome spirit and it was not long before he was employed as a scout to seek out Japanese hideouts and lead Marines through the jungle to points from which they could launch surprise attacks. He was a man of remarkable all-round initiative, with a persuasive approach to problems of human relations, who competently took charge of the Government station during the D.C's absence on tour, and did first-class work in bringing about better understanding in areas which had been soured by Marching Rule influence.

It seemed to me at the time to be somewhat incongruous that a Government servant, subject to the normal rules of Service discipline, should have been placed, as a representative in the Council of Native interests, in a position in which, in support of those interests he had not only the right but the duty to be critical of the Government if in his view such an attitude was demanded by circumstances; but to have excluded all Government servants from such membership would seriously have narrowed the field of suitable candidates and, certainly in the loss of Sitai, have deprived the islanders of a conscientious and able spokesman. Sitai had far too much character to be a "yes man". In due course he became an Administrative Officer and eventually, until his death in 1972, President of the Governing Council, the policy-making and legislative body of the Protectorate.

Among the European unofficials were Kenneth Dalrymple Hay, popularly known as Ken Hay, and Leslie Gill. Though cast by habit and circumstance in different moulds they had both become, equally with others who could be counted with them, the adopted children of the islands, all but severed from their roots, but finding in what some would regard as exile a rewarding if lonely independence. A few of them, perhaps, born under propitious stars, might have become explorers and pioneers in a wilder world, but at a stage in their journey Fate had lifted up a finger and they had paused too long.

Hay, for all his present isolation, had in the past ranged far and adventurously. During the First World War he had served with the Australian Forces in Egypt and Palestine—an experience which furnished us with memories in common—and in the second conflict had been a Coast Watcher in the Protectorate. Over the years he had spent in the islands he had acquired many interests and engaged in many enterprises. From the fruits of agricultural development he might have made a modest fortune if the fertility of the land had corresponded with that of his ideas and finance been available; but funds for experiment, whether private or public, were not an ever flowing stream. Not a few of the ventures he was able to undertake must have done well. One of them was an hotel in Honiara—a one-storey affair constructed on do-it-yourself principles, but the only one in the British Solomons; and during my time he built a soda-water factory, a cinema and a general store at which the variety of goods ranged from sticks of plug tobacco and hurricane lanterns to canteens of table silver and a selection of beauty preparations. Imposingly displayed at the door of this emporium were the names of the business houses for which Hay held agencies. A list which could not have been much shorter and probably indicated a much greater diversity of enterprise then most of the floor directories to be found on the walls of the entrance halls in modern office blocks.

Another of his plans was to convert an abandoned United States landing vessel into a swimming pool—a shark-proof amenity which would undoubtedly have been generally appreciated; but it would have been necessary to remove the object to a more suitable site and to make extensive repairs to corroded metal; and in the deep waters of finance the project foundered.

Like Silas Sitai, Ken Hay was a good scout and a good mixer. Both as a member of our Standing Committee, where his knowledge and experience were invaluable, and at the full meetings of the Advisory Council he was a staunch and faithful adviser.

Leslie Gill, a trader who remembered more prosperous days, was in many respects of more intense disposition. A man bruised in fortune by the punishment of war, lonely in a world narrowing with the disappearance of things and faces familiar. A man disappointed and even bitter at the lack of reparation for losses suffered, but without malice and, while, in Council, trenchant in his castigation of what he regarded as the vexatious delays and petty tyrannies of bureaucracy, yet able to step aside from the heat of debate and acknowledge our honest recognition of difficulties in presenting a glimpse of what he described as "the vision splendid" of the future.

He led a solitary life on one of the islands of the Western District, which he represented : there he bought copra from the Melanesians and kept a store stocked with miscellaneous merchandise. He came to Honiara only for Council meetings, and this precluded a close acquaintanceship; but as time went on I began to feel that perhaps his contacts with us had dispelled a little of the discontent that seemed to shadow the windows of his mind.

I sometimes wondered whether he was ever troubled by thoughts of another kind of shadow; for his vision was not good, and perusal of the numerous Council documents, which he used to study with great care, must have imposed a strain upon his eyes. My most frequently recurring memory of him belongs to an occasion when he came to Government House as our guest to attend the first formal meeting of the Council over which I presided. Fatigued, as he must have been after a long journey, he retired early on the night of his arrival; but some time later on my own way to bed I noticed the light still burning in his room and decided to knock and enquire whether he was comfortable and had everything he wanted. I found him sitting in a chair, a reading lamp by his side, his eyes shaded and in his hand one of the Council papers connected with a subject to be debated on the following day. He was obviously tired; but, as I was to learn later, it was not in him to say "enough" until the end of the day.

Among the unofficials was one whose commanding influence and personality would have distinguished him in any company. Bishop Alfred Hill, whose consecration as Bishop of Melanesia took place in 1954, had, as a young man, gone to sea in the service of the Melanesian Mission, and had in due course obtained his Master's certificate. Thereafter for some years he had been in charge of the Mission's principal boys' school at Pawa, situated on a small island in the Eastern District, and had earned for it a reputation for sound teaching and pride of purpose of which the Mission might well feel proud. He was a dynamic organizer and a firm disciplinarian; but his rule as headmaster was tempered by a very human understanding of the human boy. He had an eagle eye and a voice that, doubtless fortified by competition with turbulent winds at sea, would have done credit to a Regimental Sergeant-Major; and I recall the spectacle during a visit to Pawa of a small offender, guilty of some peccadillo and endeavouring to escape detection and the wrath to come, arrested in full flight at a range of well over a hundred yards, by the thunder of an inescapable magisterial summons.

I probably knew him as well as anyone outside his immediate circle, and for all his keen interest in what went on around him, his heartiness, his sailor's love of an anecdote, and his almost boyish sense of humour, the conviction grew upon me as I sometimes observed him in Council, and particularly as the day of his consecration approached, that within the inner sanctuary of his private thoughts he was a solitary. Into that sanctuary none but he could enter; but at times, in a play of fancy, I have seen a farthing dip burning on the altar of humility, and at other times the torch of faith flaming in a dungeon.

A few years ago serious illness compelled him to relinquish the bishopric of Melanesia with its unrelenting demands upon physical stamina; but this was not the end of a long voyage. He continued his ministry as an assistant to the Bishop of New Guinea, and there, among the islands whose people he had loved and served, his Pilot came on board.

Chapter XX

ROUND THE ISLANDS

IN the business of the islands an essential task was carried out by the ships of the Government fleet. They were first and foremost an administrative life-line allocated for the use of District or itinerant departmental staff and the carriage of mails and Government stores; but, if required, they accepted other cargo as well as passengers: though their "first class" accommodation was usually limited to one single cabin. They were also available for those in need of transport for hospital treatment.

For an Administrative Officer touring his District journeys in one of these vessels were not only a way of travel; they came close to being a way of life which, rewarding as it doubtless was in terms of human contacts and missions accomplished, could scarcely be described as physically comfortable, requiring, as it did at sea, a continuous exercise of the sense of balance and of muscular power necessary for combating the force of gravity. Nor in really rough weather was the consumption of a meal at all a simple matter. Cooking would almost certainly be impracticable; but the mere conveyance of food to the mouth called for considerable ingenuity, since one hand was needed to anchor oneself to some stable object and another to hold the container. The second hand could however be left free if the container was a mug, as this could be gripped and kept in position by the thighs if one sat on the floor with legs extended.

The expertise demanded by this kind of travel did not stop short at muscular dexterity and, in finding the way in poor conditions, the employment of the navigational sixth sense our boatswains seemed to possess. Having reached one's destination, one had to get ashore. I cannot recall more than half a dozen places in the Solomons where there was a landing jetty at which one of our small craft, drawing at most little more than five feet of water, could lie alongside. But the islanders had, as might have been expected, a natural aptitude for boat work.

Within the shelter of a barrier reef approach to a beach was easy provided that, as sometimes was the case at low tide, the coral bottom was not so close to the surface as to make wading essential for some part of the journey; but to land on an island encircled by a fringing reef, where there was no lagoon, could be a hazardous undertaking requiring skill of a high order, for the sea was seldom calm. As one drew closer to the shore the waves seemed to mount higher and higher as if to demonstrate their power before loosing their pent-up strength in a furious cascade of surf. The essential element in the manoeuvre was timing, and the critical moment arrived as one reached the point where the shelf of the reef curved downwards into deeper water.

At one moment one was lifted high on an incoming wave: below were the cheerful faces of helpers who had waded out to catch the boat and pull her into safety. A moment later the faces would be hidden as the boat sank into the trough of the wave that had passed her by. Up again with the green seas pouring back over the reef edge like a river flowing over the lip of a waterfall. All this time the coxswain would have been watching the sea behind, and now at his word the oarsmen would start rowing furiously and the boat surged forward onto the reef, there to be seized and steadied by a dozen pairs of willing hands before being dragged, with the surf breaking all around, towards dry land.

Other landings, if less exciting, could be equally unconventional, as when, reef conditions being unsuitable for boat handling, I was transported to the beach on a plank. On my first "State" visit to Makira, the headquarters of the Eastern District, an ancient custom was observed when, with my wife and daughter, I was required to tranship into a native dug-out canoe, which was then lifted bodily from the water and carried with ourselves inside high up onto the beach by as many stalwarts as could find arm and shoulder room beneath the burden. This procedure, I was told, was a form of V.I.P. treatment accorded in earlier days to local chiefs.

On another occasion, this time immediately following embarkation, there was a slight misadventure which, as my reflections about the Government fleet had done, kindled a memory of the past. We had just pushed off to rejoin our ship and had been rowed no more than two or three strokes when my attention was attracted by a miniature fountain springing from the bottom of the boat. This was noticed at the same time by the nearest member of the crew who, with presence of mind, slipped off his vest and, rolling it up so as to form a plug, was able to stem the flow until we had managed to regain the beach, Realizing what had happened I remembered again that day long ago at the Admiralty when, immediately before my unsuccessful interview with the Selection Board, I had been conducted by the messenger who admitted me to the building to a waiting-room and given fifteen minutes to write down what I would do if I were on board ship and ordered to lower a boat. Since something more was obviously expected than the short answer that one would do as one was told, I wrote one or two sentences about ensuring that the boat was adequately provisioned and equipped for possible emergencies; but before inspiration could carry me further the messenger had collected my paper and was reading it through. I watched his face anxiously for a sign of approval, but his comment when it came was not encouraging. "The first thing you want to go and do before you lower a boat," he said, "is to see that the bung is in."

Perhaps after all it was lack of gumption that had been my undoing that day.

In the course of our travels we covered many hundreds of miles in visits to islands in the Protectorate alone. Although at least ninety-five per cent of the Solomons population was Melanesian, there were several small outlying islands inhabited by Polynesians; but most of my contacts with that happily remembered people were made in the Gilbert and Ellice Islands, which I propose to describe in my next chapter. A visitor to the Solomons might well receive from first acquaintance with individual Melanesians the general impression of a withdrawn or even morose disposition; but any presumption so engendered would be wide of the mark as an indication of essential qualities of head and heart.

It was, however, true enough that an impassive countenance was more common than a smiling one, and that words were seldom wasted when nothing more than silence was required. This was brought home to me once when, on a tour of Malaita, the vessel I was using and that of the D.C. who was accompanying me were anchored off a village we had been visiting. From my own deck I watched one of the villagers paddle out in a canoe to the other ship and climb on board. Although several members of the D.C's crew, who were going about their duties, had obviously observed him, not one of them spoke to him or took any notice of his arrival, and after a few minutes he climbed back into his canoe and paddled off again.

I could only assume that since no word of any kind had passed the visitor had no other purpose than to satisfy curiosity. He gave no sign of being disconcerted by the lack of any response to his presence on board, and I could come to no other conclusion than that what had the appearance of a deliberate slight was in fact an indication of amicable relations. Had the crew had any suspicions of the stranger he would undoubtedly have been challenged. That they had permitted him to come and go without interference meant that they accepted his *bona fides*, and there was no need for an exchange of civilities in order to confirm what their behaviour had made obvious.

But taciturn and reserved as he could often be the Melanesian, when he gave his word, gave with it his bond. For the rest, the history of Marching Rule had revealed both his capacity for leadership and his amenability to discipline. If he said little he observed and absorbed a good deal. He was anxious to acquire knowledge and technical skills, in some of which he showed a marked aptitude. The "engineers" in our little ships seemed able to give first aid in all mechanical emergencies, and although breakdowns at sea were by no means infrequent we always managed to limp into port. In the driving seat of a motor car or a tractor the Melanesian was equally at home.

He was capable, too, of impressive displays of sustained enthusiasm. To celebrate the Queen's coronation in 1953 there were numerous observances, ceremonies and entertainments: church services, a parade of Police at which, after a salute to the

Royal Standard, coronation medals were presented, a garden party and a ball at Government House, a feast at which an ox was roasted, a firework display and an ambitiously named "Pageant of Empire", arranged by Colchester-Wemyss, the Head of Police, who also organized a torch-light procession along Mendana Avenue and past Government House, where we waited to watch it go by, of all members of the Force not on duty, reinforced by many "friends of the Force" from Honiara and elsewhere. Approaching from the distance, with something like a thousand torch-bearers, it looked like a dragon with fiery scales, but these were soon fragmented into hundreds of dancing points of light as in twos and threes, like excited children just released from school, the men streamed past, running, shouting, singing and even leaping into the air in the exuberance of the moment, their torsos glistening and gleaming like burnished bronze.

On a smaller scale than the triumphal coronation procession, but not less imaginatively contrived, were many of the manifestations of welcome with which we were greeted during our travels. At the village of Ugeli on the island of Rendova our attention was caught as we rounded the headland that protected the anchorage by a cloud of white smoke and scintillating tongues of flame ascending from a timber pylon that had been built and ignited in our honour in the absence of facilities for a salute of cannon. The landing place had been gaily decorated with flags, and as night fell golden chains of light began to spread along the shore line as lamps made out of coconut shells, which had been placed in position on both sides of the anchorage, were lit. It was also at Rendova that we first encountered the gracious custom of a presentation of gifts of vegetables and fruit made individually by each member of the village. Men, women and children came forward one by one and silently laid on the ground before us in a growing heap of produce, which was soon more than would have been adequate to adorn a parish church at a harvest festival, their contributions of sweet potatoes, plantains, heads of young green corn swathed and tasselled, papaws, limes and pineapples. The presentation had a ritual solemnity, and its simplicity and sincerity were deeply moving.

Wherever we landed we were met by the Headman of the

village and, if there was a school in the vicinity, by a party of schoolboys who sang "God Save the Queen", followed possibly by a song of welcome composed for the occasion; for musical greetings and farewells were traditional. We would then be conducted to the village centre or meeting place, often a pleasantly shaded sward of clover, where, seated in chairs placed in readiness, we would listen to the Headman, or perhaps the schoolmaster as the lettered member of the community, deliver an address of welcome, to which I would then reply.

I did not always find this an easy task. I would speak of the Queen and her concern for the wellbeing and happiness of her people, were they ever so far away, and then perhaps, slightly departing from strict geographical accuracy in order to illustrate the theme, would remind them that, the earth being round and she precisely on the opposite side of it, they could not travel in any direction without drawing a little nearer to her. It was easy to thank them for their welcome and to tell them—and Heaven knew I spoke from my heart—that we were happy to be among them and that in all matters in which they needed help I would do my best to assist them. It was not quite so easy to be certain of the kind of help they would seek or need, or the extent to which it could be readily provided.

I suppose that one way of describing poverty would be to define it as a lack of benefits enjoyed by most members of the community to which one belongs. Unsophisticated societies are usually free from the problems of the destitute and the "underprivileged" that arise in artificial and complex surroundings. If these islanders had been asked what they wanted that they didn't possess, they might, as the Marching Rule leaders had done, have fed their fancies with visions of the knowledge and power of the white man. Among those of more adventurous turn of mind there would certainly have been a desire to learn more of and, if possible, gain admission to this exciting world of opportunities and prizes that had encompassed them. So much could be inferred from the evident appeal of the "walk-about"—the Melanesian equivalent of the grand tour—and from the eager response to the slender opportunities that Protectorate education, restricted as it had been by lack of teaching staff, could offer. The Government had plenty of plans : for more schools and hospitals, teacher and technical training, improved agriculture, better ships, deeper harbours, roads, bridges . . . the list was a yard long. But many of these projects were still in the discussion or drawing-board stage; money, and above all time, would be needed before we could point to results, and as far as the people I had to talk to were concerned it was all "pie in the sky". There was so little that was immediate and tangible, and promises and expectations that might take years for fulfilment were not enough. I felt like Father Christmas without his sack of toys. What was there I could do *now*?

One thing we always did, my wife and I, and that was to shake hands with everybody in sight. Young, firm, vigorous hands; rough, horny hands; old, wrinkled hands; smooth hands, sensitive hands, little, innocent hands; hands shy and hesitant, hands resolute, hands weakened by infirmity, hands scourged and wasted by the ravages of disease. The people came up in long, orderly queues, first the men and then the women accompanied by the children including all who were able to toddle. Even the babies-in-arms who looked up at us with large brown eyes had their little hands lifted up by their proud and bashful mamas.

After taking note of any local problems or complaints and promising to look into them I would accompany the Headman in a walk round the village. It was always neat and tidy. Square or rectangular houses of traditional type were often raised from the ground on "stilts" as a protection against mud or vermin, and sometimes there was a display of pots and pans, scoured and shining, set out in orderly array on a mat outside an entrance. Roofs and walls looked trim and workman-like with their panels of plaited palm leaves, but in some villages on islands which had been within the battle area traditional materials had been abandoned in favour of planks, scraps of metal and other salvaged items, popular because it had been supposed that, being part of the white man's equipment, their strength and durability would survive indefinitely without renovation—an expectation that time had done little to justify. I found this shabby patchwork depressing : it seemed ironical that after the wreckage of war the tide of victory should, as far as these mournful experiments gave any indication, have carried with it nothing more than such dismal pieces of flotsam and jetsam. Perhaps in the eyes of some of those villagers the fine silver of the white man's world had become a little tarnished.

The proceedings would often culminate in a display of dancing, which might be traditional or specially designed to mark the occasion, and it was in such performances that the innate discipline and ingenuity of the people, attended sometimes by no mean measure of histrionic talent, found expression in mime and movement. Some of the dances, in which spears or bows and arrows were essential accessories, represented the propitiation of tutelary spirits for success in warfare, or the tribal folk-memory of some "famous victory" of the past. In a world without books dances of that kind were a living reference library of tribal lore, epic encounters and legendary tales. Others recorded contemporary events—even the story of our own visit might find its way into the choreographic archives. Dances of this kind took the place of illustrated newspapers. Sometimes the sea provided inspiration. At Pawa school the boys, under the ever ready genius of Father Hill, had organized several dances, in one of which the leading performer, representing a shark, circled swiftly with lowered head, lifted shoulder and arms extended among a shoal of smaller fishes, which scattered in terror at his approach.

Often the dancers performed in little squads, two or three abreast, advancing and retreating in perfect time and rhythm; and sometimes they would sing as they danced and stamp their feet at each about-turn. In some parts of the Solomons, as well as in the New Hebrides, a dancing squad was shadowed by a demonic figure, described as a "debil debil", who circled round it at a distance like a sheepdog rounding up a flock. He was usually plastered with black mud and held a long spear poised as for a throw. He moved rapidly, always pointing his spear, from one position to another while the dancers, showing no sign of consternation, continued their orderly backward and forward progress. Finally he would join with the others and seemingly casting aside any malevolent intentions dance off with them with every appearance of amity and good fellowship.

Times change and, as the adage reminds us, we along with

them; but custom lingers, and custom points to the origin of all beliefs that in the widest sense could be called religious. This, in the realm of folk-dancing, must be true the world over; but in the Pacific islands that I knew I believe that to witness the ritual and interpret the message of many of their dances was to meet the soul of the past and walk with it for a while.

CHAPTER XXI

GILBERT AND ELLICE

"WE really must do our best to make these people feel at home and not think they're left out of things just because their skins happen to be white."

A refreshing point of view. I must admit that I never heard such words actually spoken in the Gilbert and Ellice Islands, but they express an attitude of mind which I would cheerfully ascribe to those by whom we were greeted, wherever we travelled in the Colony, with such a jubilant effervescence of high spirits, and from whom we received so many marks of friendly hospitality. As a mind reader I lay no claim to be infallible: as a heart reader I may be no less unreliable; but it should not be for want of practice. So, accepting the risk of a misfire, I will stick to my guns.

To leave the Solomons on a visit to the Colony was, so to put it, to leave a sea and find an ocean. Within the encircling shadow of the great islands there was, stormy though the straits and channels could often be, to my mind always somehow a suggestion of a vast lake—an impression intensified on days when the winds died away to leave an untroubled expanse of blue waters extending to distant but still visible coast-lines. The Solomons once astern, there was a subtle change of atmosphere. The sea among the islands we had left might be calm or angry: beneath and before us to the ultimate horizon was the swell, restless and eternal, of the mighty Pacific.

The ship in which we travelled—whose properties and propensities I have already described—was the *Nareau*, named after the supreme deity of a Gilbertese creation myth. Although, depending upon the strength of winds and current, her speed could vary between seven knots and zero, she could at least be expected to hold her own, and under normal conditions the voyage from Honiara to Tarawa, the capital, was completed in about a week.

The eruptive genius of the Gilbert and Ellice Islands during my years in the Pacific was Michael Bernacchi, who assumed duty as Resident Commissioner of the Colony shortly after my arrival in Suva. Recently transferred on promotion from Malaya, he brought to his new task a variety of experience and a capacity for command acquired during years of service in the Royal Navy as well as in the land Forces and as a member of the post-war military administration in North Borneo. He was a stickler for discipline, a master of organization and a veritable volcano of energy. If in his atolls there had been any mountains of difficulty standing in the way of progress he would not have hesitated to lift them up and cast them into the sea.

Difficulties could scarcely be described as mountainous. Indeed, compared with the Protectorate the Colony was in a fair way to repairing the ravages of battle and invasion and making good the wastage they had caused, but there was still plenty of fuel to feed the fires of zeal. As in the Solomons, the building programme, which included the reconstruction of the Colony headquarters and the King George V school—the only one that could aim at a secondary curriculum—demanded high priority; and in all directions were enterprises of great pith and moment. At the Tarawa boat harbour, deeper lanes of entry, longer jetties, brighter lights. In other islands, schools, dispensaries, hospitals, Native Court houses and Council chambers. More vessels; for island intercourse, social and commercial, was regulated by the movements of ships, and there was no private enterprise to assist the operations. The Government also had to look after the wireless network, which was the Colony's communication cord in case of emergency. All this added up to a good deal. One could say that to be fully efficient an Administrative Officer in the Colony needed to possess, in addition to a knowledge of native language and custom, a grasp of the rudiments at least of navigation, diesel engines, motor mechanics, electrical and wireless equipment, building and carpentry, commercial book-keeping, typewriting and first aid. Bernacchi was fully efficient.

Once ashore upon an atoll it was, surprisingly, quite possible to forget temporarily that the sea was nowhere more than a few hundred yards away. I first became aware of this at Tarawa, whose lagoon, roughly triangular in shape, is enclosed on two sides by chains of islets, the third side being sheltered from the ocean by reefs. These islets, some of which are two or three miles in length, are in no place more than a quarter of a mile wide; but the tall closely growing palm trees with which they are covered make one side of the narrow strip of land invisible from the other; so that following a track by the side of the lagoon the traveller sees on one hand only an unbroken belt of trees that might, on a calm day with no sound of the sea on the ocean beaches to proclaim otherwise, just as well, as far as appearances go, be the fringe of an extensive hinterland. A different story, however, is, as I discovered later, told by the wells, whose level tends to rise and fall with the tides. The islets are separated one from another by short stretches of sand or reef, which are covered by the sea at high water, but when the tide is low can be waded over or crossed in a jeep with a determined driver.

During our first visit to Tarawa we made one or two of these amphibious journeys in order to acquaint ourselves with the way things went; but to reach the central hospital, whose removal to a more accessible site was an urgent item in the building programme, we had to spend two hours crossing the lagoon by launch to a point where the shallowing water prevented further progress except in native canoes, into which we accordingly transhipped. Two or three hundred yards from the water's edge the depth became insufficient to float even the canoes, and the final stage was completed, in the case of a High Commissioner and his lady, in chairs lashed to poles borne by stalwart orderlies, or, if the visitors were of lesser rank, by wading. Those requiring admission to hospital who were too ill to walk were floated in specially constructed flat-bottomed boats as far as they could get, and carried the rest of the way on stretchers. Unkind critics had been heard to suggest that while it remained where it was the hospital facilities were unlikely to be overburdened, since sufferers would be unwilling to face the rigours of the journey except as a last resort, in which case the likelihood of their surviving it was doubtful.

While temporarily based on Tarawa we spent two days in a visit to the neighbouring island of Abaiang. Here, also, the approach to the shore was protracted, and protocol required that I should be carried over the shallows in a florally decorated chair embellished with a canopy of leaves, which imparted to it a bowerlike appearance considered by everybody to be appropriate to the occasion. Unfortunately more thought had been given to the adornment than to the mechanical strength of the contrivance, the seat of which gave way under a thirteen stone stress when we were still a good two hundred yards from dry land. As this was by way of being a State visit, for which I had arrayed myself in uniform, I felt it would be letting down the side, as well as detrimental to my boots and overalls, to jump down and wade with the rest of the company, and I spent a highly uncomfortable five minutes supporting my weight on the arms and frame of the chair until I was deposited at my destination. I was told subsequently that the expression on my face as I attempted to smile benevolently at the appreciative crowd on the beach made an interesting study.

After this somewhat disconcerting beginning the proceedings went with a swing. We were given an enthusiastic welcome by the two communities, Protestant and Roman Catholic, which maintained a spirited rivalry on the island, and had each, not to be outdone by the other, mustered a brass band of some forty instruments to celebrate the occasion. In order to preserve harmony in every sense of the word agreement was reached that the bands would perform in turn rather than introduce their variations simultaneously, and we passed a very musical half hour while, cheered and applauded by their supporters, first one and then the other marched up and down the shining white paths of powdered coral.

The respective uniforms of the rival instrumentalists were quite dissimilar. The Protestant performers, adherents of the London Missionary Society, were dressed and ornamented traditionally and wore ceremonial dancing mats held in position round the body by belts of black human hair obligingly provided by the ladies. Their necks and brows were garlanded with flowers of frangipani. The Roman Catholics, protestant in dress if not in faith, had devised a uniform consisting of white shirts and shorts with home-made bandoliers and forage caps set at a jaunty angle. Though far less striking than that of their competitors, their attire nevertheless seemed more in keeping with the cultural associations of the sparkling phalanx of cornets, trombones, French horns and bombardons so imposingly displayed.

When these euphonious preliminaries had been completed I changed into less formal clothes, and we got down to business. One of the main objects of my visit was to meet all the Island Magistrates of the Ellice group, who assembled from time to time to discuss common problems. These Magistrates played an important part in the administration of the Colony, for they were vested with executive as well as judicial powers, and were the heads of the "Island Governments" in their respective islands. As such they presided over Island Councils, which, subject to the power of veto held by the Resident Commissioner, exercised a fairly wide control over the day to day affairs of their communities.

As a body the Magistrates impressed me as being wholly self-reliant and thoroughly equipped to carry the weight of their not inconsiderable responsibilities. They were assisted on the Councils by a certain number of *Kaubure*—men of standing who held traditional office to which they were elected by the islanders. As well as attending Council meetings the *Kaubure* performed executive duties as headmen and acted as jurors in Native Court cases —an amalgam of functions that reminded me of my own inter-woven responsibilities of Nigerian days. But the system worked; the Colony was law-abiding: the emphasis in island codes was upon consideration for one's neighbours.

The organization of medical services in a region of so many scattered communities deserves a word. The backbone of the system in all the Western Pacific territories was a cadre of locally recruited doctors and dressers in charge respectively of small island hospitals and dispensaries with a few beds for in-patients. The doctors, holding the title of Assistant Medical Practitioner, were not fully qualified Medical Officers; but a three years' course in Fiji, followed by a period of training at their own central hospital, equipped them to deal adequately with most situations that could be expected to arise—a responsibility they confidently assumed and successfully discharged. The same could be said of the dressers, who were prepared for all emergencies and ready to extract a broken fish-hook from a finger or amputate the limb of a shark-bite victim with equal assurance and, if necessary, under conditions that would have horrified a practitioner accustomed to sophisticated aids to professional efficiency.

New lamps for old! How to discover them? How to make them acceptable? How to ensure that their illumination would be clear, and steadfast to dispel the obscuring shadows of superstition without overpowering the light of customary authority or the torches of traditional pride? Such questions, not easily answered, were part of the whole complex of colonial administration. In the Gilbert and Ellice Islands the position of customary chiefs, where these were still to be found, was recognized by their appointment *ex officio* to the Councils; but though their influence was still potent and, in questions of social conduct, their prescriptions as custodians of precedent demanded and received respect, their general authority had merged with that of the Island Governments.

It was, however, in the natural genius of the people, as manifested in their festivities that the guardianship of cherished traditions seemed to be most secure. The centre of all important social occasions in each island was the *maneaba*, or assembly hall, also used as a hostel for visitors from other islands and for the feasts that were sometimes given in honour of distinguished strangers. These *maneabas*, which had no counterpart in other territories, were large barnlike buildings, rectangular in plan, with open sides and high sloping roofs, elegantly thatched with palm leaves, descending to within a few feet of the ground. It was in the *maneaba* on the islet of Bairiki at Tarawa that I first watched a display of dances peculiar to the Gilberts group.

As in Melanesia many of the dances were of ancient origin and translated the mysteries of primitive cults and rituals. They belonged to the people; they were part of their lives, and as familiar to them as the patterns of the surf on the beaches or the rustle of the wind among the coconut palms. When we arrived the atmosphere was highly charged with excitement. Standing in readiness were the performers, the men in their dancing mats, and the women in low-waisted leaf skirts dyed black and worn at the correct height to enable them to be easily swung by the hips. As well as their garlands of frangipani both men and women wore necklaces of cowrie shells, and some of them had flowers of red hibiscus bound to the back of the wrist or round the upper arm.

There was a small circle of seated musicians—the official orchestra. They played guitars or hammered with obvious and unrestrained relish upon empty biscuit tins. But the principal accompaniment was vocal—a slow chant which grew in volume as the dance proceeded. There is no rapid movement about these dances. A few slow steps forwards and backwards complete the pattern. Indeed, some so-called dances are even performed sitting on the ground with legs outstretched. Their genius is in the movements of the arms and the hands, which are extended, raised and lowered in a variety of graceful evocative gestures, suggestive now of pride and rapture, now of pleading and entreaty.

In some dances the movements are so strictly controlled and disciplined that a mere turn of the head, a sideways or downward glance, a motion of the palms or even of the finger tips, suffices to interpret and sustain the theme. But all the time the chanting grows louder until it is like the sound of a torrent or a waterfall. And as the well-nigh deafening climax draws near the onlookers start getting up to join in until at last almost every one seems to be dancing and singing. Little children with uncertain balance solemnly imitate the steps of their elders. Wrinkled old men and women, too infirm to stand, raise their thin arms and cracked voices in sympathy with the impetus of the final phase.

And then, quite suddenly, it is all over. Everybody relaxes. The dancers disperse to get ready for the next turn, the musicians wait, and for a little while there is comparative silence. But not for long : those who take part in these performances seem to be tireless, and the dances will probably continue by lamp light after sunset and far into the night.

Very different in style—particularly as affecting freedom of movement—were the dances performed in the Ellice group, which were said to be of Samoan origin. In these dances the whole body becomes the servant of the theme. The lift of the shoulders, the lilt in the step, the haughty swing of the skirt responding to the sway of the hips, the arms alive and sensitive to the extremities of the fingers, the play of the hands, poised palms upward in front of the breast or extended as if in supplication, all are invested with messages and meanings that only the drama and poetry of bodily motion can adequately express. Displays of this kind usually began with a procession of remarkably good-looking young ladies in full dancing attire, who advanced to the music of guitars with hips rotating gracefully and limbs shining under a generous application of coconut oil. They carried the usual frangipane garlands, which I soon ascertained were destined for the bared and defenceless heads of distinguished visitors. It was not long before I grew accustomed to this courtesy and even to making speeches with a garland upon my brow, though I always felt that such a quasi-imperial adornment was scarcely in keeping with a palm beach suit. Bernacchi's strong Roman features, however, when similarly crowned, looked very imposing.

Of the many dances I watched, not only in the Colony but throughout my years in the Pacific, there was one which for its charm and originality I select for special mention. This was performed, not in the Gilbert nor the Ellice Islands, but at Gardner Island in the distant Phoenix group. The six girls who took part sat on the ground in a row shoulder to shoulder facing the spectators, they inclined forwards together from the hips, tossing their heads downwards to left and right alternately, so that their long black tresses tumbled over their shoulders and lay spread out in front of them mingling in a dark rippling stream that flowed first one way and then the other. A gracious and lovely display.

Chapter XXII

NEW HEBRIDES

"OVER there," said the Resident Commissioner, extending an arm in the direction of the anchorage we were approaching, "is the donkey shot."

It was my first visit to the New Hebrides—my first, in-fact, to any of the High Commission territories—undertaken shortly after my arrival in Suva. With my wife and daughter I had just disembarked from the *Kurimarau*, and we were all being rowed across the harbour of Port Vila, the capital of the group, by a boat's crew, immaculately turned out in white vests and shorts with sailors' caps, to the private landing-stage at the small but steepish island of Iririki on top of which stood the British Residency, displaying loftily to the opposite waterfront, with its prominent advertisement of the Comptoirs Français des Nouvelles Hebrides and the drooping tricolour outside the French Club, the proud assurance of the Union Jack.

I was aware from my researches that this Anglo-French Con-dominium, described in one of the Colonial Office publications under the heading "Puzzle Piece", possessed many peculiar features. I knew that for many years the territory could be re-garded as no more than a colonial backwater; that in 1914, in the absence of telegraphic communication, the islands did not hear about the outbreak of the First World War until nearly three months after the event, and that even in 1952 there were still, notwithstanding the impact of the United States military presence while headquarters were established there during World War Two, tribes inhabiting the interiors of the larger islands and living often in small family groups on almost inaccessible hill-tops, who had had little contact with officials, missionaries or traders and were seemingly as aloof from the white man's world as they had ever been. I knew also that in the New Hebrides there were three administrations—the British Service under the British Resident Commissioner, the French Service under the French Resident Commissioner, and the Condominium Service under the joint administration of the two Resident Commissioners, who in the exercise of all their responsibilities represented their respective High Commissioners. And yet, territorially speaking, there were not three territories, but one territory : this in spite of the fact that there was no single responsible authority. It was a nice exercise in political metaphysics. In an old magazine, published in Australia in 1914, I once came across the following passage :

> "The Condominium, by which this group is governed, is a blend of French and English officials, under a Spanish President, and time alone will show what the outcome of this unique combination will be."

An interesting statement, but, as to fact, erroneous. The Condominium was certainly unique, and in many ways odd, but not quite as odd as that. But the absurdity could have been the result of a confused reading of an Article of the New Hebrides constitution which required the King of Spain to be invited to appoint a Judge as President of the Condominium Joint Court. For obvious reasons this had long been a dead letter.

All this I knew, and a good deal more. But what was one to make of "the donkey shot"? Dismissing the grotesque suggestion of a slaughtered beast of burden, I wondered with what alien and unfamiliar connotation the word, used adjectively as in "donkey engine" or even "donkey's years" could possibly have been employed. My unspoken question was answered very soon as we passed close to a handsome vessel, some sixty feet over-all, with a white hull and trim yacht-like lines. Reading the lettering upon her bows, I realized that but for the Resident Commissioner's French pronunciation I should have at once recognized his allusion to a purchase made by the Condominium for touring purposes—a ship to which had been given the name of Cervantes' hero of La Mancha. It was, however, interesting to note the reappearance of Spanish associations in the adopted spelling— *Don Quijote* instead of *Don Quixote* or the *Don Quichotte* of my bewilderment : a choice designed, doubtless, to avoid any suggestion of priority of proprietary rights in a joint undertaking. Two flagstaffs at the vessel's stern enabled the flags of the co-domini to be simultaneously displayed, so that the possibility of wearing a Spanish ensign did not arise.

The Anglo-French co-operation in the group, begun in 1887, recognized the existing interests in the islands of both nations, and by a Convention signed in that year they agreed among other things not to exercise separate control over them. By the same instrument a Joint Naval Commission was established. It consisted of the captain and two other officers of a British man-of-war and the captain and two officers of a French man-of-war, and its duty was to protect the lives and property of the subjects of the two nations. In the event of some incident which required minatory or punitive action it would certainly have accorded with the spirit, if not the letter, of the Commission's instructions that the two vessels should proceed simultaneously to the point of demonstration and fire a joint warning salvo; but I suspect that when problems of that kind arose they were dealt with, as they would have been in my time, on a basis of practical common-sense.

The constitution of the group was eventually enshrined in a Protocol signed by both Powers in 1914—a venerable instrument, which with a certain amount of patching has survived to this day. One of its Articles preserved the existence and peace-keeping functions of the Joint Naval Commission; but as far as I knew, and certainly in recent years, its assistance had never been invoked, and the likelihood of a recalcitrant being tapped on the shoulder by a Leading Seaman and told to "come along with me" was remote. One remarkable consequence of constitutional complexities was that the Condominium was in effect a foreign administration *vis-à-vis* both Britain and France, and therefore, during World War Two, not automatically dependent on the war controls, such as supply, security and censorship of either of the Powers. Nevertheless, for all its anomalies the Protocol can boast a life of nearly sixty years, with no indications of immediate collapse—a noteworthy contrast with the fate of rapidly drafted and redrafted constitutions of most of the former Colonial dependencies on their road to Independence.

The New Hebrides is defined in the Protocol as a region of joint influence in which the subjects and citizens of the two Powers enjoy equal rights of residence, personal protection and trade. Each Power retained sovereignty over its own nationals, but the New Hebridean native had no national status : he was a child with only guardians for parents. His care and wellbeing were in the hands of the Joint Administration, which, broadly speaking, was also responsible for all matters, such as works, agriculture and posts and telegraphs, that affected the community as a whole; whereas the National Services were concerned particularly with those administrative or judicial acts upon which the legal status and rights of non-natives as such had a bearing. So that if you were a British or a French national the Condominium Administration would deliver your letters and make sure that you renewed your licences; but if you increased your family and required a birth certificate or, regrettably, lapsed into crime your own National Service would take good care of you. *"Ressortissants"* of other Powers were required to opt within a month of arrival in the group for one of the two legal systems.

To clear a path through the undergrowth of a juristic jungle of that kind called for a generous measure of good will and mutual understanding at all official levels and nowhere more than at that of the two Resident Commissioners. Hubert Flaxman (later to become Chief Justice of Gibraltar, where he received a knighthood) and Pierre Anthonioz, his French opposite number, worked admirably together. Flaxman, the older of the two, had previously held the appointment of Chief Justice in the Sudan, and none could have been better qualified to solve the varied and frequently arising procedural conundrums that the operation of the Protocol presented. Anthonioz was alert, frank and positive, with more than a dash of Gallic exuberance. If any project became entangled in red tape Flaxman's knowledgeable and patient approach could be relied upon to disentangle it. Anthonioz, whose motto could well have been *"l'audace, toujours de l'audace"*, might have preferred to use a pair of scissors. He was, I soon discovered, a man of impetuous and dauntless energy, excelling at games despite a war wound that had partially disabled his right arm. Shortly before my arrival he had awakened both admiration and concern by swimming, with no heed to sharks or currents, the eight mile stretch of sea between the two promontories that bounded the entrance to Vila harbour. Although he was by no means always prepared to say "yes" to British proposals, his restlessness and dynamism, coupled with Flaxman's humour and mature judgement, provided the ingredients of an excellent partnership from which the joint administration derived humanity and strength.

In the Native life of the New Hebrides the areas to which missionary and Government influences had been unable to gain access were like witches' rags in a night sky—darkness upon darkness. But in the places where those influences had penetrated and there was light the church and the school, looked after by the Native pastor or catechist, were the focal institutions. Shortly after our first arrival in Vila we made a visit, accompanied by Flaxman and Anthonioz, to the neighbouring village of Mele, a Christian community of about five hundred persons. There, after being greeted by the local Chief, we were conducted to a position between two tall flagstaffs, from which flew the Union Jack and the Tricolour, and stood while first "God Save the Queen" and then the "Marseillaise" was sung by some sixty of the men of the village, who were drawn up in two rows facing each other, one on each side of a path leading to the central place of assembly. They were uniformly dressed in spotlessly laundered open-necked white shirts and white trousers, and as we walked forward between the ranks of this "guard of honour" they knelt, each with one knee on the ground and hands resting upon the other as a sign of greeting and respect.

It was not a posture of subservience, but of profound courtesy, as if the village were paying homage by a united act; but to my mind it was a tribute that went far beyond the recognition of personal authority, symbolizing, as I believe it did, loyalties not to persons but to ideals of guardianship and friendship as close as the two flags that flew so proudly above us. A venturesome fancy, perhaps; but truth speaks sometimes when the heart is lifted.

Before departing we were taken to the school, where we were greeted by the children, little girls in white dresses and little boys in white shirts and shorts, each holding a posy of leaves and flowers. The smallest of the little girls shyly handed a bouquet to my wife. As we drove slowly away the children cast their flowers in front of us on the track, transforming it into a carpet of green and gold and crimson.

That visit to Mele is one of the happiest of my New Hebrides memories; but among the most interesting and unusual was a day spent on the island of Tanna, in the South of the group, during a later tour. Our departure from Vila was delayed for several days by a cyclone, which narrowly missed the capital, and the sea was still far from calm when, one evening, we were advised that it would be safe to begin our journey. The *Don Quijote*, in which we had arranged to travel, had plenty of opportunity to display her seaworthiness, and not for nothing, as I quickly discovered as she forced her way through the waves, had this intrepid vessel been named after the impetuous and erratic cavalier. In the absence of windmill sails their effect was well simulated by repeated buffetings from vindictive seas; but the ultimate refinement of physical, not to mention mental, discomfort was achieved as we bounced over one of the tide-rips that bedevil these waters—an experience suggesting to the shaken passenger vainly seeking sleep on his bunk the impatient attempts of a frustrated chef to toss a too solid pancake in his frying-pan.

Although Flaxman and Anthonioz often toured the islands in company, and the strict letter of the Protocol required that in each District two Agents, as Administrative Officers were designated, one British and one French, should make periodical tours of inspection together, such officers did not invariably enter a village hand in hand. In practice there was a sensible distribution of staff that enabled officers of different nationality to perform similar duties in different parts of the same District. Bristow, the District Agent whose headquarters were on Tanna, was British.

The island had two eruptive features—a nativistic movement of the cargo-myth type, and a volcano. But whereas one, the volcano, was continuously active in a demonstrative but inoffensive way, the other was the cause of a flare-up only at fairly long intervals.

The nativistic movement, which was not confined to Tanna and had no closely definable geographical centre, was in some of its aspects not unlike the Marching Rule of the Solomons. There was the same devotion to custom, and the same intolerance of alien interference and control, together with an overlay of Messianic credences; but, as in Malaita, the fulfilment of prophecy was still awaited. The movement was, however, less positive in its aims and much less highly organized than its Malaitan counterpart; and certainly in Tanna it was directed not against the Government but against the rule of missionaries, whose proscription of dancing and other customary diversions had led to a revulsion from pastoral guidance and a reversion to a pagan way of life.

At one of the villages we visited during a drive round the island I was taken aside by one of the elders, who had been described to us as "the doyen of Tanna's old pagans, never missionized and probably a former cannibal". He was a cheerful person, and in his obvious anxiety to confide in me would, I am sure, have been as resolute to hold me as the ancient mariner, had I not, unlike the wedding guest, been ready to lend him a sympathetic ear. Chuckling and smiling as he kept my hand warmly clasped in his, and with the light of what might have been long forbidden pleasures in his reminiscent eyes, he informed me with a conspiritorial air that it was not right that people should be prevented from following the ancient customs that were part of their lives. I replied gravely to this good-natured homily that some old customs were very good, but some others had to be discouraged because they led to trouble.

Tanna's volcano has been described as the most accessible in the world. It rises abruptly to a height of twelve hundred feet from a brown and barren lava-strewn plain that stood out in vivid contrast with the rich verdure of the surrounding hills. Our ascent had been timed to take place just before sunset, so that we could watch the enhanced grandeur of volcanic activity at dusk.

The volcano erupted every few minutes, but not destructively, and the population was in no way disconcerted by distant rumblings, as of hogsheads being trundled over cobble-stones, or by the earth tremors that agitated the island at frequent intervals. It was necessary to ascend on the windward side in order to avoid noxious vapours and the erupted matter that occasionally rose above the lip of the crater. The wind, I was assured, seldom changed suddenly. At the foot of the volcano we were met by one of the French residents of the island, who had kindly motored out to give us some friendly guidance. The ascent, he said, was safe, yes, perfectly safe, but it was advisable to keep to the track and not to stand too long on the hot patches, especially if they appeared to be unstable. This seemed to me to be advice worth taking and I thanked our friend sincerely. With that we set out and reached the top of the crater after a steepish but fairly easy half-hour's climb.

The circular rim of the crater was perhaps half a mile in diameter, and the spectacle revealed as we peered over it cautiously was one that, had they ventured so far afield, might have startled even the shades of Dante. Descending steeply, the walls of the funnel converged towards a crust of lava far below. This was broken by vents, falling to invisible depths and glowing rosily in the light of subterranean fires, from which, several times while we watched, streams of incandescent fragments were rocketed hundreds of feet upwards towards the awe-stricken spectator, confused and deafened by the fury of the eruption and the avalanche of sound. It was a stupendous display, and the setting was so medievally hellish that I almost expected to find a ghostly Virgil at my elbow inviting me to explore the regions of the damned.

Chapter XXIII

DEPARTURE

I REMAINED three years in the Western Pacific and had then reached the age of compulsory retirement. It was not a long time in which to make the best use of such lessons as I had learned during twenty-six years in the Colonial Service, or for any seeds I had been able to sow to germinate. It sometimes seemed to me to be rather a pity that the fruits of experience acquired by so many senior officers should have to be laid aside just as they had become fully mature; but the rule had been made when conditions in some tropical territories could still have a prematurely ageing effect. After fifty-five a man might well have passed his prime. Moreover the field of promotion was already narrowing with the prospect of independence in sight for a number of British dependencies, and I had to count myself fortunate in the opportunities that had come my way. Of my "governorship" I could at least claim that in the British Solomons I had surveyed the ground and helped to prepare it for the foundations of buildings whose plans and proportions could be determined in the light of general progress, and varied or extended as fresh needs became apparent. In the other groups I had done my best to assist others engaged in a similar task.

On balance it was probably an advantage, though to some it may have been disappointing, that in my day it was, on the whole, unusual in the Colonial Administrative Service for those in positions of highest responsibility to complete their service where they had begun it. In some of the smaller dependencies it would clearly have been impossible for an officer to acquire the width of general experience to qualify for highest promotion; but in some of the largest territories, such as Nigeria, where indeed there have been distinguished exceptions to the usual practice, intimate knowledge of people and conditions gained over many years was extremely valuable. I have never myself regretted the changes that marked my career, and I found all my experiences useful; but I should have been happy to remain a little longer in my last administrative post.

On 7th July, 1955, we embarked at Honiara on the M.V. *Muliama*, a vessel of the Burns Philp Line, which occasionally made a round of the islands, and in which we had booked passages for Sydney en route for England. A good many people had gathered at the jetty to wish us well. For us it was a sad moment; for the islands and their people had come to be an intimate part of our lives, and we had made many friends and received much kindness during our years among them.

The day was calm and clear as we made our way along the familiar coast of Guadalcanal. Porpoises, playing the game of "I'll be first", came challenging our bows as they raced beside us in the sunlight, calling up ocean memories: hundreds upon hundreds of little white gulls hovering like bewildered snowflakes above the shores of a lonely atoll; frigate birds on the wing high over a mid-Pacific lagoon, dipping and spiralling in the brilliant air like ashes in a whirlwind. And there were memories in the forests that glided past us: satyr-like figures with lips pursed over pan-pipes, advancing with nimble steps, surely in search of a Grecian urn. Choral harmonies on village beaches. The voices of drums hollowed from the living wood, carrying their messages across the waters. Memories of people: shaking hands in the villages. Salana Ga'a in his waistcoat and peaked cap of shell money. Four thousand voices in unison: "Thy will be done. Thy kingdom come...."

We were approaching Cape Esperance when my reverie was suddenly broken into by an emanation of brilliant scintillations from the shore a little way ahead. As if the skies had miraculously opened to drench the beaches with a heavenly rain. The captain brought the vessel closer in to the land; and there, lined up on the reef on to which they had waded, and holding the pieces of looking-glass with which they had signalled to us, were the entire staff and pupils of the Roman Catholic School of Visale, situated at a short distance from the promontory. As one they waved and cheered us on our way.

Soon afterwards we had rounded the cape. The wind freshened and we were lifted gently on the shoulders of the sea as we altered course southwards towards Australia.

EPILOGUE

Mr. Speaker

Listening maketh a discerning man.
(With apologies to the shades of Francis Bacon)

After my retirement from the Colonial Service I accepted, in 1956, the offer of employment for a further three years as Speaker of the Mauritius Legislative Council, whose sittings had hitherto been presided over by the Governor of the Colony. The article which follows was published in Blackwood's Magazine *after my return to England.*

LAST DAY IN COUNCIL

THE room was not very large, and it was almost entirely filled by the enormous round table and the thirteen leather-seated chairs that encircled it. I sat down in one of them and waited, as usual, for the Clerk of the Council to tell me, or rather to intimate by his arrival with the mace, that it was time for him to lead me to the Chamber. He was rather a long time coming this morning. Perhaps, as it was the last day of the Session and there were odds and ends to be tidied up in the "lobbies", Members were being more dilatory than usual in taking their seats and making up the quorum without which business could not begin. That was not a matter with which the Speaker could interfere. So I waited.

It must have been the table that started my train of thought, pursued without heed to the impatient fanfares and strident arpeggois that forced their way through the windows of "Government House" from the commercial centre of traffic-congested Mauritius. The table—it was nearly as large as the uncarpeted space left for dancing on the floor of the fashionable restaurant that goes in for that kind of thing—was not at all in keeping with the atmosphere of this eighteenth-century "Hôtel du Gouvernement", which had been built to the orders of the famous French Governor, Mahé de Labourdonnais. That was not surprising. The table had been constructed (in sections, obviously, for by no other physical process could it have gained admission to the room) for the express purpose of facilitating the deliberations of twelve Ministers appointed under a Constitution that had been in operation only for a few months. I used the room, on days on which the Legislative Council met, by courtesy of the Governor, whose town office it was, and who presided there over the meetings of the Executive Council, now composed of the twelve Ministers, which met always in Port Louis.

Yes, the table was new, and soon there would be a new Speaker; for my contract had run its three years, and a Mauritian was to succeed me. He was about my size, and I would hand over to him the full-bottomed wig and the silk robe with which the Government had provided me. They were sometimes hot and uncomfortable, these garments, in the humid atmosphere of Port Louis; but how kind they could be to elderly contours and surfaces, concealing, as they did, and clothing with equal dignity the too expansive waistline or the skinny leg, as well as the grey hairs of advancing years or the vellumy gloss of a bald pate! The face, it was true, they could not disguise; but somehow one half expects any bewigged countenance to look a little Hogarthian, like some of the Cruikshank illustrations in Dickens; so that, unless they are villainously ugly, features can probably be left to appear on their merits.

The Clerk had come to fetch me and I was following him through the anteroom that gave access to the Throne room and the Council Chamber beyond. There were large gilt-framed mirrors in the anteroom into which one could glance in passing to make sure that one's wig was on straight. And royal portraits : King George the Third and Queen Charlotte to remind one that Mauritius became British in 1810. In the Throne room was Queen Victoria, beautifully painted in faithful and lifesize detail, down to the miniature of Albert contained in a locket on her right wrist and upside-down from the point of view of the beholder. Here, from the Governor's office to the Throne room, took place the traditional procession of Naval, Military and Civil dignitaries when the Governor arrived in uniform to address the Legislature from the Throne at the beginning of each Session. What a colourful scene it always was, I reflected, with the Chief Justice and the Puisne Judges in their grey-caped robes of scarlet; the two cassocked Bishops, Anglican and Roman, with their pectoral crosses; the Colonial Secretary in white tropical drill with gold oak-leaves on black gorgets and a gold-knotted sword-hilt under the left arm; the Navy with a trailing sword and the Army with a crimson sash; the Heads of Departments trying not to look uncomfortable in their dark morning coats, and all the wives in their summer dresses and their spring hats. The first day of Council my true love gave to me : four judges a-judging; no—scarcely that—four scarlet judges, three civil servants, two purple Bishops, one white Commander R.N. and a Governor with his A.D.C. But here is the Council Chamber. I dismiss my light-hearted fancies.

Honourable Members of Council. Mr Speaker.

I enter and, while the fifty Members and the public stand in silence, mount the three steps to the chair, a massive but handsome piece of furniture surmounted by a carved wooden canopy and thickly padded, seat, back and sides, with leather of parliamentary green. Cunningly concealed at ear level in this upholstery is a small loud-speaker, which, by the unobtrusive turning of a knob, can be used to amplify voices of indifferent timbre. A little judicious deafness in a Speaker, not to mention an occasional defect in vision, may, it has been well said, sometimes be permitted, lest, by his observing or hearing too much, the heart and spirit of debate should sink and perish in an ocean of Rules of Order that ought to sustain and not drown it. But a Speaker must be able to decide what he wishes and what he does not wish to hear, especially when, as in Mauritius, party allegiances can be a little flexible and it is not always possible to be certain of the manner in which the slings and arrows of outrageous criticism will be loosed, or the quarter they will threaten. Another aid to efficiency is a button operating a small red lamp on the table of the Clerk, who sits in front of me facing the Chamber, so that in moments of crisis or indecision I am able to attract his attention and summon him to my side for consultation without recourse to audible pleas for assistance.

I bow right, left and centre, and take my seat. The Members and the public sit, and now I am on my feet again to make what is in effect my public farewell to this assembly, holding in my hand the sheets of paper on which is typed my valedictory address. Would it be better to let them rest on the desk in front of me in case my hand should tremble ever so slightly while I am reading? No, it would be too transparent an expedient. My hand shall not tremble. . . .

"The indulgence of the House . . . the great honour and

privilege of presiding over your debates . . . support and encouragement . . . my grateful thanks.

"Three years is not long in the life of a man, still less in the history of a Council such as this, whose existence goes back for more than a century and a quarter. But these last three years have been years of great importance in the constitutional history of Mauritius . . . three years ago there was still an official executive . . . now, authority residing in the hands of Ministers supported by a parliamentary majority.

"But this is not the whole story. A Legislative Council in a democratic community does not exist solely for the purpose of giving legislative authority to the acts of the Government of the day . . . rather to be thought of as resembling an area in which athletic teams or combinations of teams of varying size and composition match their prowess and exhibit their skill. And the ultimate assessment of merit will depend upon the verdict of the spectators.

"There is yet another aspect of our Legislative Council—the personal and domestic aspect; and upon this I conclude. The 'House.' It is an expression, I submit, that we should cherish. It suggests a place where friends, whatever their politics, whatever their predilections, whatever their aversions, may gather in amity; a place where there will be mutual understanding and respect, mutual forbearance and, if necessary, forgiveness. And the memory I shall carry away with me will be of such a House as this. At heart a kindly House, a generous House, a House in which no man need fear to light a candle, a House dedicated to the worthy service of the people of Mauritius."

No, the hand did not tremble, but perhaps the heart beat a little faster. They are replying now. Kind words. His Excellency's appreciation . . . assisting us to maintain worthily the highest standards of debate . . . good fortune and happiness in the future.

Well, thank goodness that's over. I am touched, and it would never do for a Speaker to be affected by an impairment of vision that was not judicious. The Clerk calls the next item and we are down to the business that remains to be got through before the Colonial Secretary hands me the Governor's proroguing message with which the proceedings will terminate. I sit with one ear cocked, as usual, to detect any possible infringement of the rules of debate, and ready to intervene, if necessary, in order to prevent a spark of irrelevance or provocation from flaring up, as it so easily can, into a flame of discord. But this morning, it seems, I have nothing to do but listen—and, with the other half of my mind, to think.

What good fellows, when all is said and done, these Mauritians really are: the proud French; the coloureds, proud too, and sensitive; the cheerful Creoles, no wealth here but plenty of optimism and courage; the earnest, intellectual Hindus; the community-conscious, introvertive Moslems, full of faith and works; the placid and industrious Chinese, a smaller community, but where would the retail trade be without them? And, least as well as last, the small and doubtless diminishing company of the correct and conscientious English. All represented here in this long elegant room, once a banqueting chamber, with its two double rows of chairs and tables finishing up in a horseshoe at the far end in front of the public gallery, its tall windows with their heavy anti-cyclone shutters, and its handsome central chandelier, guarded on either side by more full-length royal portraits, this time of King George V. and Queen Mary. The whole, nevertheless, creating a somewhat Victorian atmosphere, contributed to by the inscription V.R. on some of the ponderous tulip-shaped glass lampshades that have successfully weathered sixty years or more of dialectical cross current.

How comes it that with all this divergence of class, creed, race and language they should play the parliamentary game so well? Perhaps because in Mauritius we have not had to do things in too much of a hurry. We did not interfere with their institutions, their customs, their language, their religion; we saw fair play; and we rode democracy, not with the curb, not with the whip and spurs, but on a light rein. . . .

We have come to the end of the Ministerial statements, and the Minister of Works gets up to move the second reading of a Bill he is in charge of.

Some people say Mauritius wants independence. Within the Commonwealth. But nowadays what is this Commonwealth? Not an imperium, not a system; not even, except in the loosest interpretation, an association. Surely a cross-section of humanity, of all humanity, something like an architect's plan which, if you study it intelligently and with imagination and sympathy, reveals the scope and purpose of the designer. Myself and the next fellow, and that man yonder; the clerk at his desk, the salesman at his counter, the labourer in the canefield, the fisherman with his net; the Christian at his altar rail, the Hindu in his temple, the Moslem as he turns to Mecca. Here it all is in this microcosm of Mauritius, this island of tall churches, ornamented mosques and red and yellow temples; of French culture and Hindu fire festivals; this island that the Arabs knew and the Portuguese visited; from which the Dutch withdrew and which the French made prosperous; to which Africans came as slaves and Indians to work, settle and multiply; which Britain seized in the wars with Napoleon and for whose destinies she is now responsible.

The Question is that the Road Traffic (Amendment) Bill be read a second time. Will those in favour saye "aye". The contrary "no". The ayes have it. Let the Bill be read a second time.

We had reached the Committee stage, and I retired while the Deputy Speaker, who was also Chairman of Committees, took the chair. Another good scout, I thought, and remembered the evening a few days before when the Members had entertained me at a farewell dinner. Deputy was master of ceremonies, and after the champagne (which in Mauritius takes the place of port on such occasions) had gone round he proposed my health with a few words I shall never forget. "You, sir, are now a part of the history of Mauritius." Literally, I suppose, it was a plain statement of truth; to the extent, at least, that my name would remain with those of my successors (before my time the Council had been presided over by the Governor) in the parliamentary records; but he intended it as a compliment, and as a very graceful, if undeserved, compliment I took it.

His words came into mind again when, a little later, I returned to the Chamber for the Report stage and Third Reading. The Committee stage had not taken long, for it was nearly lunchtime and the horse could smell the stable. What happened when one was part of the history of a place? Would one's ghost be entitled to hobnob with those of celebrated men who had been zealous for the advantage and good report of Mauritius? I thought of Labourdonnais as he appeared in the portrait that hung with those of other former Governors, French and British, in the Governor's residence at Le Réduit. Pink cheeked and peri-wigged, in his dandified, scarlet cutaway coat and breeches, his immaculate ruffles, white silk stockings and buckled shoes he looked more like a comic-opera character than the intrepid sailor, skilful administrator and gallant soldier that he was. Labour-donnais, who had governed the sister isles of Bourbon and the Ile de France, as Réunion and Mauritius were then named; Labourdonnais, the architect, the engineer, the ship-builder; Labourdonnais, the gay Governor who loved entertain-ment; Labourdonnais, the resourceful, who, when a shortage of beef threatened to deplete the island's larder, hunted stags in the forests and imported tortoises from Rodrigues; Labourdonnais, the conqueror of Madras, who had been unjustly accused, disgraced and imprisoned in the Bastille, and then, honour vindicated, released only to die, a broken man, at the age of fifty-four. I thought also of Governor Pope-Hennessy, the little Irishman who more than seventy years ago had struggled with the Colonial Office to advance the privileges and political rights of Mauritians. He it was who had secured the right of election for some of the members of the Council of Government, as the Legislature was then called. He too was suspended from office through the machinations of political enemies, but having confounded his detractors and won a libel action he was reinstated.

The Colonial Secretary came up to the Chair and handed me the Governor's message reviewing the work of the Session. I read it to the Council and came to the last paragraph :

"It is my will and pleasure that the Council should now be prorogued, and I shall by Proclamation declare this Council prorogued and order that it stands prorogued. . . ."

I bowed and left the Chamber for the last time. No, my ghost, if it ever came this way, would have no title to be seen in the company of such mighty shades as those. Anyway all ghosts were individualists, not to say exhibitionists. I should have to contrive my own act. Perhaps on the last day of every Council, when the sound of retreating footsteps and disputatious after-comment has died away, the lights in their no-longer-Victorian lamp-shades have been extinguished and the old room is dark and silent, I shall take my place in the chair vacated by the Speaker of the day and sit there, listening and thinking.

END

ACKNOWLEDGEMENTS

I WISH, first of all, to express to Viscount Boyd, for his kindness in finding time to read this book and write an introductory Foreword, the sincere thanks of one who once, to use the traditional phrase, had the honour to be his obedient humble servant.

I am indebted to Mr. B. Cheeseman, O.B.E., Head of the Library and Records Department of the Foreign and Commonwealth Office, and to Mr. D. H. Simpson, Librarian of the Royal Commonwealth Society, and their staffs, for valued assistance in the use of their extensive facilities.

Some of the material contained in Chapter XVII on the subject of "Marching Rule" in the British Solomon Islands Protectorate was included in an article published in *New Commonwealth* (now *New Commonwealth and World Development*) in 1956.

The *Excerpta Cypria*, from which quotations in the chapters on Cyprus are taken, were compiled towards the end of the last century by C. D. Cobham, who for some years was Commissioner in charge of the Larnaca District. They consist of descriptive and historical extracts and translations from the accounts of many writers who visited the island from the twelfth century to the nineteenth.

In references to the sacred law of Islam, and particularly to the law of evidence as affecting witnesses and judges, observed in the Native Courts of Moslem areas in Nigeria, I have embodied details from a summary by R. H. Ruxton of the Nigerian Service of French translations of the *Mukhtasar* of Sidi Khalil, published in 1916 by direction of Lord Lugard in a volume entitled *Maliki Law*.

INDEX

N

M